The Requirements Engineering Handbook

For a listing of recent titles in the *Artech House Technology Management and Professional Development Library,* turn to the back of this book.

The Requirements Engineering Handbook

Ralph R. Young

Artech House
Boston • London
www.artechhouse.com

Library of Congress Cataloging-in-Publication Data
A catalog record for this book is available from the U.S. Library of Congress.

British Library Cataloguing in Publication Data
A catalog record for this book is available from the British Library.

Cover design by Igor Valdman

© 2004 ARTECH HOUSE, INC.
685 Canton Street
Norwood, MA 02062

The following are registered in the U.S. Patent and Trademark Office by Carnegie Mellon University: Capability Maturity Model®, CMM®, and CMMI®.

International Standard Book Number: 1-58053-266-7
A Library of Congress Catalog Card number is available from the Library of Congress.

10 9 8 7 6 5 4 3 2 1

For you

Let's improve requirements engineering!

Contents

Foreword

Some years ago, a successful company won a contract for a fifty million dollar project. The product system had six operator consoles, another six racks of electronics equipment, and a sophisticated set of remote radios and computers. Development disciplines included software engineering, digital electronics, communications electronics, and mechanical engineering.

Customer acquisition and user groups knew what operational capability they wanted, but there had yet been no technical requirements. Early in the project, the company developed and delivered a technical specification. Customer reviewers provided dozens of changes, including six additional requirements that they interpreted from the loose operational capability statements. In later discussion, however, customer people agreed that these additional requirements, although nice to have, were too expensive to add.

Time passed. The project had political and funding problems, bouncing up and down over a period of four years like a short-hop shuttle airplane. Personnel changed several times; in one such change, the project apparently terminated and the entire acquisition group was reassigned. After two months of hiatus, a new acquisition group resumed the project.

The technical specification went through several more revisions. Somehow, the record of those six requirements remained. The record of the agreement, however, was repeatedly lost. They were reinserted repeatedly by customer reviewers. After each revision, those six requirements were again deemed too expensive to add. But the specification was never quite approved to reflect the agreement. In the throes of responding to the frequent upheavals, the developers focused on completing the design and production. The specification faded onto a dusty shelf.

Things on a dusty shelf have a way of coming back to haunt. Those six requirements came to light one last time. During system acceptance testing, customer monitors blew the dust off the specification and started a formal verification.

The result of six missing requirements was a three million dollar overrun.

Ralph Young's book provides the tools that company needed and did not have. Building on *Effective Requirements Practices* and on his years of practical experience, Ralph offers a set of tools and techniques that are essential for modern requirements analysis, written into a handbook format for continued reference. This book describes both the philosophy and practice of requirements analysis, with down-to-earth pragmatism that can help to do the job in the face of today's complex system challenges.

Human communications are imprecise. It is one aspect of nature of humanity that we fail to understand each other completely.

Recall the campfire games of your childhood. In the game "Whispers," someone starts a short statement around the campfire circle by whispering to his neighbor. In turn, each player passes on the statement, always in a whisper. After only a few transfers, the original statement is modified beyond recognition. In the game, the differences are so astonishing as to bring laughter to all.

Recall the last time you went to a restaurant and ordered from a menu. Written in front of you is a full description of the entree you want. Confidently, you tell the waiter the entree. The waiter silently sighs and starts the perennial sequence of questions about side items. "Salad or soup, ma'am?" "New potatoes or French fries?" "Green beans or succotash?" All these options were clearly written on the menu, but somehow you missed them.

Requirements are also a form of human communications, an attempt to convey complex ideas from one mind to another. Requirements are also a sparse form of communications, using bare written words to strive for precision. Like menu descriptions, requirements always fall short. It is literally impossible to write any requirement, no matter how simple, that cannot be misconstrued honestly by some recipient.

Even the word "requirement" is itself a miscommunication, for individual requirements are frequently flexible rather than required. If a trade-off promises a significant benefit to a key performance parameter, specifiers will gladly change lesser "requirements" to accommodate the trade-off.

And yet requirements are still the best method we know to convey the complexity of a technical idea. To handle this complexity, we use requirements to perform three important roles, all of which are enhanced by the tools and techniques in this book.

First, requirements are a contractual tool. This is the most commonly understood purpose. In this role, a specification defines the technical scope of a development contract. The legal impact of this role is far from small. One recent lawsuit between a prime contractor and a subcontractor hinged on the grammar of a single requirements statement, resulting in a multimillion dollar settlement. For the protection of both acquirers and suppliers, contractual requirements must be as clear as they can be.

Second, requirements are a configuration management tool. The exact form and relationship of the requirements statements uniquely define a configuration of the system. They embody the valid system functionality and bounds. By controlling the requirements, we control the configuration definition. We see the importance of configuration definition each time a new software tool fails to operate with our "open system" personal computer.

Third, requirements are an engineering tool. This essential role is frequently not understood, being overshadowed by the contractual and configuration management roles. Yet it is in engineering that requirements have their power. We use requirements during the engineering processes to do the following:

- Communicate among development team members, acquirers, users, and others;
- Describe and understand the operational need;
- Capture decisions about the technical solution;
- Define the product architecture;
- Check completion of the product elements;
- Verify completion of the product.

The problem of those six requirements happened due to many factors—the political changes to the program, the competing ideas among the customer factions, the unusual pressures of start-and-stop development, and the development team's focus on completion. That problem also happened, however, because of the lack of the requirements management (RM) methods that this book contains. A modern RM effort for the entire project would have cost a fraction of the three million dollars of overrun experienced. Even better, many other expenses would also have been avoided.

Like the children around the campfire, informality leads to miscommunications. As a campfire game, we laugh at the problems. In building today's complex system products, though, we are no longer laughing.

Eric Honour
Former President, International Council on Systems Engineering

Preface

This book is intended as a concise but thorough ready reference for requirements analysts (RAs)—those who are assigned to determine the requirements for planned systems and software, both in computing and engineering. It is a desk guide/handbook that focuses on *how* RAs can best perform their work.

The requirements are key to the success or failure of technical projects. They are the basis of all of the follow-on work. It's been my experience that most projects and organizations fail to use effective requirements practices and a documented requirements process, and also that those assigned as RAs are cast into the needed work without proper preparation, experience and training, and without a good handbook that advises them on how to perform their roles and what to do.

RAs are in a strategic position to influence the activities performed on a systems or software engineering task or project:

- The requirements are vital to the initiation, conduct, and completion of the needed work.

- They are of great importance in achieving the objectives of customers and users.

- Trained, experienced RAs are valued advisors to the program, project, or task manager and invaluable resources for other members of the team.

This book addresses all of the areas that you will need to know about in your work. Key topics include the following:

Topic

- The importance of requirements.

- Leveraging requirements-related activities to benefit your project.

- Identifying the real requirements.

- Controlling changes to requirements and new requirements.

- Use effective requirements practices, processes, methods, techniques, and tools.

- Invest in the requirements process.

- Evaluate your requirements against the criteria of a good requirement.

- Document the rationale for each requirement.

- Plan requirements-related activities.

- Use an industrial strength automated requirements tool.

- Work to improve communications. Use a project glossary and acronyms list.

- In collaboration with the task or project leaders, select a set of best practices, and then implement them effectively.

- Develop a personal professional development plan, and enhance your skills and capabilities.

- Learn and apply needed requirements analyst's specialty skills.

- Define and use an integrated quality approach.

- Evolve your own personal vision for requirements engineering.

- Address requirements risks.

Chapter 2 describes nine roles of the RA and identifies where in the system life cycle each should be applied. Requirements work requires a lot of knowledge and skills—perhaps more than most people think. Chapter 3 identifies and describes skills that you may need to use and provides a reference in this book where you can learn more about each skill.

It's important for the RA and others assigned to the task or project to understand the different types of requirements. These are described in detail in Chapter 4 and are broken down as follows:

- Business requirements;
- User requirements;
- Product requirements;
- Environmental requirements;
- Unknowable requirements.

Customer needs and expectations are analyzed and described in the following ways:

- High-level (or system-level) requirements;
- Functional requirements (what the system must do);

- Nonfunctional requirements:
  - System properties (e.g., safety);
  - The "ilities/specialty engineering requirements";
- Derived requirements and design constraints;
- Performance requirements (e.g., how fast?);
- Interface requirements (relationships between system elements).

Then the system requirements are allocated into the following:

- Subsystems (logical groupings of functions);
- Components of the system (hardware, software, training, documentation).

Checks are done to ensure the system does what it is supposed to do, incorporating the following:

- Verified requirements;
- Validated requirements;
- Qualification requirements.

The following are evident from this description of requirements activities:

- A common, shared understanding is needed on the task or project;
- Requirements-related training should be provided to three groups with somewhat different needs, so that all can benefit from industry experience and become aware of the methods, techniques, and tools that work best: (1) RAs, (2) the members of the development team, and (3) the customers and users.

These topics are addressed in Chapter 5.

The requirements gathering activities are complex and can easily become ineffective, as you likely are already aware from your experience! See Table 5.1 for a checklist that will help you in your vital roles.

Chapter 5 provides a discussion of each activity, explaining why it's important and how to get it done. References enable you to access more information, should you want it. *The intent of the book is to empower you to make a valued contribution and also to be fulfilled in your work activities.*

We hear and read a lot about "best practices." Unfortunately, they are too infrequently deployed, implemented, and institutionalized on real projects, for a variety of reasons, but most importantly, because it's hard work. Chapter 6 provides information concerning best practices for RAs, based on my own and industry experience. Obviously, one can't do everything, at least not at one time. The information in Chapter 6 will enable you to initiate discussions with your task or project team and to select the best practices that best support your project's or your organization's needs, activities, and objectives.

There is a set of specialty skills of the RA that are required at different times in your work. Chapter 7 describes these specialty skills and directs you to the section in this book where each is discussed.

Chapter 8 explains the importance of an integrated quality approach. An effectively implemented requirements process is necessary in order to have an integrated quality approach, and an integrated quality approach is required for the requirements process to work best. Chapter 8 explains what is meant by these terms and, also, how to achieve them.

Chapter 9 provides a vision for requirements engineering. You will become aware (if you are not already) that progress in requirements engineering has been slow. This book is dedicated to you, with the challenge to improve the practice of requirements engineering! This book is full of practical ideas, suggestions, approaches, and recommendations and will serve you well as a handbook in your daily work. But, only if (1) you use it, and (2) you are determined to work to make things better. This suggests that you need to be committed to making changes that improve the way we develop systems and software. Too often we don't practice what we preach. We know what we should do, but we don't do it. The bottom line is that your commitment and that of your peers and managers is required if we are to make improvements. *Use this book to guide you in your vital work.* Further, you will be able to create and implement your own professional-development plan based on the characteristics and traits you choose to further strengthen and improve. I encourage you to work in concert with your manager to evolve a plan of action to enable you to understand comprehensively your roles and, through experience and study, develop the expertise needed to impact project success rates significantly and positively.

Chapter 10 provides a summary of the book and suggestions for moving forward. The subtitle, "Knowable Requirements, Manageable Risk" suggests that we really can do a commendable job when we are empowered and apply the guidelines provided in this book. By doing so, you will be helping the computing and engineering professions to improve.

Let's acknowledge that we have a long way to go. But guidance is available concerning how to make improvements (in our policies, practices, processes, methods, techniques, and tools, for example). *In order for the profession to improve, practitioners need to take actions in their daily work that are different from what we are doing today.* Only through gradual, but committed, incremental actions will the profession advance to achieve a positive vision of requirements engineering.

Are you ready?

Please share any of your own reactions to this book, ideas, suggestions, and constructive criticisms with me at ryoungrr@aol.com. I will no doubt be hard at work on another project, and your feedback will improve any contributions I may make.

Good luck, and remember to have fun while you are doing all of this!

Acknowledgments

I continue to be very thankful to my wife, Judy, for her incredible patience, understanding, and love throughout the book writing process. Family and friends are sometimes amazed at the joy and energy I derive from writing—for me, it's as Maryanne Radmacher-Hershey characterizes it:

> Writing is the process one follows to learn what is already known deep within: it sharpens the spirit, disciplines the mind, and leads to solutions. In the spaces between words and solitude observe what happens when words and silence meet. Words matter. Pay attention. Write to learn what you know.

As for those who have supported me, how can I appropriately acknowledge reviewers and contributors who have given so generously and so much to make this a better book? Suffice it to say that many people have become close friends and valued advisors.

Speaking of advisors, there is one whose name I do not even know! Artech House Publishers engaged an advisor to review my final drafts. This person, obviously an expert in requirements engineering, chose to remain anonymous and provided constructive and helpful comments on each chapter.

Speaking of requirements-engineering experts, Ian Alexander generously provided thoughtful comments and insights in countless areas, responding in almost real time to questions, inquiries, and requests for review comments. Randall Iliff, engineering and project management mentor, also provided great insights in several areas. Jeff Grady, Earl Hoovler, Capers Jones, John Moore, Rich Raphael, and Doug Smith contributed thoughtful and useful ideas and wording.

Requirements analysts who are members of the Northrop Grumman Information Technology Defense Enterprise Solutions Requirements Working Group provided valued review comments, contributions, and lent their experiences and expertise—Terry Bartholomew, Michael Davis, David Ebenhoeh, Bob Ellinger, Jim Faust, Graham Meech, Dick Pederson, Rich

Raphael, Dave Reinberger, Ron Rudman, Charlie Rynearson, and John Waters, in particular.

Other requirements analysts who made valued contributions include Dorothy Firsching, Chris Fowler, Heather Gray, Skip Jensen, Wayne O'Brien, Joy van Helvert, Charlie Wight, and Don Young.

The graphics, illustrations, tables, and figures are critical components of any work because they convey ideas and summarize information. Thanks to Rich Raphael for creating many of those in this book, for his expertise in crafting and refining them, and for his constant willingness to help in any way possible. Olga Rosario also contributed greatly.

Many of the "artifacts" in the book benefited from additions, corrections, and review comments contributed by participants in my requirements engineering courses, tutorials, presentations, and workshops that I love to present. Thanks to all of you, particularly Pat Little.

Other friends and associates who lent a hand and mind include Barry Boehm, Grady Booch, Dennis Buede, Pete Carroll, Tom Gilb, Ellen Gottesdiener, Eric Honour, Alice Hill-Murray, Craig Hollenbach, Ivy Hooks, Ray Huber, Charles Markert, Andy Meadow, Larry Pohlmann, Olga Rosario, Penny Waugh, and Beth Werner.

Reviewers, including many of those previously mentioned, have strengthened my writings. Other reviewers include Randy Allen, Jim Hayden, and Karl Wiegers. Writing a book is clearly a team effort!

Our President of Northrop Grumman Information Technology Defense Enterprise Solutions, Kent R. Schneider, and my manager, Alan Pflugrad, have gifts for creating and maintaining a TEAMWORKS environment (read about this in Chapter 8!). It is very fulfilling and energizing to be a member of several high-performance teams through Northrop Grumman. I am thankful to Kent and Al for their leadership, support, and guidance.

I continue to be aware from my faith journey that prayer works. Thanks to treasured friends Art Banks, Tom Foss, Craig Hollenbach, and Joe Matney.

Thanks to family for their support, too—Kimberly and Mike Wallace, Ann and Jeff Young, Matt Young, and Jan and Don Hoffer.

CHAPTER

1

Contents

The Importance of Requirements

The purpose of this book is to help you improve the practice of requirements engineering. Requirements engineering is difficult. It's not just a simple matter of writing down what the customer says he wants. A fundamental problem in business is that requirements are inherently dynamic; they will change over time as our understanding of the problem we are trying to solve changes. The importance of good requirements and the underlying dynamic nature of the process mean that we must be as accurate as possible, and yet be flexible. Flexible does not mean "weak," but rather than we have a *process* for developing requirements and accommodating changed requirements as we clarify the real requirements of customers. Ineffective requirements practices are an industrywide problem. This is an area in which you can have a major positive impact. A more disciplined approach to requirements development and management is needed in order to improve project success rates. An alarming 53% of industry's investment in technical development projects is a casualty of cost overruns and failed projects.

This chapter defines the term "requirement," explains why requirements are important, and advocates planning to define the requirements strategy and activities. It suggests use of a defined and documented requirements process, that investing more in the requirements process will have a large payback, and that requirements serve a crucial role in business in managing risk. It recommends that you consider certain factors in making your career decisions. It suggests that much of the advice provided in the book is applicable to projects of all sizes.

What Are Requirements and Why Are They Important?

A *requirement* is a necessary attribute in a *system*, a statement that identifies a capability, characteristic, or quality factor of a

1

system in order for it to have value and utility to a *customer or user*. Requirements are important because they provide the basis for all of the development work that follows. Once the requirements are set, developers initiate the other technical work: system design, development, testing, implementation, and operation.

Too often, there is a tendency to want to start what is often referred to as "the real work" (developing, or programming, the software) too quickly. Many customers and project managers (PMs) seem to believe that actual programming work ("coding") indicates that progress is being made. According to industry experience, insufficient time and effort are spent on the requirements-related activities associated with system development. Industry experience confirms that a better approach is to invest more time in requirements gathering, analysis, and management activities. The reason is that, typically, coding work is started much sooner than it should be because additional time is needed to identify the *"real" requirements* and to plan for requirements-related activities (described below).

There is a significant difference between *"stated" requirements* and "real" requirements. Stated requirements are those provided by a customer at the beginning of a system or software development effort, for example, in a request for information, proposal, or quote or in a statement of work (SOW). Real requirements are those that reflect the verified needs of users for a particular system or capability. There is often a huge difference between the stated requirements and the real requirements. Analysis of the stated requirements is required to determine and refine real customer and user needs and expectations of the delivered system. The requirements need to be filtered by a process of clarification of their meaning and identification of other aspects that need to be considered. To cite a simple example, *requirements analysts* (RAs) are more familiar with the need to state requirements clearly (see the criteria for a good requirement provided below). There are many ways in which the capability, understanding, and communication of the meaning of each and every requirement may be different to a user than to a developer. Therefore, it is vital (and time saving) that all requirements be clarified through the mechanism of a joint customer/user and RA effort. Customers and users need the support of technically trained and experienced professionals, and vice versa, to ensure effective communication. Developers need to have that same understanding so that the solution they define addresses the needs in the way everyone expects. Misunderstandings of requirements result in wasted effort and rework. Another important insight is that sometimes the requirements are *unknowable* at the outset of a development effort because they are affected by the new capabilities to be provided in the new system. This suggests the need to plan for new and changed requirements—to provide a degree of flexibility.

Identifying the real requirements requires an *interactive and iterative* requirements process, supported by effective practices, processes, mechanisms, methods, techniques, and tools. This book provides a description of *how* the RA can use these in performing the needed work. In a previous book, *Effective Requirements Practices* [1], I describe *what* should be done and provide an extensive set of references to many of the best publications in the industry literature. This book is intended to provide a concise handbook that serves as a desk reference guide for the RA or engineer and requirements manager in engineering and computing. It also provides updated references.

The requirements process need not be complicated or expensive. However, a requirements process is *required* for a project of any size. It's most important that a project or organization *have* a defined and documented requirements process. The nature of the specific components of the defined process can be improved based on experience.

Why Plan?

It's well known and understood by most people that a bit of planning goes a long way. For example, before leaving on an automobile trip, checking a map to locate the destination and, perhaps, even planning a route may be time well spent. Yet, we frequently charge ahead with the doing with little or no planning, don't we? It's human nature to want to get on with the needed work without doing much planning.

Systems development and software development managers and practitioners are familiar with several types of plans: project plan, systems engineering management plan (SEMP), quality assurance (QA) plan, configuration management (CM) plan, software development plan (SDP), test plan, and so on. However, the concept of a *requirements plan* may be new to you. Leveraging requirements-related activities has great power and effect. Writing a requirements plan maximizes value. A requirements plan defines how the real requirements will evolve and how the requirements activities will be addressed.

Writing a requirements plan (RP) facilitates an understanding of the activities and efforts that need to be undertaken to implement an effective requirements process for a particular development effort. Additional details concerning the requirements plan are provided below.

A Suggested Strategy

I suggest a strategy that includes (1) writing a requirements plan, (2) designing or tailoring a requirements process for your project, (3) investing in the requirements-related activities in the system life cycle, and (4) utilizing the effective requirements practices, mechanisms, methods, techniques, tools, and training that are described in this book.

Requirements Activities in the System Life Cycle

Managers often think of requirements-related activities as consisting primarily of gathering requirements and managing changes to those requirements throughout the life cycle. In reality, there are several other requirements-related activities that need to be addressed in the *system life cycle:*

▸ *Identifying the stakeholders:* This includes anyone who has an interest in the system or in its possessing qualities that meet particular needs.

▸ *Gaining an understanding of the customers' and users' needs for the planned system and their expectations of it:* This is often referred to as *requirements elicitation.* Note that the requirements can include several types. Types of requirements are discussed in Chapter 4. Requirements gathering techniques are discussed in Chapter 5.

▸ *Identifying requirements:* This involves stating requirements in simple sentences and providing them as a set. Business needs or requirements are the essential activities of an enterprise. They are derived from business goals (the objectives of the enterprise). Business *scenarios* may be used as a technique for understanding business requirements. A key factor in the success of a system is the extent to which it supports the business requirements and facilitates an organization in achieving them.

▸ *Clarifying and restating the requirements:* This is done to ensure that they describe the customer's real needs and are in a form that can be understood and used by developers of the system.

▸ *Analyzing the requirements:* This is done to ensure that they are well defined and that they conform to the criteria of a good requirement (provided below).

▸ *Defining the requirements in a way that means the same thing to all of the stakeholders:* Note that each stakeholder group may have a significantly different perspective of the system and the system's requirements. Sometimes this requires investing significant time learning a special vocabulary or project lexicon. Often it requires spending considerable time and effort to achieve a common understanding.

▸ *Specifying the requirements:* This requires including all of the precise detail of each requirement so that it can be included in a specification document or other documentation, depending on the size of the project.

▸ *Prioritizing the requirements:* All requirements are not of equal importance to the customers and users of the planned system. Some are critical, some of relatively high priority, some of normal or average priority, and some even of lower priority. It is important to prioritize all of the requirements because there is never enough time or money to do *everything* we'd like to do in our developed systems. Prioritizing the requirements provides the opportunity to address the highest priority first and possibly release a version of a product later that addresses lower-priority needs. Prioritizing helps ensure that an appropriate amount of investment is made in meeting various customer needs.[1]

▸ *Deriving requirements:* There are some requirements that come about because of the design of a system, but do not provide a direct benefit to the end user. A requirement for disc storage might result from the need to store a lot of data, for example.

▸ *Partitioning requirements:* We categorize requirements as those that can be met by hardware, software, training, and documentation, for example. Often this process turns out to be more complex than we anticipate when some requirements are satisfied by more than one category.

▸ *Allocating requirements:* We allocate requirements to different subsystems and components of the system. The allocations may not always be satisfied by just one subsystem or component.

▸ *Tracking requirements:* We need the capability to trace or track where in the system each requirement is satisfied, so that we can verify that each requirement is being addressed. This is most often accomplished through use of an automated requirements tool.

▸ *Managing requirements:* We need to be able to add, delete, and modify requirements during all of the phases of system design, development, integration, testing, deployment, and operation. The *requirements repository* consists of a set of artifacts and databases. It is described in Chapter 5.

▸ *Testing and verifying requirements:* This is the process of checking requirements, designs, code, test plans, and system products to ensure that the requirements are met.

▸ *Validating requirements:* This is the process for confirming that the real requirements are implemented in the delivered system. The order of validation of requirements should be prioritized since there is a limited amount of funding available.

Investment in the Requirements Process

The industry average investment in the requirements process for a typical system is 2% to 3% of total project cost. It should be evident from the

---

1. See A. M. Davis, "The Art of Requirements Triage," *Computer* (March 2003), for a discussion of the concept of "requirements triage." Davis defines requirements triage as the process of determining which requirements a product should satisfy given the time and resources available. He provides extensive guidance and suggestions that help prioritize requirements. Three product development case studies and 14 recommendations are provided.

information already presented that this amount of investment is inadequate and in fact is the root cause of the failure of many projects. Data from the U.S. National Aeronautics and Space Administration (NASA) described in [2] provide a clear and powerful message: projects that expended the industry average of 2% to 3% of total project cost/effort on the (full life cycle) requirements process experienced an 80% to 200% cost overrun, while projects that invested 8% to 14% of total project cost/effort in the requirements process had 0% to 50% overruns [2, p. 9]. (Obviously, our goal is not to have overruns at all; however, a smaller overrun is preferable to a larger one!) This book describes how to achieve an appropriate level of investment in the requirements process and the associated benefits.

A Process Approach

Over the past two decades, there has been considerable discussion of the value of a "process approach." By a process approach, I mean developing and using a documented description—a process flowchart and an accompanying process description (PD)—of a set of activities that results in the accomplishment of a task or achievement of an outcome. Based on my experience, there is great value to using a process approach:

- Those who support the activity document the actions or activities involved in getting something done.

- Once documented, there is a common (shared) understanding of what is involved.

- The documented process can be understood by all who are involved.

- Those involved, having a common understanding, can suggest improvements to the process (enabling *continuous improvement* and empowering those who are involved to contribute ideas for making the process better).

Several general process models have been developed. For example, the Capability Maturity Model (CMM®) [3] developed by the Software Engineering Institute (SEI) at Carnegie Mellon University in the late 1980s provides an industry standard framework for assessing the maturity/capability of a development process. The current version of this model is called the Capability Maturity Model Integration (CMMI®) [4]. Its success is due to the model's capability to discern whether software is being developed more effectively. One can tell whether the development effort is "better" or "worse" over time. Some PMs may question the value of process improvement, believing that it diverts resources from their main responsibility of satisfying the customer needs and that process improvement costs too much money. Industry data maintained by the SEI reflect a 7:1 return on investment (ROI) from process improvement.[2] Other industry data consistently report 40% to 50% rework on development projects. Reducing rework is a lucrative target for process improvement efforts. Reducing rework can provide the resources to undertake process improvement initiatives.

Also, requirements process models are available; for example, one is provided in my earlier book and available on my Web site (www. ralphyoung.net); the spiral model for requirements engineering; and a model is provided in *Mastering the Requirements Process* [5].

The Requirements Plan

A requirements plan should be developed by the RA early—either during the proposal preparation phase or soon after a decision is made to proceed with a development project or task. The purpose of the requirements plan is to determine and document how the real requirements will be evolved and how the requirements-related activities in the system life cycle (listed and described above) will be addressed. Following is a list of suggested topics for this plan and a description of each topic:

> • *Purpose (of the requirements plan):* This was defined in the preceding paragraph.

> • *Contract/project summary:* A high-level summary of the objectives of the system or software should be provided. This section can be extracted from other documents such as a *vision and scope document* that may have been written previously to describe the overall intent.

> • *Background:* This section should describe the situation that led to the decision to develop the system or software. It should identify the major stakeholder groups—those who have an interest in the system, such as the customer (the person or organization providing the funds to pay for the project or its end products), various categories of users, developers, and major suppliers.

> • *Evolution of the requirements:* A *mechanism* should be agreed upon between the customers/users and the development team to review the stated requirements and evolve the real requirements. Customers may resist this effort, believing that they already have a "good" set of requirements. The RA should be familiar with industry experience concerning how many projects have failed and how many more have been seriously and negatively affected by a failure to invest in this critical step [1, p. 48]. A *mechanism* is a way to get something done or to achieve

---

2. See B. K. Clark's "Effects of Process Maturity on Development Effort," Center for Software Engineering, University of Southern California, 1999, at www. ralphyoung.net/goodarticles, for an excellent summary of the benefits of process improvement.

a result. The recommended mechanism to evolve the real requirements is a cooperative or joint team composed of one or a few representatives of the users and a similar number of technically proficient developers. The members of the *joint team* should review the requirements to ensure that they meet the criteria of a good requirement provided in Table 1.1. Also the rationale for each requirement (why it is needed) should be documented. Industry experience is that by taking this one step, up to *half* of the requirements can be eliminated.

> *Roles and responsibilities of the project's personnel involved in requirements-related activities:* Even on a *small project*, it's likely that more than one person will be involved with requirements-related activities. It's helpful to clarify and document these roles, so that everyone understands his or her unique and common responsibilities. For example, someone should be designated to provide requirements training (the content of this training is described in Chapter 5). Another person will be responsible for the automated requirements tool. Yet another person may have responsibility for the key processes to be utilized on the project, including the *requirements process*. Still another may be responsible for designing the architecture (the underlying structure of the system or software). Since the requirements and the architecture impact each other, a recommended requirements practice is to iterate the requirements and the architecture repeatedly—this results in stronger requirements and a more robust architecture [1, pp. 131–158].

Table 1.1   Criteria of a Good Requirement

Each Individual Requirement Should Be
Necessary: If the system can meet prioritized real needs without the requirement, it isn't necessary.
Feasible: The requirement is doable and can be accomplished within budget and schedule.
Correct: The facts related to the requirement are accurate, and it is technically and legally possible.
Concise: The requirement is stated simply.
Unambiguous: The requirement can be interpreted in only one way.
Complete: All conditions under which the requirement applies are stated, and it expresses a whole idea or statement.
Consistent: It is not in conflict with other requirements.
Verifiable: Implementation of the requirement in the system can be proved.
Traceable: The source of the requirement can be traced, and it can be tracked throughout the system (e.g., to the design, code, test, and documentation).
Allocated: The requirement is assigned to a component of the designed system.
Design independent: It does not pose a specific implementation solution.
Nonredundant: It is not a duplicate requirement.
Written using the standard construct: The requirement is stated as an imperative using "shall."
Assigned a unique identifier: Each requirement shall have a unique identifying number.
Devoid of escape clauses: Language should not include such phrases as "if," "when," "but," "except," "unless," and "although." Language should not be speculative or general (i.e., avoid wording such as "usually," "generally," "often," "normally," and "typically").

▶ *Definition of the requirements process to be used:* As noted above, a documented requirements process is essential. A process may be thought of as a flowchart (indicating the steps performed and the person or organization that performs each step) accompanied by a narrative PD that indicates, for example, the name of the process, its customers, inputs to the process, outputs from the process, tasks performed in the process, the person or organization performing each task, and some measures (metrics) that can be used to evaluate the quality of the products produced by the process and the performance of the process. Experience shows that it's a good practice to involve the major stakeholders of a process in its construction. This approach encourages understanding, completeness, and *buy-in* to the defined process, as well as commitment to using it.

▶ *Mechanisms, methods, techniques, and tools to be utilized:* Several examples of each category will be described throughout this book. Obviously, some are more appropriate in some cases than others, and some are particularly useful in specific situations. The specific mechanisms, methods, techniques, and tools should be determined and documented, and the project team should be familiarized with those selected and the rationale for their selection.

▶ *Integration of proven effective requirements practices:* Experience has shown that use of a set of proven effective requirements practices can make a huge difference on a project [1]. For example, the practice of investing time and effort to define the real customer needs has already been recommended. Recommended "best" requirements practices will be described throughout this book and are summarized in Chapter 6. Select and document a set of requirements practices that will serve your project well.

▶ *References:* There will be a set of documents that are key references for the requirements process. Examples include documents that describe system goals and objectives, lists of requirements of different users, standards that the customer has specified be applied, policies that are applicable, and so forth. These references should be listed, and the location where each can be accessed should be indicated.

▶ *Recommended strategy:* Based on analysis of the above information, a strategy should be developed and set forth to optimally leverage requirements-related aspects of the project. Elements of the strategy might include the following:

  ▶ The partnering strategy;[3]

---

3. The term "partnering" is often used to suggest a close, coordinated, effective working relationship. Here I refer to a defined process of partnership effort in a project. I encourage you to familiarize with the references at [6] and to consider use of the partnering process. You may find (as I have) that it holds one of the secrets to project success.

- The "upfront process" to be used (to understand real customer needs and the environment, understand and document the scope of the project, define external interfaces, define system components, and define the outline for specification of the system);

- Determining what drives the requirements (regulations; higher-level specifications; standards; policies; existing systems and processes; constraints, such as cost, schedule, technical viability; customer and user needs and expectations);

- Definition of a project requirements policy;

- Definition of the requirements process (flowchart and PD) (A sample requirements process is provided in [1] and on my Web site (www.ralphyoung.net). You may be able to utilize it to tailor a requirements process for your environment or project.);

- Mechanisms to be utilized (e.g., the joint team and others that are recommended in this book);

- Training concerning requirements for the project team (including the customer);

- Selection of an appropriate automated requirements tool and how it will be used;

- Definition of the target architecture;

- Plans to deal with new and changed requirements (e.g., use of a mechanism to control them, as well as versions, releases, and builds);

- Understanding of risks inherent to the requirements, as it's likely that lack of full understanding of some requirements creates major project risks;

- Definition of guidelines for system development based on requirements considerations.

- *Appendixes:* These might include the following:

  - Requirements process (flowcharts and PDs);

  - Partnering process approach [6];

  - Draft project requirements policy;

  - Action plans and timelines for needed efforts (e.g., selection of a requirements tool).

Factors Affecting Your Career Decisions

I recommend that you meet with your PM very early, perhaps even before your assignment to the project is finalized. Discuss with him or her perspectives concerning requirements. After digesting this book and my previous one, you should have a sufficient understanding of requirements practices to allow you to conclude whether you can be effective in your role.

▸ Does the PM believe that requirements, requirements practices, investing in the requirement process, controlling requirements changes and new requirements, and minimizing rework are important?

▸ Do you sense that he or she will support you in the many roles in which you can potentially contribute to the project (see Chapter 2)?

▸ Does he or she seem concerned about people, about motivating people, acknowledging their efforts, empowering them, and supporting them?

▸ Does he or she have a good reputation in the organization as a PM?

▸ Is he or she concerned about personal and professional growth?

▸ Is he or she willing to delegate responsibility?

The point is that you are about to commit a portion of your professional life to a project. Take the time and effort to satisfy yourself that your time will be well spent. You should perceive that a new position will provide you with learning experiences, opportunities to make valued and needed contributions, to work with peers whom you respect, to derive self-satisfaction and fulfillment, and to have fun at work.

A Comment Concerning Small Projects

Many people feel that the approach that is used on medium and large projects is an inappropriate guide for small projects—that the practices, policies, mechanisms, methods, techniques, and tools can't be applied. My experience is that professional judgment can be used to scale down and apply key practices to achieve good results on small projects. I encourage members of small projects, tasks, or teams to benefit from what they can learn from the experiences of larger projects by tailoring the approach, rather than use smallness as an excuse for not taking advantage of industry lessons. See [7] for additional insights.

Summary

This chapter has focused on the importance of requirements and provided an introduction to the critical role of the RA (the roles of the RA are further detailed in the next chapter, and the skills and characteristics of an effective RA are described in Chapter 3). It should be apparent from the material presented already that there is great power and effect in leveraging requirements-related activities in engineering and computing. An alarming 53% of industry's investment in technical development projects is a casualty of cost overruns and failed projects. Major contributing factors are a lack of user input (13%), incomplete requirements (12%), and changing requirements (12%).[4] The user community and particularly project management do not realize the value of investing in the requirements process. I suggest that it is not "okay" for an RA to be aware of this and not to discuss the implications with his or her PM. As a concerned professional, you have the responsibility to bring these facts and your recommended approach to your PM and to ask him or her to support an effective requirements process that incorporates effective requirements practices. RAs, engineers, and managers are in a strategic position to improve industry's performance. This book provides focused and specific guidance that can have a huge payoff. By applying the approach recommended in this book, you can have a very positive impact on your project and organization.

Case Study

This first case study reports on a workshop involving facilitated discussions among a group of PMs concerning the top reasons they believed systems and software projects had difficulties, based on their experience. Here are the top reasons that were reported by a set of PMs:

1. The requirements for the project are not explicit.

2. Requirements changes are made/accepted without addressing the concomitant cost, schedule, and quality impacts.

3. A requirements process is not used.

4. There is no mechanism (such as a joint team) to reach agreement on the definition of the requirements and to manage the requirements through the project life cycle.

5. The "real" customer needs are not defined.

6. There is no mechanism to maintain communication between the parties involved in the project.

7. Known, familiar, proven methods, techniques, and tools are not utilized.

8. The customer is not involved as a partner throughout the project life cycle.

I recommend that you keep these reasons in mind as you digest this book. Ascertain what you might be able to do or to recommend that will help overcome these problems.

---

4. The Standish Group, *The CHAOS Report* (Dennis, MA: The Standish Group International, 1995). See https://secure.standishgroup.com/reports/reports.php?rid=1.

References

[1]   Young, R. R., *Effective Requirements Practices*, Boston, MA: Addison-Wesley, 2001.

[2]   Hooks, I. F., and K. A. Farry, *Customer-Centered Products: Creating Successful Products through Smart Requirements Management*, New York: AMACOM, 2001.

[3]   Paulk, M. C., et al., *Capability Maturity Model for Software*, Version 1.1, February, 1993, SEI, Carnegie-Mellon University, Pittsburgh, PA, 1993.

[4]   CMMI Web site at www.sei.cmu.edu/cmmi.

[5]   Robertson, S., and J. Robertson, *Mastering the Requirements Process,* Harlow, UK: Addison-Wesley, 1999.

[6]   Markert, C., "Partnering: Unleashing the Power of Teamwork," 2002, briefing available from markert@facilitationcenter.com. See also Frank Carr et al., *Partnering in Construction: A Practical Guide to Project Success,* Chicago: American Bar Association Publishing, 1999.

[7]   See Paulk, M. C., "Using the Software CMM with Good Judgment," ASQ *Software Quality Professional* 1(3) (June 1999): 19–29, at www.sei.cmu.edu/publications/articles/paulk/judgment.html.

The Roles of the RA

Chapter 1 emphasized the importance of requirements. It was noted that customers, managers, and developers undervalue requirements engineering. The RA is in a strategic position to improve the practices in use on projects and in the organization. The analyst can have a positive impact on project success and also facilitate the organization's improvement results by performing in several roles. Making the RA's role explicit contributes to a smoother process. The RA's role can be linked readily to business goals, such as increasing customer satisfaction with the delivered work products; reducing the time to market of products; meeting cost, schedule, and quality objectives; and utilizing the human resources of the enterprise more effectively. The RA's role needs to be understood and valued in the minds of PMs and the technical communities (both computing and engineering). Table 2.1 summarizes the roles of the RA, noting the life-cycle phases in which each role is performed.

Suggested Roles of the RA

1. *Work collaboratively with customers, users, and system architects and designers to identify the real requirements for a planned system or software development effort to define the problem that needs to be solved.*

The concept of the real requirements was explained in Chapter 1. Experience has shown that the number one problem in requirements engineering is the failure to identify the real requirements prior to initiating system development activities. Anyone who has had some experience in developing systems or software will agree that identifying the real requirements is a significant problem. With respect to this role, the RA needs to create an awareness of the problem and also provide a

15

Table 2.1   RA Roles and Life-Cycle Activities

RA Role	System Initiation	System Analysis and Design	System Component Design	System Implementation	System Integration, Test, and Evaluation	System Operations and Support
1. Work collaboratively with customers, users, and system architects and designers to identify the real requirements for a planned system or software development effort to define the problem that needs to be solved.	X	X	A	A	A	A
2. Work effectively with customers and users to manage new and changed requirements so that the project stays under control. Install a mechanism to control changes.			X	X	X	X
3. Be alert to new technologies that may help.			X	X		X
4. Facilitate the project in reusing artifacts and achieving repeatability.	X	X	X	X		X
5. Assist the project and its customers in envisioning a growth path from the first release or version of a product through a set of staged releases to the "ultimate system or products."	X	X	X	X	X	X
6. Advise the project (and customer) of methods, techniques, and automated tools that are available to best support requirements-related project work and activities.	X	X				X
7. Use metrics to measure, track, and control requirements-related project work activities and results.	B	X	X	X	X	X
8. Be able to facilitate discussions and to mediate conflicts.	X	X	X	X	X	X
9. Study the domain of the area in which the system or software is being used.	X	X				X

The life-cycle phases shown in the top row are not intended as a recommendation for a waterfall life-cycle model. Rather, the use of the phase terminology is intended to depict the activity being performed; this activity is equally applicable to virtually all life-cycle models (e.g., spiral, rapid application development, incremental, rational unified process), although the life-cycle phase names will differ.

A—Continue to identify real requirements for subsequent releases and revisions, maintaining configuration control.

B—System initiation or "project or task startup" is a confusing time. The experienced RA will be able to lend assistance. For example, the RA should provide a briefing to the project team that includes the topics noted in Table 5.4.

Source: Richard Raphael.

suggested strategy to overcome the problem. This is a concrete example of a situation that we know can be improved, but most often we don't act on this knowledge. We are impatient to get started on the so-called real work of programming. We are content to allow the development effort to proceed without taking the extra effort to evolve the real requirements. Note that I have used the word "evolve." This work involves more than identifying requirements. The essential task is to use the stated requirements articulated by customers and users as a base, couple this with a thorough understanding of the business objectives, and iterate to evolve requirements that meet the criteria for a good requirement and address prioritized real needs for the system or software. Activities involved in performing this work include the following:

- Identifying the stated needs of customers and users. This involves reviewing things previously written about the proposed system, interviewing customers and users, studying relevant legislation, and so forth.

- Studying the business objectives for the proposed effort.

- Collaborating with customers and users in a joint or cooperative environment to analyze the stated requirements, evolve better requirements, and prioritize them (see the suggested techniques that follow).

- Involving system architects in requirements development. Iterating the draft or proposed requirements will result in a candidate architecture with better requirements and a more robust architecture. For example, systems need to be able to accommodate changing business needs. The architecture should be designed and developed accordingly, or else the delivered system soon will be outdated.

- Utilizing an industry-strength automated requirements tool to support this work.

The RA should work within the project organization to win the support of the PM in gaining commitment to investing added time and effort to evolve the real requirements. Here is a great opportunity for the RA to take responsibility and, drawing upon industry experience, convince project management and developers to invest more time and effort in the requirements process. Fortunately, data is available to help us manage by fact rather than by intuition or the way we have always done things. Refer to *Effective Requirements Practices* [1, p. 62] for these data.

Consider using collaborative requirements elicitation techniques that work well in group sessions. Examples of good requirements elicitation techniques are requirements workshops, electronic-based groupware or electronic collaborative development tools, high-level data flow diagrams, high-level IDEF0 diagrams (especially for business modeling), and high-level use case diagrams (especially to distinguish requirements that are outside the system versus behavior expected from the system). All of these work well on a whiteboard, are easy to understand, and allow everyone present to participate. See Dean Leffingwell and Don Widrig's *Managing Software Requirements: A Unified Approach* [2] for good discussions of these and other techniques and how to use them. David Hay provides a useful comparison of techniques that can be used in *Requirements Analysis: From Business Views to Architecture* (see [3, p. 194] and the preceding discussion).

2.   *Work effectively with customers and users to manage new and changed requirements so that the project stays under control. Install a mechanism to control changes.*

The next most serious problem in requirements engineering (after the failure to identify the real requirements) is failure to control requirements that are identified after system development (programming) begins, both new requirements and changes to existing requirements. Here we distinguish between critical requirements (those that would have an impact on cost, schedule, or the development effort if changed) and noncritical requirements, such as a derived requirement that further defines the system being built, but serves to clarify a higher-level requirement and does not affect cost, schedule, or functionality. All stakeholders should welcome a "no-impact" requirement that further clarifies the system.

Again, we have data from industry experience to guide our actions: a 20% change in requirements will result in a doubling of project-development costs [4]. Therefore, it's critical that a mechanism be put in place to evaluate and adjudicate changes to requirements. Without an effective mechanism to control changes to requirements, the project will soon be out of control in terms of schedule and cost. Several things must be done:

▸ The importance of controlling changes to requirements must be explained to customers, users, and developers so that the partnership commitment to project success is maintained.

▸ Developers must be trained not to accept unauthorized requirements changes. All requests for changes, no matter how trivial, must be funneled through the change control mechanism.

▸ The change control mechanism should be a joint team that includes empowered decision makers representing the customer and the developer. The joint team should meet frequently enough to have a reasonable number of change requests to consider. A target metric of 0.5% requirements volatility is recommended to guide decisions made by the joint team once a baseline of validated requirements has been established.[1] "Whoa," you say, "that's not much!" Right! This is another

---

1. Chapter 10 of *Effective Requirements Practices* provides several ideas, suggestions, and recommendations for controlling requirements changes.

reason to invest the needed time to evolve the real requirements prior to starting the development activities.

-) Partnering with your customer, evolve ways to deal with change. We know the world is changing while we're developing the system. What are some ways to deal with this without jeopardizing project success? Consider using releases, versions, and upgrades. Package increments of requirements upgrades and changes in subsequent releases or system upgrades.

-) Ensure that your contract provides for additional time and budgeting for all changes. This is a mechanism to maintain good relationships throughout the contract work—to partner for success. Changes cost time and money. This should be recognized up front and reflected in the contract.

3. *Be alert to new technologies that may help.*

A role that is often underutilized is advising our customers concerning evolving technology. While this is not solely the responsibility of the requirements analysts or engineers, many involved in developing systems for customers would be well advised to spend additional time and effort learning about new technologies and how they can be applied to our work. Customers are typically focused on what the system needs to do. We can serve them best by being familiar with evolving technologies that improve *how* the needed system is designed. This suggests that RAs will benefit from having system designers review their work products. Concurrently with requirements elaboration, involve a small team of designers to review the real requirements for cost, schedule, technology, and risk impacts. Use trade studies—the Decision Analysis Resolution (DAR) process in CMMI® terminology—to evolve alternatives. Keep the customer involved in these activities, so that when opportunities arise, the customer is there to partner with you in making recommendations for decisions. An excellent reference that describes the process of utilizing new technologies is Everett M. Rogers's *Diffusion of Innovations* (4th ed.) [5].

4. *Facilitate the project's reuse of artifacts and achieving repeatability.*

There has been a lot of discussion in the industry literature about reuse. Reuse has two meanings: (1) to take object X (e.g., an object, subroutine, or COTS software) that was done by Y and use it directly in another project, and (2) to tailor[2] a developed work product (a specification, a plan, or process, for example). Many organizations have invested in reuse strategies only to conclude that they are not viable or practical. Others are wary of

---

2. By "tailoring," we mean modifying, extracting pieces from, elaborating, or adapting a process or document for another use. Reuse of tailored artifacts saves time and money and is an advantage of a process-oriented approach.

reuse because they believe it precludes unprecedented solutions and incorporates the errors of the reused work products.

We can consider requirements themselves as reusable artifacts. Books that discuss reusable requirement patterns include *Data Model Patterns: Conventions of Thought* [6] (for a relational viewpoint) by David C. Hay, *Analysis Patterns* (for an object oriented viewpoint) by Martin Fowler [7], and *Design Patterns* by Eric Gamma, et al. [8]. Michael Jackson's problem frames (described in his book by the same name [9]) are in essence highly abstract requirements patterns that can be connected, nested, and built into real world models. The point is that many requirements are not unique; they have already been identified in someone else's environment and problem space.

I have found in my writing activities that starting with an example work product gives me ideas about format, structure, content, and resources to reference or contact. An example work product you might want to consider is a requirements plan. As emphasized in Chapter 1, I advocate development of a requirements plan for any system or software development effort. This idea may be new to you, and it would be very helpful and instructive to review one developed previously in order to consider its potential value to your work. Another example from my experience is reusing documented processes. If the organization or another project has a documented process for doing something, why not tailor it as needed and then reuse it, rather than create one's own process? Others who have performed the process in practice have incorporated their experience and the lessons they have learned using it. Related to this is the value of peer reviews. I advocate a peer review of every work product. (The extent of the peer review—the number of people requested to review the work product and the time invested to perform the peer review and report on defects and make suggestions—is a function of the importance of the work product.) If one can reuse the peer review process and checklists of another organization, this provides a jump-start in getting the process designed, accepted, deployed, implemented, and institutionalized.

An Example of Process Reuse

In teaching requirements courses and tutorials, I'm always interested to learn how many of the participants are using a documented requirements process on their project or in their organization. Typically, this turns out to be 15% to 20% of the participants. A sample requirements process is provided in *Effective Requirements Practices* [1, pp. 110–118]. This process has been tailored, deployed, and implemented on more than 50 projects. Its integration with the system architecture process is described later in the book [1, pp. 136–146].

Suggestion: Tailor this sample requirements process for your project or organization. Involve the stakeholders to make the changes that best serve their needs. Provide both flowcharts and narrative PDs as described in *Effective Requirements Practices*. Periodically update the documented process with continuous improvement ideas and suggestions.

5. *Assist the project and its customers in envisioning a growth path from the first release or version of a product through a set of staged releases to the ultimate system or product.*

This role is related to role 3. The RA can serve an important and valuable role in helping customers to envision and evolve a series of releases or versions of products. This approach is particularly appropriate in the situation in which requirements are not well understood at the outset or the requirements are changing rapidly. This suggests that an "incremental development approach" should be used, in which the full system is implemented over a period of time through increments of delivered functionality. In a sense, no system is ever done, so we have to help everyone see system development as a journey. Independently of the system development methodology used (waterfall, incremental, spiral, evolutionary, etc.), there has to be an agreed-upon process for managing changes and determining the scope of individual projects. No matter how much discussion and testing is done, there are some missing requirements that won't be discovered until the system is in production.

6. *Advise the project (and customer) of methods, techniques, and automated tools that are available to best support requirements-related project work and activities.*

This is an important role. Experience has shown that methods and techniques vary in their applicability and effectiveness and that often automated tools purchased by projects and organizations are not used or are underutilized. Chapter 11 of *Effective Requirements Practices* [1] reports on industry experience and provides several recommendations. Chapter 8 of *Effective Requirements Practices* [1] recommends that the methods and techniques that are used by a project be familiar to the project participants and proven in their respective industry. It's not advisable to undertake a project with unproven, unfamiliar methods and techniques. The development work is challenging enough without introducing the complexity of methods or techniques that are not familiar and haven't been used successfully on previous projects in the organization. At the project level, the team should stick with the tools, processes, and techniques with which its members are familiar. At the organizational level, the project should try to use the tools, processes, and techniques that are known and proven in the organization. When contractors are brought into an existing effort, they should adapt to the tools that the customer already has in place (assuming they are working effectively). If the last five projects were done with tool X, and everyone is satisfied with the usefulness of the tool, then when you arrive, there are good reasons to use it. Note that a resource issue may be involved. Ideally, an RA would be a leveraged resource, moving from project to project and taking her experience with her. However, often in practice, a project team is built (or already exists) and someone from the current team with domain knowledge is tasked with being the RA. While tried-and-true techniques and tools exist, they may be unfamiliar to this person, requiring a lengthy and sometimes painful learning curve, with significant disadvantages to the project. This argues for the organization to provide a set of experienced RAs that will provide a high return on the investment made to identify them, train them, and provide them with experience.

I also recommend challenging customer directions to use specific methods or techniques that are not familiar to the project team or not previously proven in practice. For example, a customer might direct that an object-oriented (OO) development approach be employed (see [10] for thoughtful guidelines on this topic) or that a particular automated tool or tool suite be used. It's valuable to be in a position to be able to advise your project and your customer of the methods, techniques, and automated tools that will best support the specific development situation. Draw on industry experience and don't pretend that "everything will work out."

7. *Use metrics to measure, track, and control requirements-related project work activities and results.*

The industry literature concerning metrics is vast. I'd estimate that perhaps 20% of it provides helpful counsel. It's easy to get into a situation of performing measurement activities for their own sake, rather than to help evaluate project work and take corrective actions. I recommend using a few useful metrics. I have developed the following axiom in my work over the years:

> The things that are measured and tracked and that management pays attention to are the ones that improve.

This suggests that it's not sufficient to have a few useful metrics—they must be tracked, and they must be used by management to guide project decisions.

There is a set of measures or metrics that should be used by all projects. See *Effective Requirements Practices* [1, pp. 255–261] for specific suggestions.

There is another level of sophistication that should be used by mature projects and organizations. As used here, "mature" means that processes have been defined, documented, implemented, used, institutionalized, and continuously improved over a period of at least two to four years. This involves quantitative management (QM) of cost, schedule, quality, and process metrics and baselines in support of specific business objectives. It is fulfilling to see projects and organizations move from the situation in which QM is not well understood to one in which QM is effectively used to achieve business objectives. This is especially satisfying to process engineers, because executives can see first hand the value of process improvement in meeting business needs.

8. *Be able to facilitate discussions and to mediate conflicts.*

This role stresses the "people skills" of the RA. We've learned that being well qualified technically is important, but that it's also necessary to have strong, well-refined people skills. Experience has shown that two heads are better than one—whenever we take the time to explore ideas and approaches with others, we get even better ideas and approaches! Ergo, we can drop the point of view that "we know best." And we can make great use of this principle by becoming good facilitators and mediators. There are courses available to assist (e.g., negotiating skills, team building, communications, relationships, and leading). Much can be gained by practicing these skills in our daily work. Having a "win-win" perspective is helpful—in fact, Barry Boehm et al. have developed a win-win requirements development approach in work done at the University of Southern California. See http://sunset.usc.edu/research/WINWIN/winwin_main.html.

9.   *Study the domain of the area in which the system or software is being used.*

Be able to grasp, abstract, and express ideas quickly in the users' language. If the RA does not understand the user domain almost as well as the users do, he risks limiting his role to that of an order taker. I have seen different groups come and go whose specialty was communication, consensus building, and so forth. Populating those groups was a set of people who were trained facilitators, but who were not technically proficient. They moved from project to project so frequently that they never achieved any deep domain understanding. For example, what if, on a network communications project, the only way an RA can explain any concept to the users is by giving analogies with building military aircraft? Answer: reduced effectiveness and credibility.

Summary

The RA performs several important roles on a project and in an organization. Nine important roles were identified and described in this chapter. The first two are paramount and essential to project success. Accordingly, study these, become proficient in them, and assist your project and organization in adopting, implementing, and institutionalizing related practices. Organizations should consider taking specific steps to develop and leverage their RAs, such as (1) ensuring that experienced RAs are assigned to each project; (2) providing appropriate training for RAs; (3) assigning experienced RAs to mentor new employees, junior RAs, and interns; and (4) having an organizational requirements working group to share expertise and provide a resource to the organization. The RA should be a trained, experienced, and strong performer. Unfortunately, I've seen many cases where the new employee or the summer intern is dispatched "to get the requirements." The role of the RA needs to be understood and valued in the minds of PMs and the technical community. At this point, you may feel overwhelmed with your responsibilities, as Figure 2.1 suggests. Be assured that with study and experience, you will provide a very positive contribution to the efforts that you support!

Figure 2.1 The challenges of the RA.

Case Study

This is the story of a project that failed because neither the customer nor the contractor knew how to handle requirements. It is a negative example. Although the people involved were professionals and were well intentioned, things went horribly wrong because effective requirements practices were not applied.

The project approach was one that is used with alarmingly frequency and can be characterized as "get started programming and we will find out what they want as we proceed." The customer, a military organization, handed the contractor a shelf-load of rules and regulations ("regs") saying, "These are the requirements." The programmers, all on-site employees of a contractor, were ready to start, and they did. Representatives of the military organization were aware of the project, but they did not participate in it until it was time to review the finished code.

While the code was being written, the contractor undertook to convert the regs to a set of shall statements. This was faithfully and painstakingly done, but as the code emerged, it was found that the verification of the shall statements—matching them to parts of the different code modules—was virtually impossible. They simply did not map.

Another complication encountered was a complete breakdown in communication between the contractor and the subcontractor producing the code. It wasn't that they did not understand each other; they simply did not communicate. The subcontractor viewed any inquiries as interference, and in an atmosphere of hostility, communication simply died.

As the code came into review by the customer, the military representatives were heard to say again and again, "No, that's what we do, but that's not how we do it." And as the modules came into test by the contractor, they failed repeatedly. The right things had been written the wrong way, and they did not work.

After months of struggle, the first of about 20 modules was almost ready for release. It was still a little shaky, and lots of people were unhappy with it, but it was close to acceptance from the contractor's perspective. However, the customer gave up because relationships between the two parties had become broken during the code development period. Not only was the process broken, but also the platform and the operating system were outdated and inadequate. Three million lines of code were abandoned, the hardware was scrapped, and the whole project was started all over again.

What had gone wrong?

- There was no partnership between the customer, contractor, and subcontractor.

- There was no communication.

- There was not an atmosphere of mutual respect.

- There was no workable requirements plan.

- There was no mechanism for joint resolution of problems.

The project was begun anew, on a different platform, in a different language, by a different mix of subcontractors. An improved set of requirements practices was used, which included the following:

- Mechanisms (similar to the joint team discussed in Chapter 1) to facilitate partnering, identifying real needs and requirements, and prioritization of requirements;

- An approach that involved the users in the development effort, provided for collaboration with them, and gained the buy-in of the users to the project approach;

- Use of methods including use cases that facilitated understanding and effective communication of user needs and requirements;

- Incorporating appropriate and updated technology that better served the customer and the users.

References

[1]   Young, R. R., *Effective Requirements Practices,* Boston, MA: Addison-Wesley, 2001.

[2]   Leffingwell, D., and D. Widrig, *Managing Software Requirements: A Unified Approach*, Reading, MA: Addison-Wesley, 2000.

[3]   Hay, D. C., *Requirements Analysis: From Business Views to Architecture,* Upper Saddle River, NJ: Prentice Hall, 2003.

[4] Hooks, I., "Writing Good Requirements: A One-Day Tutorial," Sponsored by the Washington Metropolitan Area (WMA) Chapter of the International Council on Systems Engineering (INCOSE), McLean, VA, Compliance Automation, Inc., June 1997.

[5] Rogers, E. M., *Diffusion of Innovations*, 4th ed., New York: The Free Press, 1995.

[6] Hay, D. C., *Data Model Patterns: Conventions of Thought*, New York: Dorset House, 1996.

[7] Fowler, M., *Analysis Patterns: Reusable Object Models*, Reading, MA: Addison-Wesley, 1996.

[8] Gamma, E., et al., *Design Patterns*, Reading, MA: Addison-Wesley, 1995.

[9] Jackson, M., *Problem Frames: Analyzing and Structuring Software Development Problems*, London, UK: Addison-Wesley, 2001.

[10] Webster, B. F., *Pitfalls of Object-Oriented Development*, New York: Hungry Minds, Inc., 1995.

CHAPTER

3

Contents

Skills and Characteristics of an Effective RA

This chapter describes the desired skills and characteristics of an effective RA. As emphasized in the previous chapter, the RA fulfills several critical project roles. On many projects, the RA is a part-time individual who is otherwise engaged as PM, product manager, system engineer, developer, or in some other capacity. On other projects, there may be a full time RA or even several RAs and a requirements manager. The size of the project and the perceived complexity of the needed requirements-related activities, as well as the funding available, are the major determinants of the number of RAs and their needed skill levels. The roles of the RA may be divided among those available to do the needed work, also considering current skills, interests, and desired development needs. Whatever the situation, RAs should consider themselves key resources, able to contribute to the project in the roles described in the previous chapter. The RA requires a unique blend of skills that reflects knowledge and real-world orientation, as well as the ability to interpret and satisfy customers', users', and management's intent. Some of the skills are intrinsic in the way an individual works (such as analytical and interpersonal skills) and others are learned (e.g., facilitation skills).

Skills of the RA

As a framework for this chapter, refer to Table 3.1, RA's Skills Matrix.[1] A list of RA skills is provided. Three levels of RAs are shown:

[1]. With thanks to senior RA Michael Davis of Northrop Grumman IT for providing this artifact. The responsibility for modifications to the original version is mine.

Table 3.1 RA's Skills Matrix

Line Number	RA's Skills Matrix	Reference	Entry/ Junior-Level Analyst	Mid-Level Analyst	Senior-Level Analyst
1	Types of requirements	Ch. 4	K	X	X
2	Criteria of a good requirement	Ch. 1	K	X	X
3	Customer/user involvement with requirements joint team	Ch. 1	K	X	X
4	Identifying real requirements (from the stated requirements)	Ch. 1	K	X	X
5	Anticipating and controlling requirements changes	Ch. 1	K	X	X
6	Office automation tools	Tutorials	X	X	X
7	References concerning requirements (books, articles, standards)	See Bibliography	K	X	X
8	Requirements attributes	Ch. 5	K	X	X
9	Requirements baseline	Ch. 6	K	X	X
10	Training in systems engineering (e.g., life cycles, risk management)	Ch. 5	K	X	X
11	Requirements justification/rationale	Ch. 5	K	X	X
12	Requirements management tools (e.g., DOORS, RequisitePro)	Ch. 5	K	X	X
13	Requirements peer review/inspection/walk-through	Ch. 5	K	X	X
14	Requirements syntax	WBR, Ch. 7	K	X	X
15	Requirements traceability	Ch. 5	K	X	X
16	Requirements verification and validation (V&V)	Ch. 5	K	X	X
17	System/subsystem/software-level requirements	Ch. 5	K	X	X
18	Developing and using metrics for requirements activities/processes	Ch. 2	K	X	X
19	Technical writing of requirements deliverables (RTM, SRS, IRS)	Ch. 4	K	X	X
20	Development, implementation, and use of requirements processes	Ch. 5		K	X
21	Familiarity with Microsoft Project	Tutorial		K	X
22	QA of requirements	Ch. 9		K	X
23	Requirements allocation (to components, applications, packages)	Ch. 4		K	X
24	Requirements change control and change notification	Ch. 6		K	X
25	Requirements repository	Ch. 5		K	X
26	Requirements errors (missing, incorrect, infeasible, out of scope)	Ch. 6		K	X
27	Requirements defect notification	Ch. 6		K	X
28	Requirements dissemination to customers/users/developers/testers	Ch. 4		K	X

Table 3.1 RA's Skills Matrix (continued)

Line Number	RA's Skills Matrix	Reference	Entry/ Junior-Level Analyst	Mid-Level Analyst	Senior-Level Analyst
29	Requirements elicitation	Ch. 5		K	X
30	Requirements identification	Ch. 5		K	X
31	Use case development (with customer/user and based on user's guides)	Ch. 7		K	X
32	Requirements in customer/user decision-making process	Ch. 1		K	X
33	Requirements interaction with CM	Ch. 6		X	X
34	Requirements negotiation	SL, EG1		X	X
35	Requirements ownership	WBR, EG2		X	X
36	Requirements prioritization	Ch. 5		X	X
37	Requirements review board (RRB)/configuration review board (CRB)/configuration control board (CCB)	Ch. 7		X	X
38	Requirements rough-order-of-magnitude (ROM) costs	Ch. 7		X	X
39	Requirements specifications	Ch. 7		X	X
40	Evaluating requirements for risks	Ch. 7			X
41	Training the requirements processes	Ch. 5			X
42	Requirements impact estimation (IE) table	Gilb			X

Knowledge of = K   Experience with = X

References:

REH = Young, R. R., *The Requirements Engineering Handbook,* Norwood, MA: Artech House, 2004.
WBR = Alexander, I. F., and R. Stevens, *Writing Better Requirements,* Boston: Addison-Wesley, 2002.
SL = Lauesen, S. *Software Requirements: Styles and Techniques,* pp. 346–347.
EG1 = Gottesdiener, E., *Requirements by Collaboration: Workshops for Defining Needs,* Reading, MA: Addison-Wesley, 2002, pp. 122–128.
EG2 = *Gottesdiener, E., Requirements by Collaboration: Workshops for Defining Needs, Reading,* MA: Addison-Wesley, 2002, pp. 89–94.
Gilb: See material at www.result-planning.com.

    1.   Entry/junior-level analyst;

    2.   Mid-level analyst;

    3.   Senior-level analyst.

A "K" is used in this table to suggest that knowledge of the skill is needed at a particular level of analyst expertise. An "X" suggests that experience in using the skill is needed at a particular level. A mapping is provided to sections in this book or to other sources where each skill is addressed. Additional references are provided in those places.

As with any framework or model, use this matrix as a guide, not as a specification. It will help you evaluate your suitability for a project role and provide a guide to and resource for strengthening and improving your skills.

Obviously, one could add other skills. However, the matrix serves as a guide and suggests that there is a lot to learn in order to be an effective RA. It is one thing to read about (gain knowledge of) skills and quite another thing to garner experience in applying the skills in a project environment that involves actual customers and users.

A junior or entry-level analyst (those with less than two years of experience) should be familiar with the following:

- The types of requirements (described in detail in the next chapter);

- The criteria of a good requirement (provided in Chapter 1);

- Office automation tools [e.g., Microsoft (MS) Office or Corel WordPerfect suite];

- The concept of using a requirements process;

- Some of the references concerning requirements-related activities;

- The purpose of requirements verification, and so forth.

She should understand that a rationale should be provided for each requirement (why the requirement is needed in the system or software).

A mid-level analyst (those with two to four years of experience) should have knowledge of more of the aspects and activities of requirements engineering, coupled with additional experience in applying this knowledge. High on this list are requirements activities involving customers and users (such as the concept of a joint team), utilizing a requirements process, and familiarity with an industry-strength requirements tool. The mid-level analyst should be proficient with peer reviews and inspections and should ensure that all of her own work products are peer reviewed. She should understand the value of bidirectional traceability of the requirements and be learning how to develop a requirements traceability matrix (RTM).

A senior-level analyst (those with five or more years of experience performing requirements-related activities) should have both knowledge of and experience with using all of the skills in the matrix. She should be familiar with all of the roles described in the previous chapter and have well-developed interpersonal skills and characteristics as described later in this chapter. She should understand the value and importance of independent QA and have a thorough understanding of CM activities. She should be able to recommend and use requirements metrics and be able to apply metrics to requirements processes. She should be able to provide training sessions for more junior RAs and for other members of the project team. She should have a good familiarity with systems engineering and the system life cycle and an understanding of the many requirements-related activities that need to be performed throughout the system life cycle.

Figure 3.1 summarizes the progression of the RA.

Another important document is the RA's position or job description, provided in Table 3.2.[2]

This is a concise and useful summary of the role of the RA. It describes the position, summarizes skills that are needed (although not in as much detail or precision as Figure 3.1), indicates knowledge that is needed, suggests several responsibilities, indicates some measures of performance, and provides three useful references on which this artifact is based. I suggest that you utilize this artifact to clarify your role and to develop position requisitions of prospective RAs. Tailor it to reflect your responsibilities. Utilize it in your performance reviews to discuss professional-development activities that will enhance your skills with your manager.

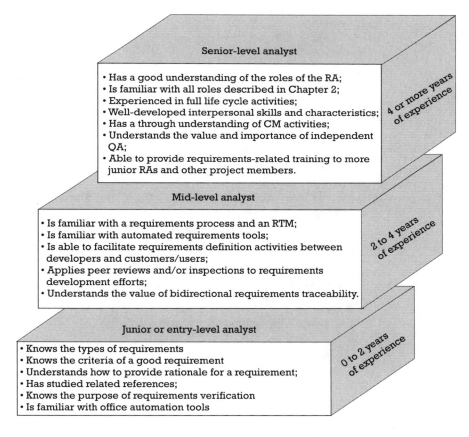

Senior-level analyst
- Has a good understanding of the roles of the RA;
- Is familiar with all roles described in Chapter 2;
- Experienced in full life cycle activities;
- Well-developed interpersonal skills and characteristics;
- Has a through understanding of CM activities;
- Understands the value and importance of independent QA;
- Able to provide requirements-related training to more junior RAs and other project members.

4 or more years of experience

Mid-level analyst
- Is familiar with a requirements process and an RTM;
- Is familiar with automated requirements tools;
- Is able to facilitate requirements definition activities between developers and customers/users;
- Applies peer reviews and/or inspections to requirements development efforts;
- Understands the value of bidirectional requirements traceability.

2 to 4 years of experience

Junior or entry-level analyst
- Knows the types of requirements
- Knows the criteria of a good requirement
- Understands how to provide rationale for a requirement;
- Has studied related references;
- Knows the purpose of requirements verification
- Is familiar with office automation tools

0 to 2 years of experience

Figure 3.1 Professional growth of the RA is based on cumulative experiences. (*Adapted from:* Michael Davis.)

2. With thanks to Karl Wiegers for allowing me to participate in the development of versions of this artifact.

Table 3.2 RA Job Description

Description	The RA or engineer is the individual who has the primary responsibility to elicit, analyze, validate, specify, verify, and manage the real needs of the project stakeholders, including customers and end users. The RA/engineer is also known as a requirements manager, business analyst, system analyst, or, simply, analyst. The RA serves as the conduit between the customer community and the software development team through which requirements flow.
	An RA is involved at some level throughout the entire system or software development life cycle. Upon establishment of the requirements baseline, the focus is shifted towards the management of the requirements specification and verifying the fulfillment of all requirements.
	The requirements engineering function is a project role, not necessarily a job title. The role may be performed by a dedicated RA or split among multiple team members who have other primary job functions, such as a PM or product developer. The RA is responsible for ensuring that the tasks are performed properly.
Skills Needed	Interviewing skills to talk with individuals and groups about their needs and ask the right questions to surface essential requirements information.
	Listening skills to understand what people say and to detect what they might be hesitant to say.
	Analytical skills to evaluate critically the information gathered from multiple sources, reconcile conflicts, decompose high-level information into details, abstract up from low-level information to a more general understanding, distinguish presented user requests from the underlying true needs, and distinguish solution ideas from requirements.
	Facilitation skills to lead requirements elicitation workshops.
	Observational skills to validate data obtained via other techniques and expose new areas for elicitation.
	Writing skills to communicate information effectively to customers, marketing, managers, and technical staff.
	Organizational skills to work with the vast array of information gathered during elicitation and analysis and to cope with rapidly changing information.
	Interpersonal skills to help negotiate priorities and to resolve conflicts among project stakeholders (such as customers, product management, and engineering).
	Modeling skills to represent requirements information in graphical forms that augment textual representations in natural language, including using modeling languages already established in the development organization.
Knowledge Needed	An understanding of contemporary requirements elicitation, analysis, specification, verification, and management practices and the ability to apply them in practice.
	Familiarity with requirements engineering tools and other resources.
	An understanding of how to practice requirements engineering according to several software development life cycles in a team environment.
	Knowledge of product management concepts and how enterprise software products are positioned and developed.
	Application domain knowledge is a plus to have credibility with user representatives and be able to work effectively with them.
Responsibilities	Work with the PM, product manager, or project sponsor to document the product's vision and scope.
	Identify project stakeholders and user classes, document user class characteristics, and identify appropriate representatives for each user class and negotiate their responsibilities.

Table 3.2   RA Job Description (continued)

Responsibilities	Elicit requirements using interviews, document analysis, requirements workshops, storyboards, surveys, site visits, business process descriptions, use cases, scenarios, event lists, business analysis, competitive product analysis, task and workflow analysis, and viewpoints.
	Write requirements specifications according to standard templates, using natural language simply, clearly, unambiguously, and concisely.
	Decompose high-level business and user requirements into functional requirements and quality requirements, specified in an appropriate level of detail suitable for use by those who must base their work on the requirements.
	Define quality attributes, external interfaces, constraints, and other nonfunctional requirements.
	Represent requirements using alternative views, such as analysis models (diagrams), prototypes, or scenarios, where appropriate.
	Lead requirements analysis and verification, ensuring that requirement statements are complete, consistent, concise, comprehensible, traceable, feasible, unambiguous, and verifiable and that they conform to standards.
	Participate in requirements prioritization.
	Participate in peer reviews and inspections of requirements documents.
	Participate in peer reviews of work products derived from requirements specifications to ensure that the requirements were interpreted correctly.
	Enter, manipulate, and report on requirements stored in a commercial requirements tool.
	Define requirement attributes and facilitate their use throughout the project.
	Manage requirements traceability information and track requirements status throughout the project.
	Identify requirements errors and defects, and write requirements defect identification and notification reports.
	Manage changes to baselined requirements through effective application of change control processes and tools.
	Establish and implement effective requirements practices, including use and continuous improvement of a requirements process.
	Assist with the development of the organization's requirements engineering policies, procedures, and tools.
	Implement ways to reuse requirements across projects.
	Identify ways to assist product management in product planning through requirements development and analysis.
	Propose new product features and updates.
Measures of Performance	Evaluation from product and project management on overall product quality and effectiveness in the marketplace of the requirements after the product has been developed.
	Feedback from key customer or marketing representatives on the way in which the requirements engineering process was conducted.
	Customer satisfaction measures.
	Satisfying or exceeding requirements development schedules, resource constraints, and quality goals.
	Control of requirements creep attributable to missed requirements and leakage of "unofficial" requirements into the project.

Table 3.2   RA Job Description (continued)

References	Ferdinandi, Patricia L., *A Requirements Pattern: Succeeding in the Internet Economy*, Boston: Addison-Wesley, 2002, Chapter 8.
	Wiegers, Karl, "The Habits of Effective Analysts," *Software Development* 8(10) (October 2000): 62–65.
	Young, R. R., *Effective Requirements Practices*, Boston, MA: Addison-Wesley, 2001, Chapters 4 and 5.

Notes:

Each team that uses this job description needs to weight the various skills and knowledge that are pertinent to its job. Certain skills listed might be critical for one requirements engineer job and unimportant for another.

Each person considering hiring an individual to be a requirements engineer needs to consider which of these skills are intrinsic to the way the individual works (e.g., analytical and interpersonal skills) and which can be learned (e.g., facilitation and listening skills).

The users of this generic job description will need to modify some of the terminology to reflect their specific environments (e.g., corporate information-systems development, commercial product development, contract development).

This job description needs to be tailored to match the experience level for the position.

Source: Karl Wiegers et al.

Characteristics of an Effective RA

In addition to learned, or "hard," skills, there is a set of personal characteristics that will serve the RA well. You may feel that some of these characteristics are themselves really skills. I won't argue this with you—let's agree that all of the skills and characteristics noted are helpful and useful. Table 3.3 summarizes the desired characteristics described below as countermeasures you can apply to overcome barriers you are likely to encounter.

Table 3.4 provides suggestions for how to strengthen these characteristics.

Consider the following characteristics, which you may choose to continue to refine, as well as the suggestions and resources proffered to help.

1. Engage in continuing education to acquire expert knowledge of requirements engineering and requirements practices. Chapter 1 described the many components of the requirements process, a set of activities that are performed throughout the system life cycle of a project. My earlier book [1] provides a comprehensive set of references in the requirements literature as of 2001 (many more recent references are provided in this book). For each of the 10 recommended practices described in the earlier book, a few key references are provided at the end of each chapter, together with a short summary of the information provided by the reference. Ongoing study, such as attending training seminars in areas related to expertise, assignment, and activities, is helpful. Journals such as *IEEE Software*, *CrossTalk*, *Software Development Magazine*, and *INSIGHT* provide informative articles and reviews of related books that you might purchase and study. These are both informative and motivational—they

Table 3.3 Desired RA Characteristics as Countermeasures to Likely Barriers

Barriers You May Encounter	Characteristics as Countermeasures
[A] Lacking a thorough knowledge of requirements engineering, requirements processes, and requirements errors methodologies can cause the RA to be less effective than is needed.	[1] Engage in continuing education to acquire expert knowledge of requirements engineering and requirements practices. [7] Initiate learning, applying, and using effective practices; seek sponsorship for requirements-related activities from the PM; be committed to project success. [13] Maintain a good knowledge of evolving technology and how it can be applied to meet customer needs.
[B] The end product does not meet the customer's needs. There are different ideas and opinions as to what the real requirements are.	[2] Be a good listener, communicator, and writer. Carefully document decisions and action items. [3] Have good facilitation and negotiation skills. [4] Be persistent and persevering. [5] Be proactive in engaging customers and users, coworkers, and project management. [15] Desire to make a difference in your professional work.
[C] Management does not always understand what is being built and what resources are needed to achieve the end product.	[6] Develop the ability to communicate effectively with management. [10] Develop the ability to estimate the time and other resources required to accomplish technical work.
[D] The requirements process does not support the project's needs.	[8] Develop and maintain an attitude of continuous improvement. [14] Set achievable goals and meet them. define and describe methods to achieve the project's goals in a requirements plan. [16] Develop your ability to contribute to the project's risk process.
[E] Strong personalities and strong opinions can derail the effectiveness of good requirements development and management.	[2] Be a good listener, communicator, and writer. Carefully document decisions and action items. [9] Take responsibility for your views, attitudes, relationships, and actions, and maintain respect for others.
[F] People often try to do more than is called for and to make ad hoc changes during work product development.	[11] Maintain focus on keeping the main thing the main thing. Install a mechanism to control new requirements and changes. Don't invent requirements independently and avoid gold plating. Avoid requirements creep.
[G] Project personnel can become too vested in the work product solution to analyze and decompose requirements effectively.	[12] Develop the ability to think outside the box to provide creative approaches that might not occur to people who are close to the problem and the legacy system.

Source: Richard Raphael.

provide encouragement to strengthen one's own understanding. Also, there are several Web sites that offer reviews of requirements-related books (see for example Ian Alexander's Web site [2]) and "goodies" (reusable requirements-related artifacts) available at Karl Wiegers' Web site [3]. Attending conferences such as the annual Institute of Electrical and Electronics Engineers (IEEE) Conference on Requirements Engineering [4] or the annual conference

Table 3.4 Characteristics of an Effective RA and Suggested Activities to Strengthen Them

Characteristic	Suggested Activities
1. Engage in continuing education.	Read requirements engineering literature, attend professional meetings and conferences, visit Web sites, hold office in professional associations.
2. Good listener, communicator, and writer.	Attend seminars in listening skills, communications, and writing; practice making presentations and writing.
3. Good facilitation and negotiation skills.	Practice facilitating meetings, coordinating workshops, and managing process design sessions.
4. Persistent and persevering.	Practice evolving real requirements from stated requirements.
5. Proactive i.n engaging others.	In performing daily assignments, think deliberately about (1) suggestions for making things better, and (2) appropriate venues and approaches for making them. Practice. Ask for feedback, and act on it.
6. Ability to communicate effectively with management.	Practice looking at your responsibilities from the perspective of your manager and senior management. Write down your perspective and management's perspective. Work to understand differences and modify your communications accordingly.
7. Learn, apply and use effective practices.	Select a practice that you believe will improve a work situation. Gather support for trying it out ("piloting" it). Consider steps you and the project or organization can take to give the pilot the best chance of success. Implement the practice. Follow through to ensure it takes. Assess the value of implementing the practice after one month.
8. Develop and maintain an attitude of continuous improvement.	Practice the Plan-Do-Check-Act (PDCA) cycle at the conclusion of meetings. Document the suggestions that are offered. Follow up on suggestions to the extent feasible and possible. If this works, explore other opportunities to inculcate an attitude of continuous improvement, such as by documenting processes and improving them.
9. Take responsibility for your views, attitudes, relationships, and actions.	Make known to coworkers an error you have made, in the spirit of contributing to doing things better. Convey that your intentions were good and that you have worked toward learning from the error. Also, work to recognize the value provided by all coworkers.
10. Develop the ability to estimate work requirements.	Estimate the time you think you will require to accomplish work tasks assigned to you. Track the actual time consumed, noting distractions. Consider changes you might make in your work habits to be more productive. Over time, try to have estimates be closer to actuals.
11. Maintain focus.	Embrace the concept of real requirements. Understand how these are different from stated requirements. Suggest prioritizing requirements on your project, and evolve an approach to collaboratively prioritizing a set of requirements. Evaluate the impact of this approach.
12. Strengthen your ability to think outside the box.	Meet with stakeholders to consider previously unconsidered potential solutions to vexing problems. Use the brainstorming technique to get three ideas from each participant. Multivote on the ideas suggested. Consider the potential value in seriously pursuing one or more ideas.
13. Strengthen your knowledge of available technology.	Schedule a brown bag to consider technology possibilities. Invite a system architect and other "technologists." Discuss possible ways to accomplish some system objectives by incorporating new technologies.
14. Set achievable goals and meet them.	Plan your work for the next month. Set a few specific objectives for some things that you believe are really important to accomplish. Keep these specific objectives foremost in mind over the next month. Manage to the specific objectives (i.e., ensure that you accomplish them).
15. Strive to make a difference in your work situations.	Explore with your manager how the tasks for which you are responsible at work might make a difference to the project or organization. Identify some specific achievements, and then pursue them in earnest. Solicit your coworkers' and your manager's support in achieving them.

Table 3.4 Characteristics of an Effective RA and Suggested Activities to Strengthen Them (continued)

Characteristic	Suggested Activities
16. Contribute to your project's risk process.	Volunteer to serve on the project's risk management team. If your project does not have one, suggest that the project consider initiating a risk process. Identify the top risks, prioritize them, and develop risk mitigation plans for those considered to be the most serious risks. Monitor the risks.

Source: Richard Raphael.

of the International Council on Systems Engineering (INCOSE) [5] is another way to strengthen knowledge, learn about old and new techniques, meet others who are working in this area, and find out about the latest offerings available from vendors. Consider becoming a member and active participant in professional associations and societies such as INCOSE, IEEE, the American Society for Quality (ASQ), the Society for Software Quality (SSQ), the International Association of Facilitators (or associated local organizations), and the Requirements Engineering Specialist Group (RESG) in Europe [6]. Often, professional organizations offer evening meetings, lunchtime sessions, or Saturday tutorials that provide opportunities to learn and to meet colleagues. For example, the Washington, D.C., chapter of INCOSE provides superb opportunities to share experiences, glean lessons learned, and find sources of information, as do many other local and regional chapters [7]. Actively seek opportunities to write articles and make presentations. The old adage that no one learns more than the author, teacher, or presenter is true.

2. Be a good listener, communicator, and writer. Good communication skills are important. It is important to understand the needs and expectations of different stakeholders. Learn to listen carefully so as to hear what users and customers are trying to say, even if they aren't very good at expressing it. You need to be able to verify understanding by repeating back your interpretation of statements. You need to be able to write clearly and concisely so that the requirements are documented according to the criteria of a good requirement provided in Chapter 1. Steven Gaffney's Web site and his seminars have been valuable resources for me—see the workshops and materials available at his Web site [8].

3. Have good facilitation and negotiation skills. Among the most effective requirements gathering techniques is the requirements workshop. See Ellen Gottesdiener's *Requirements by Collaboration* [9] for a thorough treatment of this important technique. The RA often may find him- or herself facilitating groups of people in such venues. It's important to be able to encourage the identification of ideas, while not allowing one or a few people to dominate the discussion. Often, you'll find yourself needing to negotiate to achieve consensus

among individuals with divergent views. There are workshops you can attend to learn and hone these skills. As noted above, there are professional resources available to strengthen facilitation skills. See the Web site for the International Association of Facilitators for ideas [10].

4. Be persistent and persevering. Since customers and users provide us their stated requirements, it's vital that RAs be persistent and persevering so that the real requirements are evolved. It's not enough to depend on being able to proffer the excuse that "we built the system that you requested." If the stated requirements are not acceptable, do not wait until you have completed the system and the users reject it. Cut the risks to your project by improving the requirements as early as possible. The risks include doing wasted technical work, and of course having the system rejected (with all the legal and commercial risks that result). Identifying the real requirements is the one most important thing that the RA can do to contribute the most to customers.

5. Be proactive in engaging customers and users, coworkers, and project management. You'll soon appreciate that it's not enough just to go with the flow. The performance of the RA's roles demands that you be proactive. Customers and users need your initiative and persistence to help them evolve the real requirements. Your coworkers need your proactive support to help them select and use effective processes, practices, methods, techniques, and tools. Project management needs you to speak for approaches that will best serve the project, for example, investing more in the requirements process, identifying the real requirements, and providing a mechanism to control new requirements and changes to requirements.

6. Develop the ability to communicate effectively with management. Too often, differences in perspective prevent good communication. Management views information technology (IT) as a means to achieve business objectives. Systems and software engineers view their work in terms of work products that must meet specified requirements. As noted earlier, it furthers neither your career nor the project or organization to say yes, when impossible commitments only guarantee failure in the future. Dorothy McKinney offers suggestions in her article "Six Translations between Software-Speak and Management-Speak" [11]. Another insight is that sometimes RAs must concern themselves not only with their own management, but also with the customer's management.

7. Initiate learning and applying effective practices, and be committed to project success. One needs to be willing to learn and use effective practices. Learning comes from experience and study. Applying practices on projects requires training to familiarize people with them; mentoring people in their use; tracking their effectiveness; and ensuring that their deployment and use is effective. A serious

problem is that, most often, new and improved practices aren't given a real chance because it is human nature to revert to using practices that are already in place.[3] One needs to be committed to project success and to advising when things need to be done differently or better.

8. Develop and maintain an attitude of continuous improvement. Related to the commitment described above is the idea of maintaining an attitude of continuous improvement. The RA should encourage the project to embrace mechanisms to instill the attitude of "getting ever better." At my company, we end every meeting with an evaluation of how the meeting went: what worked and what could have been done better. We call this "doing PDCA" in honor of Dr. Deming and Walter Shewhart's contributions to continuous process improvement and our adoption of their teachings. Similarly, at the end of each cycle of activities, consider having a workshop to gather feedback concerning how things went. Use the ideas and suggestions generated to improve how the work is done (i.e., to improve the process that is being used). These mechanisms (in addition to providing good ideas) serve to help everyone buy in to the procedures used, because participants help shape them—"I helped improve that process!"

9. Take responsibility for your views, attitudes, relationships, and actions. By taking responsibility, one establishes a sense of accountability. You'll tend to exhibit pride in your work. You'll not let personalities and individual characteristics deter you from having good relationships with everyone. Your actions will make a valued contribution. You will be setting an example for others. You'll be a leader.

10. Develop the ability to estimate the time and other resources required to accomplish technical work. One of the difficulties in making estimates of technical work is that these estimates are needed early in order to develop projections of the number of staff required to complete the project. (The number of staff, their seniority, and their roles are required to develop an estimate of the cost of the project.) The difficulty is compounded by the fact that the real requirements are not yet known. So, we often find ourselves making estimates without an accurate basis for them. This can lead to a lot of work that is not productive and also to confusion caused by the inability downstream to meet the estimates.

The RA can contribute to the estimation process by (1) working with users in the joint team environment to identify the real

---

3. See Watts Humphrey's "Why Don't They Practice What We Preach" for insights concerning this problem and suggestions for how to deal with it. See www.sei.cmu.edu/publications/articles/practice-preach/practice-preach.html.

requirements, and (2) working with PMs and the development staff to make estimates of the time and other resources required to accomplish the technical work. Using data based on previous experiences ("managing by fact") is best.

Coworker John E. Moore in the Defense Enterprise Solutions (DES) business unit at Northrop Grumman IT is a valuable resource. As project management (project planning, project tracking, and integrated product management) "process owner," Dr. Moore has developed a "Brickchart" capability within MS Project that facilitates tracking progress for tasks.[4] Another coworker, Rich Raphael, developed the Risk Manager's Assistant (RMA), a straightforward database tool that supports standard risk management processes and programs.[5] Both of these are easily learned and useful project-management tools. See the discussion in Chapter 5 concerning risk management. As an RA gets more experienced performing requirements analysis, the RA should also be evaluating each new or changed requirement for any risk that it may add to the project. As projects get more complex and as customers become more mature in specifying their needs, each new or changing requirement risks adverse impact on the project. Note that the CMMI®, as part of the introduction to the requirements management (REQM) process area (PA), specifies that one should "refer to the risk management (RI) process area for more information about identifying and handling risks associated with requirements."

11. Maintain focus on keeping the main thing the main thing. One of the pitfalls in developing systems and software is that we try to do too much; another is that we try to incorporate changes as we work. Customers and users will ask, Can you do this? Will the new system do that? We don't like to say no. We participate in creating a perception that the new system will be all things to all stakeholders. In so doing, we jeopardize our ability to fulfill these commitments and the success of the effort.

The RA can serve a critical role here. Very early, the RA should facilitate establishing the concept that all requirements are not equally important and that it's the responsibility of all stakeholders to prioritize needs collaboratively and to focus the intent of the project (to keep the main thing the main thing). As suggested by Neal Whitten in "Meet Minimum Requirements: Anything More Is Too Much" [12], the RA should work to identify the minimum set of requirements required to accomplish the business objectives. This goal can be facilitated by doing the following:

---

4. Contact Dr. Moore at john.moore@ngc.com.

5. Contact Mr. Raphael at RRaphael@ngc.com.

- Establishing and following a process of prioritizing all requirements;
- Establishing the concept of follow-on releases or versions that will address lower-priority requirements and requirements that are identified during development of increments of functionality later in the development process;
- Ensuring that a mechanism is put in place and used to control new requirements and changes to requirements.

These activities can have an enormous positive impact on keeping the train on the tracks. One of the major causes of rework is changes introduced after technical work has been completed or is well underway.

Another aspect of this desired characteristic is that the RA should not invent requirements independently and should avoid "gold plating," that is, adding features and capabilities to systems and software when they are not required by the real requirements. The RA or developer might think he knows something that will be "way cool" for the users that could turn out to be unwanted or very disruptive to the project (e.g., if increased costs are incurred to provide it).

12. Develop the ability to think outside the box to provide creative approaches that might not occur to people who are close to the problem and the legacy system. One of the advantages an RA brings to a new assignment is that he does not have the same vested interest that a user or customer has and, therefore, can act as an impartial or unbiased agent. The RA arrives without expectations, without necessarily having much knowledge of the domain, and without being attached to any particular outcome. Unhindered by years of association with a problem domain and unconfined by the constraints of the legacy system, you are free to think more freely about what needs to be done and how it can be addressed best. Leverage these opportunities to think of new and different ways the system objectives might be addressed.

13. Maintain a good knowledge of evolving technology and how it can be applied to meet customer needs. Some experienced RAs believe that a strong technical background is very helpful for an RA. As mentioned earlier, understanding current technologies is not solely the responsibility of the RA, but we can contribute to the system design by involving architects in reviews of the requirements and by assisting them in developing technical solutions. Another reason this is important is that incorporating some new technologies creates new requirements that must be considered. Other experienced RAs believe that a strong technical background is not as important to the RA as the other characteristics, especially when eliciting requirements and understanding the real needs and expectations of customers and users. These people believe that a strong technical

perspective may actually inhibit the RA and that utilizing a person with a more general background is a better approach.

14. Set achievable goals and meet them. This is related to the characteristic of maintaining focus. The RA should set achievable goals and meet them. Having a documented requirements plan and process and following them will help.

15. Desire to make a difference in your professional work. We shouldn't be content to just go to work or to put in a set number of hours at our jobs. Rather, it should be one of our values to want to make a difference in our professional work. It's vital that control of the project be maintained. Having this value affects others and inspires us to become increasingly effective in our own roles.

      Occasionally, we find ourselves in a situation in which we are powerless to make a difference. For example, I participated on a project for a period of several months during which I sensed that I made an important, needed, and valued contribution. Suddenly, the PM seemed to withdraw his support for my role. I discussed the situation with him and was unable to change it. It was time for me to move on to a different project. Sometimes we need to take the responsibility for change and act on it.

16. Develop your ability to contribute to the project's risk process. Every project should have a risk process to identify, evaluate, prioritize, and mitigate existing or potential risks. Consider participating in your project's risk management team and process. Requirements-related risks are important to the project. You can contribute to the dialogue that will help your project deal with its risks successfully.

Summary

Suggested skills of the RA are listed and categorized in an RA's skills matrix (Table 3.1) according to those needed by a junior-level, mid-level, or senior-level analyst. This matrix will help you evaluate your suitability for a specific project role. You may use it as a guide to further strengthen and improve your skills or as a reference to sources of information concerning each skill. Table 3.2 provided an RA job or position description that should help you clarify the many ways in which the role of the RA can be leveraged to benefit both your project and your organization. Making the RA's role explicit helps a project to run more smoothly. The RA's role needs to be understood and valued in the minds of PMs and the technical community—this job description should help! Sixteen characteristics of an effective RA were presented and described. Suggestions are provided concerning how to strengthen these characteristics. Consider these in the context of your own personal and professional development, as well as of your current assignments and responsibilities, and select one or a few characteristics to strengthen each year. Yes, being an effective RA involves learning many skills and having many desired personal characteristics. This chapter, coupled with thoughtful introspection, should provide a useful road map.

Case Study

A requirements engineering consultant was invited to assist a particular location of a large U.S. Government organization. Senior management at that location indicated, "millions of dollars had been wasted" in repeated efforts to develop systems and software solutions internally. The consultant met with senior management, managers, users, and developers to gather information and gain an understanding of the situation. Following analysis and development of a tailored requirements course, he presented formal training for all stakeholders that addressed existing problems in the organization from the perspective of relevant industry experience. On the surface, there seemed to be a sincere desire on the part of all stakeholders to improve the situation, although many issues existed. The training addressed how these issues could be resolved. At the conclusion of the training, the senior manager concluded that the situation could not be improved. Many of the other participants in the training were perplexed by this conclusion: they felt they were off to a fresh start.

Analysis: The senior manager himself was the key issue that prevented the situation from improving. Although there were issues relating to all parties, management was willing to allow parochial interests of users, an overly bureaucratic development process, and power struggles of some key stakeholders to paralyze efforts and render improvement of the situation impossible. In Dr. Deming's framework, there were "too many red beads."[6] Users and the development organization were powerless to improve the situation without management's support and management's expectation for better results. Management must enable and empower its workers (all the rest of us) in order for work to be productive and effective. Industry studies report that lack of appropriate senior management support is a factor in most IT failures. This vignette has much to offer senior managers. Industry experience is that senior management must sponsor and support IT and systems/software development initiatives if they are to be successful. See the discussion in Chapter 8 and a recent *Harvard Business Review* article, "Six Decisions Your IT People Shouldn't Make," [13] for further insights and specific suggestions. The RA can be helpful here by offering these insights, suggestions, and industry experience to his or her management team and by helping to clarify the specific roles that senior management should provide.

---

6. Be sure to familiarize yourself with Dr. Deming's teachings. See, for example, Mary Walton's *The Deming Management Method* (New York: The Putnam Publishing Group, 1986). In Chapter 4, Walton explains how Dr. Deming used "The Parable of the Red Beads" in his seminars to drive home that the workers in any organization [most of us] are powerless without management's support.

References

[1] Young, R. R., *Effective Requirements Practices,* Boston, MA: Addison-Wesley, 2001.

[2] Alexander, I. F., and Richard Stevens, *Writing Better Requirements,* Boston: Addison-Wesley, 2002, www.easyweb.easy.net.co.uk/~iany/index.htm.

[3] Wiegers, K., Web site, at www.processimpact.com (for requirements-related "goodies" and other useful information).

[4] IEEE Requirements Engineering Conference , Web site, at conferences.computer .org/RE.

[5] INCOSE national organization's Web site, at www.incose.org/se-int.

[6] Requirements Engineering Specialist Group (in the United Kingdom), Web site, at www.resg.org.uk.

[7] INCOSE WMA Chapter, Web site, at www.incose-wma.org/info.

[8] Gaffney, S., Web site, at www.StevenGaffney.com.

[9] Gottesdiener, E., *Requirements by Collaboration: Workshops for Defining Needs.* Reading, MA: Addison-Wesley, 2002.

[10] International Association of Facilitators, Web site, at www.iaf-world.org.

[11] McKinney, D., "Six Translations between Software-Speak and Management-Speak," *IEEE Software* 19(6) (2002): 50–52. See www.computer.org/software.

[12] Whitten, N., "Meet Minimum Requirements: Anything More Is Too Much," *PM Network* (September 1998), p. 19.

[13] Ross, J. W., and P. Weill, "Six IT Decisions Your IT People Shouldn't Make," *Harvard Business Review* (November 2002): 85–91.

Contents

Types of Requirements

It's important for the RA or requirements engineer to settle on definitions of the types of requirements that he will use consistently. He should advocate consistent meanings for these types on his project and in his organization. Much confusion can be avoided by agreeing on a set of definitions and by not using certain terms. In this chapter, we'll review several types of requirements and suggest definitions for them. We'll suggest why some terms shouldn't be used and provide other guidelines. One important reason for agreeing on the definitions of the types of requirements is to avoid lengthy and heated debates about terminology while we are working together. Establish a project glossary that everyone can live with (even if some definitions are not everyone's favorites) and utilize it in your work. Consider the glossary provided with this book as a starting point, and tailor it as needed.

First, let's recall our simple and useful definition of a requirement from Chapter 1. A *requirement* is a statement that identifies a capability, characteristic, or quality factor of a system in order for it to have value and utility for a user. A requirement is well defined and more specific than a *need,* which is a capability desired by a user or customer to solve a problem or achieve an objective. The authors of the Systems Engineering Capability Maturity Model (SE-CMM®) [1] were insightful when they created Process Area 06, "Understand Customer Needs and Expectations." The purpose of this process area is to elicit, stimulate, analyze, and communicate customer and user needs and expectations and translate them into a verifiable set of requirements.

Views of Requirements Types

Next, let's provide three different ways to organize requirements types. These views will help you put your work into context and perspective. The views are provided courtesy of Jeffrey O. Grady, author and instructor of systems engineering and requirements courses. The definitions of the various types are provided later in this chapter.

Table 4.1 provides the first view. Here requirements types are divided into hardware and software. Hardware requirements are then characterized as either performance requirements or constraints. Performance requirements define how well the system must perform a requirement. Constraints are further characterized as interface requirements, specialty engineering requirements, and environmental requirements. Software requirements are characterized as either functional or nonfunctional. Functional requirements specify an action that a system must be able to perform. A nonfunctional requirement specifies system properties, such as reliability and safety (see the discussion of "ilities and specialty engineering requirements" below).

Figure 4.1 provides a more detailed context for the RA. The requirements types that are noted are production process requirements (e.g., the physical facilities needed), requirements of the products to be provided by the system or software, the requirements of the processes utilized to produce the products (e.g., the testing process), and operational and logistics support requirements (e.g., equipment, training, and procedures). All of these requirements must be identified before work on the detailed system design is started. While the product engineers are developing specifications for the product elements, the manufacturing engineers must define the manufacturing requirements, the logistics engineers the logistics requirements, and the verification engineers the qualification requirements. While doing so, these engineers must communicate among themselves and jointly resolve the best aggregate expression of the requirements from the product and process perspective.

It's important to note that several steps or walk-throughs of the identified real requirements must be made[1] to ensure, for example, the following:

Table 4.1 Requirements Types

Hardware requirements:
Performance requirements
Constraints:
Interface requirements
Specialty engineering requirements
Environmental requirements
Software requirements:
Functional requirements
Nonfunctional requirements

Source: Jeffrey O. Grady. Used with permission.

---

1. Industry practitioner and advisor Ellen Gottesdiener, president of EBG Consulting, Inc., recommends three or four iterations of requirements development, each incorporating a formal or informal review by internal and external customers. Her experience emphasizes the value and importance of identifying the real requirements before starting other work.

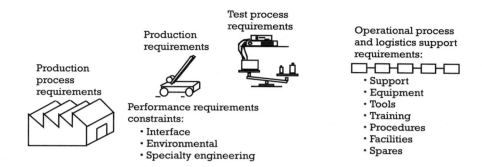

Figure 4.1   Another view of requirements types.

▸ The requirements are mutually consistent;

▸ The requirements are prioritized (there is never enough time and money to do everything).

Figure 4.2 provides a total requirements taxonomy. Grady describes his figure as follows:

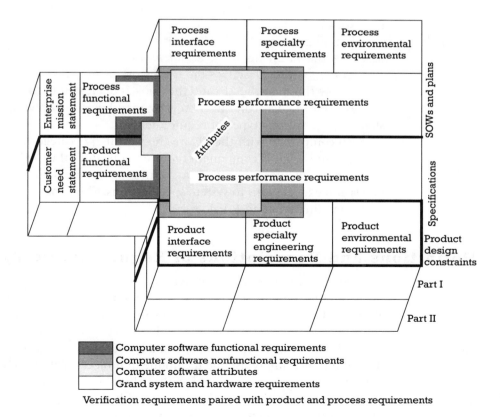

Figure 4.2   Total requirements taxonomy. (*Source:* Jeffrey O. Grady.)

The top layer corresponds to development requirements, often called *design-to* requirements that must be clearly understood before design. The lower layer corresponds to product requirements, commonly called *build-to* requirements. The requirements above the heavy middle line correspond to process requirements captured in statements of work and plans. The process requirements fall into program plans and procedures. The product requirements are captured in program specifications starting with the ultimate requirement, the customer need. We need effective methods to expand the need statement into a more refined view of the customer need, thus defining more detailed performance requirements. In addition, we must identify additional requirements called constraints of three kinds that require special models. The specifications we create may have to be released in two parts: (1) development or performance specifications, and (2) product or detail specifications. The former kind drives design and qualification. The latter kind drives acceptance [8].

Another view with which the RA should be familiar is provided in Electronic Industries Association (EIA) Standard 632 [2], Section 4, ("Requirements"), and in IEEE Standard 12207 [3], Section 5.3.2 ("System Requirements Analysis") and Section 5.3.4 ("Software Requirements Analysis"). You should digest these standards and consider the categories that are suggested.

Another approach is the Zachman Framework (ZF) [4, 5]. John Hay describes the ZF in his book *Requirements Analysis—From Business Views to Architecture* [6]. Hay describes the RA's work as moving from rows one and two to row three on the ZF, and the book is dedicated to the analytic techniques used in each column. A review may help in clarifying and understanding the various types of requirements.

Also compatible with the ZF are the CMMI® [7] categories of customer, product, and product component requirements. Both the CMMI® and the ZF treat requirements analysis as a continuing progression from customer needs and expectations to system specifications. This progression is useful in understanding what an RA does.

Definitions and Descriptions of Requirements Types

The remainder of this chapter provides definitions and descriptions of many types of requirements. I reiterate my earlier suggestion that you establish a glossary of terms to be used on your project. Working with the other developers, add words and definitions of them that you can all support as you proceed with your work. Don't spend a lot of time coming to consensus on the definitions: simply use the technique in project meetings of each person indicating her or his agreement with a thumbs up, down, or sideways to reach agreements that people can live with. I've suggested that some of these terms (requirements types) provided below should not be used because they tend to confuse people and create misunderstandings that jeopardize successful completion of work activities. These are just my own opinions and biases based on my experience. You may have different opinions and that's okay!

Table 4.2 provides an RA's view of many of the types of requirements. It may help you to gain and apply a helpful understanding of the different types of requirements.

Business Requirements

Business requirements are the reason for developing systems and software in the first place. Business requirements are the essential activities of an enterprise. Business requirements are derived from business goals (the objectives of the enterprise or organization). Business scenarios may be used as a technique for understanding business requirements. A key factor in the success of a system is the extent to which the system supports the business requirements and facilitates an organization in achieving them. If our systems and software do not support the business requirements effectively and efficiently, they have no reason for being. Businesses exist to make money

Table 4.2   An RA's View of Requirements Types

Customer needs and expectations:
Business requirements;
User requirements;
Product requirements;
Environmental requirements;
Unknowable requirements.
These are analyzed by the requirements analyst and described in different ways:
High-level (or system-level) requirements;
Functional requirements (what the system must do);
Nonfunctional requirements:
System properties (e.g., safety);
The "ilities/specialty engineering requirements."
Derived requirements and design constraints;
Performance requirements (e.g., how fast?);
Interface requirements (relationships between system elements);
The system requirements are allocated into:
Subsystems (logical groupings of functions);
Components of the system (hardware, software, training, documentation).
Checks are done to ensure the system does what it is supposed to do, incorporating:
Verified requirements;
Validated requirements;
Qualification requirements.

for stockholders; organizations exist to meet the needs of their members. It's vital that we consider our systems and software development work totally within the context of business and organizational objectives.

Stated Requirements Versus Real Requirements

We have already clarified the difference between these:

> ▸ Stated requirements are provided by a customer at the beginning of a system or software development effort.

> ▸ Real requirements reflect the verified needs for a particular system or capability. Note that some real requirements may be identified that the customer and users omitted in the stated requirements. In fact, identifying omitted requirements is a key task of the RA.

User Requirements

Users are the individuals or groups that use a system or software in its environment. User requirements are their verified needs for that system or software.

High-Level or System-Level Requirements

To enable comprehending a needed system, we refer to the high-level or system-level requirements. This term relates to those requirements that are foremost in importance, capture the vision of the customer, enable defining the scope of the system, and allow estimating the cost and schedule required to build the system. (Some system architects believe that the requirements specification should contain every performance requirement.) It's recommended that a workable number of requirements (on the order of 50 to 200) system-level requirements be identified for a large system. In Chapter 8, we will discuss a set of business drivers that may be considered high-level customer requirements, which often are not expressed.

Business Rules

Business rules[2] provide the basis for creating the functional requirements. They are as follows:

> ▸ The policies, conditions, and constraints of the business activities supported by the system;

> ▸ The decision processes, guidelines, and controls behind the functional requirements (e.g., procedures);

---

2. This discussion is summarized from materials developed by Ellen Gottesdiener, including "Capturing Business Rules," "The Value of Standardization of Business Rules," and "Turning Rules into Requirements." These materials are available at her Web site, www.ebgconsulting.com.

> • Definitions used by the business;

> • Relationships and workflows in the business;

> • Knowledge needed to perform actions.

One guideline to follow is to document the business rules correctly and early. Active sponsorship and leadership by your customer are required to achieve this, because there will likely be "undiscussables," unclear and conflicting business policies and rules, which need to be clarified and resolved in order to provide an adequate basis for the development of the real requirements for the system or software. It's important to identify business rules that are inconsistent, in conflict, inefficient, redundant, nonstandardized, noncompliant with regulations or company policy, or that have no owner.

Business rules must be captured explicitly by the RA and baselined during requirements analysis. Focusing on business rules as the core functional requirements speeds requirements analysis and promotes validation and verification. The RA should use the "Documenting Business Rules" process described in Figure 4.3 to select or tailor a taxonomy and a business-rule template for any given business problem. The template provides a standard syntax for writing business rules in natural language (English).

If you find yourself in a situation where help is needed, consider contacting Ellen Gottesdiener (ellen@ebgconsulting.com) to facilitate a business-rules requirements workshop.

Functional Requirements

Functional requirements is an important category of the real requirements. Functional requirements describe what the system or software must do. A function is a useful capability provided by one or more components of a system. Functional requirements are sometimes called behavioral or operational requirements because they specify the inputs (stimuli) to the system, the outputs (responses) from the system, and behavioral relationships between them. The document used to communicate the requirements to customers, system, and software engineers is referred to as a functional

The RA collaborates with:

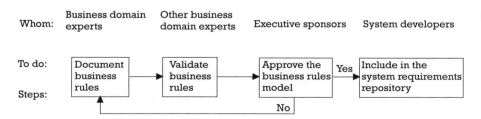

Figure 4.3 Documenting Business-Rules Process. (*Adapted from*: Ellen Gottesdiener.)

document (FD) or specification. This refers to a comprehensive collection of the characteristics of a system and the capabilities it will make available to the users. It provides a detailed analysis of the data the system will be expected to manipulate. It may include a detailed definition of the user interfaces of the system.

Nonfunctional Requirements

Nonfunctional requirements specify system properties, such as reliability and safety.

Derived Requirements

A derived requirement is one that is further refined from a higher-level requirement or a requirement that results from choosing a specific implementation or system element. In a sense, all requirements are derived from the system need; thus, the derived distinction tends to have little significance. However, many systems engineers distinguish between externally identified requirements and requirements that are derived under the control of the engineer.

Design Requirements and Design Constraints

For most system development efforts, design requirements/constraints appear right at the beginning of the system formulation. Here are examples of why it's difficult to separate requirements engineering from design activities:

- New systems are often installed in environments that already have other systems. The other systems usually constrain the design of the new system. For example, a requirement (design constraint) may be that the system to be developed must obtain its information from an existing database. The database has already been designed and parts of its specification will usually be included in the requirements document.

- For large systems, some architectural design is often necessary to identify subsystems and relationships. Identifying subsystems means that the requirements engineering process for each subsystem can go on in parallel.

- For reasons of budget, schedule, or quality, an organization may wish to reuse some or all existing software systems in the implementation of a new system. This constrains both the system requirements and the design.

- If a system has to be approved by an external regulator (e.g., systems in civil aircraft), it may be necessary to use standard certified design that has been tested in other systems.

Performance Requirements

One of the most difficult challenges in system development is defining and meeting the performance requirements (sometimes referred to as dependability requirements). The performance requirements define how well the functional requirements must perform. Performance requirements analysis components are beyond the scope of this book, but are described by Jeffrey O. Grady in *Systems Requirements Analysis* [8, pp. 238, 313, and 324]. Grady also provides a set of guidelines helpful in the identification of performance requirements [8, pp. 323–324]. Dependability requirements correspond to system-level needs for availability, security, performance, reliability, and safety.

Interface Requirements

Another difficult challenge in system development is finding and defining the interface requirements. Interface requirements analysis identifies physical and functional relationships among system elements and between system elements and the system environment. One project team member should be assigned principal responsibility for assuring coordination of interface requirements. See [8, pp. 270–297] for a good discussion of interface analysis and techniques.

Verified Requirements

Verified requirements are real requirements that are met or satisfied in the design solution.

Validated Requirements

Validated requirements are requirements that are implemented in the delivered system. See Jeffrey O. Grady's *System Validation and Verification* [9] for clear definitions of these terms, detailed information concerning how to use these fundamental problem-solving tools, and practical methods for each step of the process.

Qualification Requirements

Qualification refers to the verification or validation of item performance in a specific application and results from design review, test data review, and configuration audits.

The "Ilities" and Specialty Engineering Requirements

One often hears references to the "ilities" of a system, sometimes called quality attributes, such as the following:

- Designability;
- Efficiency;

- Human engineering;
- Modifiability;
- Portability;
- Reliability;
- Testability;
- Understandability;
- Capacity;
- Degradation of service;
- Maintainability;
- Memory;
- Timing constraints;
- Modifiability;
- Usability.

These are the nonfunctional or nonbehavioral requirements of a system or the software. See Alan Davis's *Software Requirements: Objects, Functions, & States* [10, pp. 307–340] for a detailed discussion and suggested techniques.

Unknowable Requirements

Experience has shown that there are requirements that are unknowable at the beginning of a system development effort. Some requirements become apparent only as the system evolves. We discover that we have a requirement that we could not envision previously.

Such unknowable requirements may be real requirements, which must be included.

Product Requirements

These are requirements of the products that are produced by a system.

Process Requirements

There are requirements that exist because of the processes being used to develop the system or software.

Logistics Support Requirements

These are requirements that exist because of such things as tools, training, procedures, facilities, and spares. One often hears of them in references to the integrated logistics support (ILS) requirements.

Environmental Requirements

These are requirements that result from the physical setting and social and cultural conditions of the system development effort and the setting in which the system or software will be used.

System, Subsystem, and Component Requirements

This refers to requirements associated with different levels of the system. The system is the highest level and is divided into subsystems; the subsystems are made up of components, such as hardware, software, training, and documentation.

Terminologies to Avoid

Source or Customer Requirements

One sometimes hears people refer to source requirements or customer requirements. I prefer instead to specify the source of the requirement—that is, from whom or where the real requirement was identified—as an attribute[3] of a real requirement. Having the source identified for each real requirement enables us to go to the person or document for questions and clarifications. I suggest avoiding use of the terms *source requirements* or *customer requirements*.

Nonnegotiable Versus Negotiable Requirements

A nonnegotiable requirement implies that if it is not met, the system is of little use. Clearly, the requirement is a real requirement. A negotiable requirement implies that it's really okay if it's not satisfied in the delivered system. Clearly, negotiable requirements are not real requirements. This classification is not useful. Neal Whitten's article, "Meet Minimum Requirements: Anything More Is Too Much" [11] is instructive. Meeting minimum real requirements is in everyone's best interests, because this approach reduces risk, cost, schedule, complexity, and so forth. Keep in mind the CHAOS Report [12] conclusion that 45% of system features provided in developed systems are never used once!

---

3. See Young's *Effective Requirements Practices* [13, pp. 85–87] for a discussion of the attributes of a requirement and a sample requirements attributes matrix one might use in a requirements tool such as the Dynamic Object-Oriented Requirements System (DOORS). Examples of attributes of each requirement include unique ID, source, owner, rationale (why the requirement is needed), priority, status (approved, pending approval, rejected, being reconsidered), cost, difficulty, stability, assigned to, location, author, revision, date, reason, traced-from, traced-to, root tag number, history, verification, validation, release, module, and others that depend on the specific needs of your project. See also step 19 in Chapter 5.

Key Requirements

The term *key requirements* is sometimes used to refer to requirements that are important in order to understand a system's essential capabilities or functions.[4] It is appropriate to analyze requirements in terms of their benefit-to-cost ratio, risk, or the estimated time and effort needed to address them, so that we can have informal discussions within the joint team to negotiate the requirements to be included. However, I suggest avoiding use of this term, because it's unclear.

Originating Requirements

In *The Engineering Design of Systems: Models and Methods* [14], Dennis Buede uses the term *originating requirements* to refer to the requirements initially established by the system's stakeholders with the help of the systems-engineering team. The term is not as clear as the term *real requirements,* and therefore I suggest not using it.

Other Guidelines

- Avoid using vague terminology, such as "usually, often, typically, generally, user friendly, versatile, flexible, reliable, and upgradeable," in writing requirements.

- Avoid putting more than one requirement in a requirement (often indicated by the presence of the word "and").

- Avoid clauses like "if that should be necessary."

- Avoid wishful thinking: 100% reliability, running on all platforms, pleasing all users, handling all unexpected failures.

See Alexander and Stevens's *Writing Better Requirements* [15] for excellent guidelines based on extensive experience.

Examples of Requirements Types

The following scenario provides examples of the requirements types discussed above that will facilitate an understanding of the different types.

ABC, Inc. has experienced phenomenal growth over the last three years due to mergers and acquisitions of companies that are similar or complementary in nature. To enhance ABC's competitive position, management

---

4. Industry expert Ian Alexander advises that it is practice of the United Kingdom (UK) Ministry of Defense (MoD) to use very few "key requirements"—there might be five for a warship, for example. "These become the most strongly sought goals for the system: if all else fails, these goals remain, and the other requirements can be evaluated in their light. It might not suit everybody but it contains something of the essence of prioritisation." Personal communication to the author, January 18, 2003.

desires an HR system to identify employees with needed skills and training across all company locations.

ABC management has determined that developing a new comprehensive HR system across the company would be cost prohibitive. Instead, management wishes to leave the legacy systems of each acquired company in place and integrate the data contained in them into an IT framework. The framework will consist of an IT infrastructure at headquarters, the public telephone network, and communications equipment at each company location necessary to support the framework processes.

The framework, code named SATURN (for Skills and Training Unified Referral Network), will not replace any of the legacy systems of the individual companies that ABC has acquired. The presentation of the new companywide employee data will be transparent to the local user. In other words, each local user will see the selected employee information for the whole company in the same format as it would be if stored locally on their own legacy system.

In addition, SATURN will be able to determine whether all legacy systems are available at the time a query is made. Should a particular legacy system be unavailable for any reason, the user will be notified so that a query can be made at a later time. Each query should be complete and all available information returned to the user within one minute. The SATURN system should be able to support up to 20 concurrent users without any degradation of performance.

The following Table 4.3(a–d) provides examples of requirement types for the development of the SATURN system. Table 4.3(a) provides requirement examples for the hardware/software requirements view shown in Table 4.1. Table 4.3(b) provides examples for the more detailed context described in Figure 4.1. Table 4.3(c) provides examples from the total requirements taxonomy view described in Figure 4.2. Finally Table 4.3(d) provides examples for the RA view of requirements described in Table 4.2.

Summary

It's apparent from this discussion that there are a lot of different types of requirements. It helps to agree to use a selected few types. Agree within your project team on the types that will be most useful. Use your project glossary, which provides defined and agreed-upon terminology. Use simple, understandable words. Write requirements that meet the criteria of a good requirement (see Chapter 1). Study the references provided for this chapter if you aren't already familiar with them.

Case Study

We had a known requirement for Web site performance. It involved a finite set of user scenarios that had to be executed by a specific number of

Table 4.3(a)   Hardware/Software Requirements View Examples

Hardware Requirements	
Performance	The SATURN system shall complete all retrievals and display the requested information, within one minute of the user entering the query.
	Up to 20 concurrent users may use the SATURN system without any degradation of response time.
Interface requirement	The SATURN system shall operate through a commercially available browser such as Internet Explorer or Netscape.
Specialty engineering requirement	The SATURN system shall run on commercial off-the-shelf (COTS) hardware using the Microsoft Windows Operating System.
Environmental requirement	The SATURN system shall operate on single-phase commercially available power with a line voltage in the range of 110 volts, plus or minus 20 volts AC.
Software Requirements	
Functional requirement	The SATURN system shall retrieve basic identifying information for all employees meeting the specified criteria.
Nonfunctional requirement	The SATURN system will generate error messages when a query fails to run to completion or a legacy system is not responding within the allotted time.

Source: Terry Bartholomew. Used with permission.

Table 4.3(b)   More Detailed Context Requirement Examples

Production process requirement	The SATURN system shall be available for use by all HR representatives at each company facility.
Product requirement	The SATURN system shall retrieve basic identifying information for all employees who meet the predetermined skills and training criteria.
Test process requirement	Test HR records for verifying the SATURN system will consist of a special set of personnel records at each company location specifically created with artificial data.
Operational process requirement	The SATURN system will have the same look and feel at each company location that users of the system at that location are familiar with and, therefore, shall require no training.

Source: Terry Bartholomew. Used with permission.

Table 4.3(c)   Total Taxonomy View Requirement Examples

Process functional requirement	The SATURN system shall be developed to provide companywide access to employee skills and training information to all HR representatives.
Process interface requirement	Skills and training information from all company locations will be available to all other company locations.
Process specialty requirement	To ensure complete skills and training information are captured among the legacy systems, a data model shall be created.
Process environmental requirement	SATURN shall be developed using joint application development (JAD) teams composed of users (HR representatives), developers, and system testers.
Process performance requirement	The SATURN system shall be ready for system acceptance testing within 180 days of project inception.

Table 4.3(c)   Total Taxonomy View Requirement Examples (continued)

Product functional requirement	The HR user shall be able to retrieve employee skills and training data by predefined categories.
Product interface requirement	The SATURN system's look and feel shall be identical to each local legacy system.
Product specialty requirement	The SATURN system shall use relational database technology.
Product environmental requirement	The SATURN system shall not require that additional heat, ventilation, and air conditioning (HVAC) capacity be installed at any location.
Product performance requirement	The SATURN system shall operate with 97% reliability, 24 hours a day, 7 days a week.

Source: Terry Bartholomew. Used with permission.

Table 4.3(d)   RA View Requirement Examples

Customer Needs and Expectations	*Examples*
(Requirements Analysis Input)	
Business requirements	Managers need access to timely and accurate data on personnel in order to meet operational needs.
User requirements	The user needs the capability to search on personnel across the entire company by predefined skill sets.
Product requirements	Data formats shall be translated across legacy system boundaries into the format supported by the local user's system.
Environmental requirements	There shall be no operational impact on any user other than the impact on information retrieval caused by having a larger population of employees from which to select.
System Requirements Specifications (Requirements Analysis Output)	
High-level (or system-level) requirements	The SATURN system shall maintain cross-references for information types contained in the legacy systems. For example the field called "education_level" in one system is the same as "education" in another.
	The SATURN system shall convert data from each legacy system to the data expected by the local user. For example a masters degree in one system might be reflected in another system as "grade 17."
Functional requirements	The local user shall be able to search all legacy systems in a predefined local, regional, or national geographical area for personnel meeting a specified skill set.
Nonfunctional requirements	The SATURN system shall make use of the public switched network (PSN) and not require dedicated lines of communication.
Derived (or design) requirements and design constraints	The SATURN system shall use public key infrastructure (PKI) communications security.
Performance requirements	The SATURN system shall support up to 20 simultaneous users without any noticeable degradation of service.
	The SATURN system shall return all available skill sets to the user within 1 minute of initiating a search.
Interface requirements	The SATURN system shall present a look and feel consistent with each local office's legacy system.

Source: Terry Bartholomew. Used with permission.

simultaneous users. Our test machine was much smaller than our production machine was going to be, and in fact, one of our requirements was to determine the size and configuration of machine(s) we needed to meet the performance requirement. It turned out that there was no reasonable way to extrapolate measured performance on our test box to the expected performance on a variety of possible production boxes. Moreover, we could not even begin to execute the test scripts on our test box until we had essentially completed development of all of the functionality. Neither of these facts was known when we committed to a delivery date. In effect, we had a derived requirement that we did not realize: in this scenario, we needed several months of stability after development of version 1 and prior to release of version 1 in which we could test, measure, procure a new box, and tune it. Lesson learned: schedule commitments shouldn't be made until the requirements are understood.

References

[1] Engineering Process Improvement Collaboration (EPIC), *A Systems Engineering Capability Maturity Model*, Version 1.1. Pittsburgh, PA, Software Engineering Institute, Carnegie-Mellon University, 1995, at www.sei.cmu.edu/pub/documents/95.reports/pdf/mm003.95.pdf.

[2] EIA Standard 632, "Processes for Engineering a System," Arlington, VA, 1998.

[3] IEEE Standard 12207, "Software Life Cycle Processes," New York: IEEE, 1998.

[4] Zachman Framework Web sites (e.g., see www.zifa.com).

[5] Inmon, W. H., J. A. Zachman, and J. C. Geiger, *Data Stores, Data Warehousing, and the Zachman Framework: Managing Enterprise Knowledge*, New York: McGraw Hill, 1997.

[6] Hay, J., *Requirements Analysis—From Business Views to Architecture*, Englewood Cliffs, NJ: Prentice Hall, 2002.

[7] CMMI Web site, at www.sei.cmu.edu/cmmi.

[8] Grady, J. O., *Systems Requirements Analysis*, New York: McGraw-Hill, 1993.

[9] Grady, J. O., *System Validation and Verification*, Boca Raton, FL: CRC Press, 1997.

[10] Davis, A. M., *Software Requirements: Objects, Functions, & States*, Upper Saddle River, NJ: Prentice Hall, 1993.

[11] Whitten, N., "Meet Minimum Requirements: Anything More Is Too Much," *PM Network* (September 1998), p. 19.

[12] The Standish Group International, Inc., *CHAOS Chronicles 2003 Report*, West Yarmouth, MA: The Standish Group International, Inc., 2002, at www.standishgroup.com.

[13] Young, R. R., *Effective Requirements Practices*, Boston, MA: Addison-Wesley, 2001.

[14] Buede, D. M., *The Engineering Design of Systems: Models and Methods*, New York: John Wiley & Sons, 2000.

[15] Alexander, I. F., and R. Stevens, *Writing Better Requirements*, London, UK: Addison-Wesley, 2002.

Gathering Requirements

The need to gather requirements is initiated by a request from an internal or external customer. Requests can come in many forms, including a request for proposals (RFP) [1], an SOW, or an informal or formal inquiry describing a capability that is needed. The request initiates a set of requirements gathering activities. It's vital for the RA to have a thorough understanding of these activities and to gain experience in performing related tasks.

My experience has taught me the following:

▸ A lot of time and effort is wasted in the project startup phase and in performing requirements gathering activities. There are a number of reasons for this:

1. The project is just getting organized and things are confused.

2. There is no road map or checklist of startup activities.

3. Not all staff are present; some are still being recruited.

4. There isn't much pressure to meet the schedule yet.

5. The customer and users are also trying to get organized and get started.

6. The staff who will be working on end-product development may not fully understand the customer's objectives and, consequently, may not be able to appreciate the customer's expectations.

7. An effective proven procedure for the requirements gathering steps is not available or used.

▸ If the requirements gathering effort is not effective, the stage is set for much additional time and effort to be wasted when technical work is initiated and performed as a result of poor requirements. For example, at one large telecommunications company, 100% of planned development costs was budgeted for rework of developed software based on previous experience that the stated requirements would not be what was actually needed.

Thus, the RA can play a vital role by ensuring that the requirements gathering activities are planned and performed well (effectively). He or she can do a lot to ensure that the train (the project) stays on the tracks by suggesting and recommending effective practices, methods, techniques, and tools and by assisting the PM, customers, users, and members of the project team. His or her role is not limited strictly to requirements-related activities; rather the RA is a valuable advisor to the PM and all others on the project team. Take a few moments to review the nine roles of an RA (described in Chapter 2):

1. Work collaboratively with customers, users, and system architects and designers to identify the real requirements for a planned system or software development effort to define the problem that needs to be solved;

2. Work effectively with customers and users to manage new and changed requirements so that the project stays under control; to install a mechanism to control changes;

3. Be alert to new technologies that may help;

4. Facilitate the project in reusing artifacts and achieving repeatability;

5. Assist the project and its customers in envisioning a growth path from the first release or version of a product through a set of staged releases to the ultimate system or product;

6. Advise the project (and customer) of methods, techniques, and automated tools that are available to best support requirements-related project work and activities;

7. Use metrics to measure, track, and control requirements-related project work activities and results;

8. Facilitate discussions and to mediate conflicts;

9. Study the domain of the area in which the system or software is being used.

These roles provide the context for this chapter. The first step is to plan the approach.

Plan the Approach

I've suggested previously the tremendous value of spending some time (in any endeavor) to plan the approach. Write (document) the planned approach to address the requirements-related work in a project requirements plan. As is the case with other plans, the requirements plan can be (and should be) revisited and updated frequently during the project. Some of the critical aspects of this plan are summarized in the checklist provided in Table 5.1 and discussed below. Note that all aspects are not necessarily always perfomed sequentially; some may be performed concurrently. Note that some aspects are iterative (done repeatedly based on the availability of new or different information). Retain flexibility in your approach (always) to allow new information to shape refinements in the approach.

Table 5.1   Checklist for Project Requirements Gathering Activities

Done?	Step	Action or Activity
	1	Review related historical information
	2	Review related organizational policies
	3	Identify the stakeholders of the project
	4	Develop a strategy to involve customers and users throughout the development effort
	5	Write (and iterate) a project vision and scope document
	6	Develop a requirements plan
	7	Provide for peer reviews and inspections of all requirements-related work products
	8	Initiate a project glossary and a project acronyms list
	9	Decide on the life-cycle approach to be used on the project
	10	Begin tailoring of the corporate (or other) requirements process
	11	Establish a mechanism to evolve the real requirements from the stated requirements
	12	Provide requirements-related training for project participants, including customers and users, and for RAs
	13	Rewrite the high-level system or software requirements as you proceed through the initial steps
	14	Initiate development of the real requirements based on the stated requirements
	15	Initiate documentation of the rationale for each requirement
	16	Establish a mechanism to control changes to requirements and new requirements
	17	Perform the verification approach and validation planning
	18	Select the practices, methods, and techniques that will be used to gather the requirements
	19	Begin consideration and selection of an automated requirements tool, identification of the attributes that will be needed for each requirement, and the composition of the requirements repository
	20	Select and acquire the automated requirements tool
	21	Load the initial real requirements into the selected requirements tool, label each requirement uniquely, and initiate assignment of appropriate attributes information to each requirement
	22	Perform requirements gathering
	23	Involve system architects and designers in reviews of the requirements
	24	Develop the traceability strategy to be used
	25	Identify the requirements that will be met in the first release or initial products (prioritize real requirements)
	26	Establish an approach for a proof of concept, prototype, or other approximation of the work product
	27	Incorporate requirements best practices and garner management support for effective requirements engineering (including an integrated quality approach)
	28	Complete requirements gathering for the first release

Each of the steps of the requirements gathering approach is discussed below, and several suggested references are provided to point you to additional information. Think of these steps as a procedure for implementing two of the three subprocesses of the requirements process: Assess New/Changed Requirements and Control Changes; and Understand Customer Needs and Expectations, RE100 and RE200 in the terminology of *Effective Requirements Practices* (see [2, pp. 114 and 115] for the actual process flowcharts). As always, tailor (modify) the approach as needed to your particular situation and your project and organizational environment—you may be able to eliminate some of the steps or you may want to add steps.

It's likely that you will benefit from having copies of the flowcharts in front of you so that you can consider changes you would like to make. You might want to visit my Web site (www.ralphyoung.net); go to the "Reusable Artifacts" button, and look for "Sample Requirements Process." This will enable you to print four flowcharts, a macro- (high-level) process and three micro- (lower-level) or subprocesses to the macro flow. Note the link on that Web page for the "Process Descriptions" that explain the four flowcharts (process purpose, standards and references, related processes, customers of the process, customer requirements, entrance criteria, inputs, outputs, exit criteria, responsibilities, tools, resources, and suggested metrics). Digesting these artifacts will provide you with a lot of ideas.

1. *Review related historical information.*

In any effort, there are materials available that need to be read, digested, and analyzed. Examples of such information include descriptions of the legacy system(s), statements concerning needs for new capabilities, white papers, descriptions of related systems developed by other organizations, research studies, people with whom you might meet to garner insight (such as proponents or advocates of a needed capability or new system), and so forth. Be open and thorough in looking for and reviewing materials. Organize the materials you find in a way that helps you gauge their relative importance and value and also allows retrieval of information when it is needed. Think about the materials in the context of the other steps in the requirements gathering approach listed in Table 5.1.

2. *Review related organizational policies.*

In any organization, there should exist a set of organizational policies concerning how systems and software development is to be done. Find these policies; read and digest them. Ensure that you understand them and can apply them in your work. Ask coworkers and your manager for clarification, if needed. If policies exist and no one pays close attention to them, this itself is a continuous improvement opportunity for the organization—get QA and process engineering folks involved. Find out if a library exists of related processes, sample plans such as project plans and others, metrics that should be used, methods, techniques, automated and manual tools that are available, lessons learned (or at least observed) from other (previous) projects, and so forth. Ensure that you have a comprehensive knowledge of the resources available to you to do your work. Look for templates, checklists, presentations, and files of familiarization and training sessions that may help. Before embarking on a task to create an artifact, check to see if one already exists that you can reuse or at least use as a guide. Try to avoid reinventing the wheel, that is, recreating an artifact when a template or example already exists. If someone has already done what you are about to do, chances are that you can save time and effort by knowing about it.

3.   *Identify stakeholders of the project.*

A stakeholder is anyone who has an interest in the project and anyone who will be touched by the system. Think of customers (those who are paying for the work), users (people who will actually use the system), advisors (such as legal experts or regulators who have relevant information about the requirements), project groups that are involved in developing the system (such as systems engineering, software engineering, QA, CM, project control, documentation, training, testing, and so forth.). Just as in designing a process, there are always more stakeholders than we think of initially. Ian Alexander suggests using a "Stakeholder Analysis Template" [3] to identify stakeholders. John Boardman Associates (JBA) developed the template (e-mail: ian@jba.net). Figures 5.1 and 5.2 depict the roles of stakeholders and the viewpoints of the roles.[1]

The systems engineering approach suggests developing a concept of operations (CONOPS) that focuses on the goals, objectives, and general desired capabilities of a new or improved system or product.[2] Operational scenarios (sequences of events expected during the operation of system products) are developed (see the discussion of scenarios as a requirements gathering technique later in this chapter). These include the environmental conditions, usage rates, inputs to the system (sometimes referred to as expected stimuli), and outputs (responses). Operational scenarios are the ideal framework for mission/business/user requirements and are also helpful in identifying and clarifying system aspects.

---

1. See also Chapter 13 of Sommerville and Sawyer's *Requirements Engineering: A Good Practice Guide* (New York: John Wiley & Sons, 1997), which provides a systematic approach for collecting requirements from multiple viewpoints, called PREview. A related Web site, www.info.comp.lancs. ac.uk/publications/index.phtml, is well worth a visit.

2. EIA 632, "Processes for Engineering a System," provides a comprehensive, structured, disciplined approach for all life-cycle phases. The systems engineering process is applied iteratively throughout the system life cycle. The operational concept facilitates separating mission requirements from other system requirements, identifying scenarios that dictate the interaction between the system and other systems (including people), and focuses heavily on the inputs and outputs of the system.

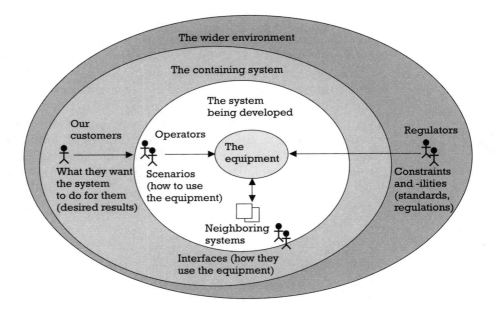

Figure 5.1   Roles of stakeholders. (*Source:* John Boardman Associates (JBA). Used with permission.)

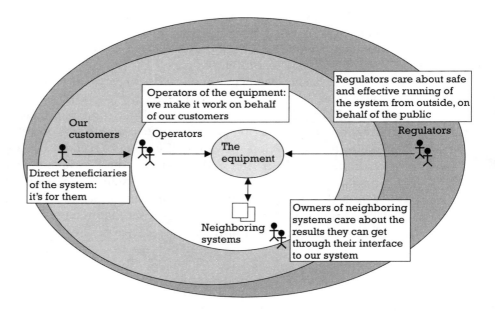

Figure 5.2   Viewpoints of roles. (*Source:* John Boardman Associates (JBA). Used with permission.)

Helen Sharp [4] suggests using a recursive approach to identify stake-holders—ask your initial point of contact for a list of stakeholders, then ask each person on that list who else has a stake, and so forth, until you are not finding any more stakeholders (sometimes this approach is referred to as "peeling the onion"). She suggests naming four groups of baselines stakeholders—users, developers, legislators, and decision makers—and then exploring the network of stakeholders around the baseline. Ellen Gottesdiener [5] suggests including "indirect users" (or "secondary users")—people who will come in contact with the system's outputs (such as files and reports) or with system by-products (such as decisions).

Understanding the customer makeup and internal politics is important. For example, if the proposed system will replace existing systems, each owned by an established (read "entrenched") group, and the change is being forced from above, the strategy used to involve customers might be far different from that used if the proposed system is to integrate with several existing systems and leave them essentially intact. An ideal situation might be to build a new system for a single customer, but frequently projects have multiple customers. A challenging situation from one RA's experience was a system that had three separate agencies as customers: two strong willed ones and a meek one. Trying to sort out the politics was far too complicated for most reasonable people. A second contractor that had a significant negative impact on project efforts further complicated the situation. In the final analysis, understanding the project from the perspective of various organizations' involvement may be as important as understanding stakeholders' needs.

4.   *Develop a strategy to involve customers and users throughout the development effort.*

Experience shows us that projects that involve customers and users throughout the development effort are more successful. The reason is that there exists effective communication. Without effective communication, the customer/user and the developer lose sight of each other and their perspectives. While this task is not primarily the role of the RA, it is critical to the successful performance of the RA's tasks that this strategy be developed and implemented. Advocate as part of the project team that the strategy be pursued.

One strategy to involve customers and users is "partnering." See Insert 5.1 and *Effective Requirements Practices* [2, pp. 30–41], for a discussion of this approach. This could well be the nugget that empowers your overall strategy. I have used partnering, and I can tell you that it works very well.

Another strategy is to use requirements workshops and other requirements gathering techniques that involve customers and users interactively in the decisions that are made. It's best if the customer and users are intimately involved throughout the entire life cycle. Another technique to help with this is to include customers on a project change control board (CCB) to facilitate their being actively involved throughout development activities. Note that many commercial products are designed toward target audience needs rather than those of a finite group of stakeholders. Focus groups and other techniques are used to generate a model of customer behavior that

Insert 5.1—Description of Partnering

Partnering is a structured process designed to create an atmosphere of commitment, cooperation, and collegial problem solving among organizations and individuals working together on a project. An environment of mutual safety and trust is essential to effective partnering. Partnering uses an outside, trained facilitator to develop vision statements, common goals, guiding principles, issue-resolution procedures, and evaluation methods to help ensure project success. The process is normally initiated at a workshop at the beginning of the project. At the workshop everyone is considered equal. No participant or organization should be allowed to dominate the workshop process. All parties need to recognize that partnering is the building of the team with the objective of achieving commitment to project success.

Partnering does not change the parties' contract obligations. It does facilitate the manner in which the contracting parties treat each other during the course of contract performance. It creates a climate in which the interests and expectations of the contracted parties are more readily achievable. To this end, a written charter is created during the workshop that states the parties' common interests in reducing time-consuming and costly disputes, as well as improving communications to the benefit of all parties.

All contracting parties have an economic interest in the success of the project. Just as customers are concerned with getting good value for their money, suppliers are in business to make a fair profit for the services they provide. When a supplier is squeezed for profit, the quality of the work and business relationships can suffer or be destroyed, creating hostility and expensive protracted litigation of claims. Driving good suppliers out of business is not in anyone's best interest. The long-term goal of every owner should be to keep good contractors in business so that competitive bidding is as robust as possible in the future.

Partnering should include the ultimate users of the system. Customers need to be involved in the partnering process from start to finish. They provide valuable information about their project needs and can participate in problem-solving sessions at the workshop and follow-up meetings, and may gain a better understanding of where their dollars are going when contract modifications are required. A typical goal of the partnering team is to deliver a quality project to the customer that meets the customer's functional needs and financial constraints. Customer satisfaction is an essential ingredient in virtually all partnering efforts.

The costs for partnering generally include one to three days of the participants' time at the start of a project to conduct the workshop and any follow-up sessions later. There are also the facilitator's fees for these meetings. These costs are small, however, when a project is delivered within the customer's budget, at a profit for the supplier, and

---

Insert 5.1—Description of Partnering (continued)

ahead of schedule. The time required is small in comparison to the time saved over the course of the project. At the initial workshop, many partnering teams will identify and resolve potential problems. This can prevent weeks or months of delay later in the project. During the project, the team uses partnering procedures to work together to avoid other schedule delays and to achieve project goals.

Anyone who has a direct impact on the success of the project should be a participant and attend the initial partnering workshop to become a team member. Participation in the workshop assures an understanding of the team's common goals and mutual vision. When an individual is not present at the workshop, partnering may have no meaning to that person.

Follow-up sessions are sometimes delayed or canceled because of the pressures of project performance and completion schedules. This prevents the partnering process from working effectively when it is most needed. It takes a strong commitment to partnering to ensure that follow-up sessions take place when everyone is otherwise busy. To avoid this problem, a schedule for the follow-up sessions should be established during the initial workshop. Dates can be set to meet all team members' schedule requirements.

Subcontractors should participate to inform the other participants of their interests and value to the project. Subcontractors will, in turn, learn and appreciate what is important to the other project participants. Subcontractor participation in the workshop can help prevent disputes during performance.

Two essential elements of a successful partnering relationship are trust and communication. If any team member feels that other team members are taking advantage, trust will be adversely affected. Team members should be encouraged to communicate this feeling to the others plainly and promptly when the issue arises.

Source: Chales Markert, partnering facilitator.

---

then serves as a placeholder. This model must be validated and verified just as one would do with any other step of the requirements process, but frequently it is very poorly crafted and only later are the actual market preferences discovered.

5. *Write (and iterate) a project vision and scope document.*

This document needs to be only a few pages long, but it is very important, because it helps all stakeholders gain a better understanding of the planned system or software. The document should present the following:

▸ The business requirements and related business objectives for the system;

▸ The vision of the solution, consolidated from the various stakeholders, and described in terms of what is needed to meet the business objectives;

▸ The scope of the system that is envisioned in terms of what it should and should not include.

Karl Wiegers provides an instructive and insightful discussion about why this document is important and a detailed outline of what it should include in *Software Requirements* [6, pp. 81–93]. I suggest that you iterate the project vision and scope document because it will become more useful as you and others gain a more comprehensive understanding of the planned system. You'll find that the vision may change a little and the scope a lot. Beware of requirements growth (also known as requirements "creep," where requirements are added without having RM controls in place). Weinberg [7] utilizes the term *requirements leakage* to refer to unofficial requirements being added when they are not really needed—see the discussion of this important issue in *Effective Requirements Practices*, [2, pp. 221–229]. Again, this demonstrates the value of planning and reinforces the value of investing in early requirements activities, before the other technical work is launched.

6.   *Develop a requirements plan.*

I have stressed the importance of planning with regard to any activity, and requirements activities are no exception. You are familiar with several types of plans for a project, such as the project management plan (PMP), SEMP, SDP, QA plan, CM plan, training plan, and others. Use the suggested table of contents for a project requirements plan provided in Table 5.2 to help you to document needed requirements-related activities and what will be done and to discern holes and needs [8].

Ellen Gottesdiener's experience [5] is that the experienced RA will plan for three to four iterations through the requirements development process. Both internal and external customers should follow each iteration with a formal or informal review. This approach may seem excessive, particularly if you are new to gathering requirements. Ellen Gottesdiener's experience lends credence to the value of investing in the requirements process to identify the real requirements prior to starting other work. This can be a major factor in reducing rework (rework represents 40% to 50% of total costs of most projects). Make sure that all stakeholders buy into the approach you have defined. While there are excellent reasons to plan and conduct multiple iterations of the requirements, it is likely that you will have to defend the time and resources needed to accomplish this.

7.   *Provide for peer reviews and inspections of all requirements-related work products.*

Table 5.2   Sample Table of Contents for a Project
Requirements Plan

Purpose
Contract, Project, or Task Summary
Use of the System Engineering Process
Suggested Strategy for Addressing Industry Requirements Problems
The Project Requirements Process
Importance of the Requirements Process in Overcoming Requirements Problems
Requirements Process, Mechanisms, Practices, Methods, Techniques, and Tools to Be Used on the Project
Suggested Approach to Involve Customers and Users
Industry Requirements Best Practices
References Consulted
Appendixes
A   Tailored Requirements Process (flowcharts and process descriptions)
B   Partnering Process Briefing
C   Criteria of a Good Requirement
D   Guidelines for System Development Based on Requirements Considerations

In the first place, ensure that there is an effective peer review process that is actually used throughout your project. If one is not in place, work with your manager and the PM to adopt and use this industry best practice. Provide them the discussion in *Effective Requirements Practices* [2, pp. 248–250]. *Work hard to advocate use of peer reviews and inspections. They will save time, money, and effort and also improve quality and customer satisfaction.* Use Wiegers's *Peer Reviews in Software: A Practical Guide* [9] to implement a peer-review and inspections approach that best fits your project. (Although the title of Wiegers's book says "software," the information about peer reviews in the book applies to any work product.) On request, Northrop Grumman IT DES [10] can provide two 2-hour training courses and associated support to launch your project's or organization's peer-review process:

1.   "Peer Review Participant Training";

2.   "Peer Review Moderator Training."

Contact peer review process owner Penny Waugh at PWaugh@ngc.com for information.

Some projects receive the advice not to do peer reviews and inspections of requirements-related documents on their projects. Not having peer reviews is an inexcusable project risk in my opinion. Experience has shown that no work product should be developed, no matter how simple it is, without being reviewed by at least one peer who is knowledgeable about the subject of the work product. The point is that (1) the words that I use may

or may not communicate my intent effectively; (2) others may have a
different perspective; (3) any work product will benefit from the ideas,
suggestions, and corrections provided by others; and (4) time and money
are saved when defects are identified earlier than they otherwise would
be. The challenge is to find people independent enough to provide a
fresh set of eyes, yet familiar enough with the general topic and process to
avoid excessive review overhead or making meaningless or misleading
comments.

8.   *Initiate a project glossary and a project acronyms list.*

One of the issues in my own experience that has jeopardized teamwork, caused far too much discussion (read, confusion, frustration, and
delays), and even destroyed many good interpersonal relationships is that
we technical people tend to have very strong opinions about definitions
of particular words, and we tend to resist moving forward when we
don't know or understand an acronym that is being used. I strongly recommend and advocate that each project develop a project glossary and
a project list of acronyms. These artifacts should be created as early as possible, for example, as part of the project vision documentation, and
expanded as the project matures. In addition to acronyms, the basic
nomenclature associated with an emerging system concept can have a
major impact on design freedom. (Functional versus physical language
choices in particular have great benefit early in the project life cycle.)
Include words and acronyms that are acceptable to and used by the customers and users— for example, we refer to knowledge of the customer's
area as domain knowledge or expertise; persons who are extremely
knowledgeable in a particular area are referred to as subject matter experts
(SMEs). In the interests of the project work being accomplished expedi-
tiously, let's do the following:

> ‣ *Agree on definitions of the words we use that we all can live with.*
> This doesn't require that the consensus definition is each person's
> favorite definition of the word, only that all of us on our project
> team can live with the wording of the definition. Suggestion: use
> a thumbs-up("I support it"), thumbs down ("I can't live with it"),
> or thumbs sideways ("I can live with it") technique in project meet-
> ings to gain consensus quickly. If people have issues ("thumbs
> down"), ask, "What will it take to convince you to be able to live
> with the approach or definition that most people find accept-
> able?" If you have a TEAMWORKS environment, you should be
> able to achieve consensus on most topics easily. (A TEAMWORKS
> environment is a work setting where working together as an
> effective team is valued and appreciated and where coworkers pro-
> actively support one another. See Chapter 8 for further discussion
> concerning teamwork.) If you can't, perhaps you have a "spe-
> cial cause of variation," such as an obstreperous person or different

perspectives.[3] I have no golden cure for special causes of variation, only that we should look constantly for root causes of issues and problems, use our many venues to brainstorm countermeasures, prioritize countermeasures according to their perceived effectiveness, implement them, and then evaluate whether the countermeasures have had the desire impact on the root causes. If they haven't, it's time to identify and select other countermeasures.

▸ Develop a project acronyms list that includes all of the acronyms that are encountered by all of those working on the project. This can be accomplished by putting the list of acronyms on a shared server so that everyone can have access to it and adding acronyms as they are encountered. Also, anyone encountering an acronym can use this resource to try to find out what the acronym stands for. It makes no sense whatever for project meetings, training sessions, briefings, and so forth, to become bogged down because someone doesn't know an acronym!

9. *Decide on the life-cycle approach to be used on the project.*[4]

This decision may seem to you to be outside your purview. However, in my experience, most projects don't give this decision enough consideration. Most often, projects tend to hobble through the design and development activities without making the life-cycle approach explicit. A specific life-cycle approach should be selected by the project. This decision is important because different life-cycle models have strengths and weaknesses, and some are more appropriate for particular domains.[5] A key question is, What fraction of the final design would you say is known at this point? Projects with only minor changes to existing designs are very different from those that require fundamental work. Study Table 5.3 and Figures 5.3 to 5.6. Review related information provided in the references by Reed Sorenson [11] and Barry Boehm [12]. If you are considering the spiral model approach, read Boehm and Hanse's "The Spiral Model As a Tool for Evolutionary

---

3. Ian Alexander reports from his consulting experiences that coworkers often insist on using specific words in ways that preclude common understanding and that delay and even prevent progress in reaching consensus. He believes the root cause of this serious problem is not obstreperousness, but rather that people have different perspectives about things. This emphasizes why it is so important to have a TEAMWORKS environment, as well as to use mechanisms (such as thumbs up, down, or sideways and a project glossary) to reach consensus and move on.

4. With thanks to Rich Raphael of Northrop Grumman IT DES for developing these materials and providing analysis of life-cycle models and illustrations of them.

5. The U.S. undersecretary of defense for acquisition, technology, and logistics, E. C. Aldridge Jr., published a memorandum dated April 12, 2002, expressing a preference for evolutionary acquisition strategies relying on a spiral development process. A point of contact for further information is Skip Hawthorne (skip.hawthorne @osd.mil). The memorandum acknowledges that there is "confusion about what these terms mean and how spiral development impacts various processes such as contracting and requirements generation that interface with an evolutionary acquisition strategy."

Table 5.3 Comparison of Life-Cycle Models

	Waterfall	Incremental	Evolutionary	Spiral
Description	Emphasizes completion of one phase of development before proceeding to the next phase; freeze the products of one phase before proceeding to the next phase. Must use a formal change mechanism to make requirements changes.	Performs the waterfall in overlapping sections.	The development stage is done as a series of increments. Each increment builds a subset of the full system. An increment is a full life cycle of analysis, design, coding, testing, and integration. It may be delivered to the user, but not necessarily. If it is delivered, there may be some finishing: optimization, packaging, and the like, after the build.	Divides system development into four basic activities: planning, risk analysis, engineering, and evaluation. Within each spiral loop, risks are identified and attempts to mitigate risk are made before proceeding to the engineering activity of the spiral.
Strengths	Patterned after process models in other disciplines, making it easy for managers to understand and accept. In this model each phase is defined by a set of functions, goals, milestones, and deliverables, making the process highly visible and the project easier to track. Since requirements and specifications are determined at the outset, the PM is better able to determine his or her resource needs and establish schedules.	Requirements do not have to be fully specified/clarified at onset. As each increment is completed, requirements are clarified.	Is focused on early and continuous delivery of requirement-defined stakeholder value. Allows detailed requirements to emerge gradually.	Avoids some of the difficulties of existing software models by using a risk-driven approach. Tries to eliminate errors in early phases. Provides mechanisms for QA. Applicable to other kinds of projects. Works well for a complex, dynamic, innovative project. Reevaluation after each phase allows changes in user perspectives, technology advances, or financial perspectives.
Weaknesses	Does not work very well in situations where the requirements are not well defined at the beginning of the process.	There is a tendency to push difficult problems to the future in order to demonstrate early success to management.	Requires cultural mind-set change from conventional methods.	Lacks explicit process guidance to determine objectives, constraints, and alternatives.

Table 5.3 Comparison of Life Cycle Models (continued)

	Waterfall	Incremental	Evolutionary	Spiral
Weaknesses	The model's major weakness is the costliness of changing requirements. The farther a project proceeds, the more costly a change in requirements becomes. The customer does not see a working product until late in the life cycle. By the time the customer gets a chance to review the product, any errors or omissions are very costly to correct. Real projects seldom flow sequentially. Although reiterating is possible, reiteration tends to cause confusion as the project advances.	Difficult to manage and measure project because one cannot ascertain when all requirements will be complete.	Requires some training and experience to apply the method effectively.	Provides more flexibility than convenient for many applications. Risk assessment expertise: The assessment of project risks and their resolution is not an easy task. A lot of experience in projects is necessary to accomplish tasks successfully.
Domain of applications	Systems that have well-defined requirements at the outset and systems where the costs and schedules need to be determined up front.	Well-suited for systems where the requirements cannot be specified.	Well-suited for systems where the requirements cannot be specified prior to start of life-cycle development activities.	Complex, dynamic, innovative, ambitious projects carried out in internal teams (not necessarily limited to software).

Source: Richard Raphael. Used with permission.

Acquisition" [13], which explains enhancements to the original spiral model that now are considered essential to its use. Note that the win-win approach is the subject of ongoing work by Boehm and others. Make information available to other members of your project team (including the customer), have discussions, and reach consensus on the life-cycle model that best meets the needs of your project. Be aware that some requirements are unknowable until customers and users start using the system. This concern is best addressed by using an incremental development approach.

Some industry experts question whether the evolutionary and spiral models are really different. Boehm himself discusses "evolution" in describing the spiral model. Some industry experts believe that the incremental and evolutionary models are very different and incompatible—it's very

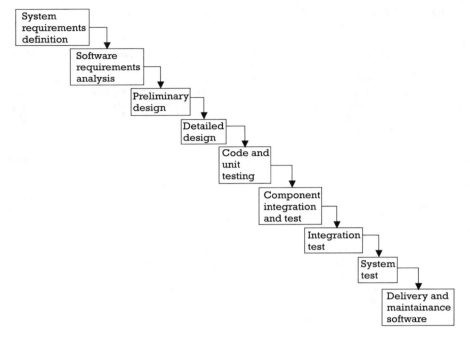

Figure 5.3   Illustration of the waterfall model.

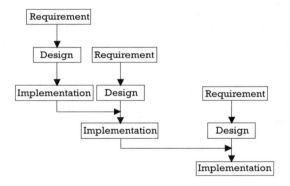

Figure 5.4   Illustration of the incremental development model.

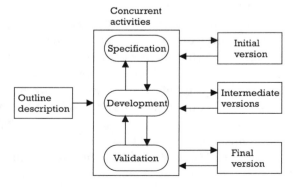

Figure 5.5   Illustration of the evolutionary model.

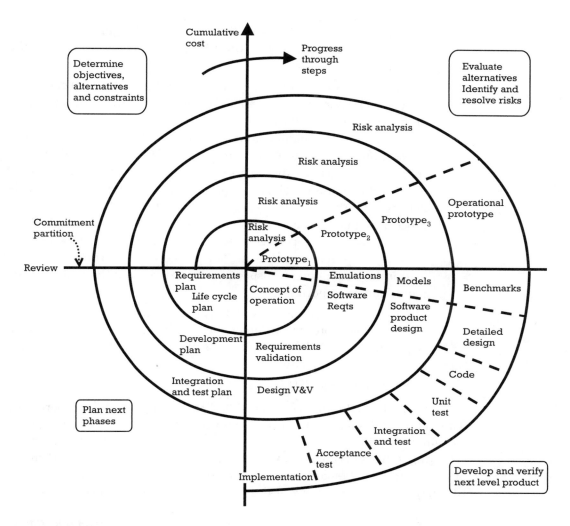

Figure 5.6 Illustration of the spiral model. (*Sources:* [12, 13].)

tricky to allow evolution when attempting to maintain an unchanged architecture, while adding components to it incrementally. Another view is that all of the models cited are applicable to some aspect of many projects—think of them as alternate views of the same thing, and the more viewing angles that are considered, the better the understanding! To an extent, it's like arguing over whether a top or side view is better.

10. *Begin tailoring the corporate (or other) requirements process.*

I've mentioned earlier the importance of using a documented requirements process. The essential point is that you will be following a process in any case, whether it is a documented process or not. Experience has shown us that using documented processes is a vastly superior approach for the following reasons:

- Lessons learned from industry and corporate experience, as well as from previous projects in your organization, can be incorporated into the process.

- There is less risk of having to perform rework (the industry average for rework on systems and software development projects is 40% to 50% of the total project's effort and cost; proactively reducing rework is an opportunity to save money, time, and effort and to increase customer satisfaction and quality at same time). Requirements engineering consultant and industry expert Karl Wiegers estimates that 80% of the rework effort on a development project is traceable to requirements defects [14]. This suggests strongly that investing in the requirements process can finance substantial levels of process improvement activities. For example, Wiegers recommends formal inspections of every requirements-related document. See Wiegers's two articles [15, 16] concerning requirements inspections for advice about how to provide requirements inspections.

- There is a higher probability that you will be able to improve the process as you proceed through the project activities if the process is documented. "Whoa!" you say, "I don't even know where to go to 'get' a requirements process!" Yes, you do! See my Web site (www.ralphyoung.net).

Incidentally, tailoring is a critical skill that is being lost as the experience base retires and is replaced by people who are self-taught or whose insight is acquired only from software marketing brochures or industry standards. Tailoring is the application of experienced-based insight to arrive at an intelligent match of standard process elements and situational challenges. I strongly suggest peer review of the tailoring approach wherever possible.

11. *Establish a mechanism to evolve the real requirements from the stated requirements.*

As you begin the process of identifying more detailed requirements, you'll need to establish a mechanism to evolve the real requirements from the stated requirements (see Chapter 4 for clarification of the differences). In *Effective Requirements Practices*, I refer to this mechanism as the joint team (see [2, pp. 46–53] for a discussion of the joint team). It doesn't really matter what you call this mechanism. What's needed is one or a few representatives of the customer who are empowered to make decisions concerning requirements to meet with a similar number of empowered people from the project to review all of the requirements to do the following:

- Ensure that each requirement reflects real customer and user needs. You'll find that many of the stated requirements are not real requirements.

- Ensure that each requirement meets the criteria of a good requirement. You'll find that this step will require a lot of work. Knowing that

there are important reasons for each of the criteria, you'll understand that this work is highly leveraged and invaluable. If you
don't understand the reasons for one or more of the criteria, take some
time to study the criteria and satisfy yourself that each criterion is
essential.

> Provide a rationale for each requirement (why it is needed). Industry
> experience is that up to half of the stated requirements can be elimi-
> nated by performing this one step. Stop to think for a minute about the
> work that this one step potentially can save the project ("proactively
> reduce rework"). Realize also that this effort could well make the differ-
> ence between project success and failure. Discuss this with your man-
> ager and the PM. Help the project benefit from a TEAMWORKS
> approach by applying team approaches in your own work activities (see
> Chapter 9 for a discussion of teamwork).

> *While performing this work, focus on product benefits (necessary real require-
> ments), not features of the work products.* We can provide a ton of features,
> all of which take time and money to develop and include in the system,
> but we need to focus on minimum requirements (remember, "Any-
> thing more is too much!" [Neal Whitten]).

> Make an intentional effort to discover real requirements that are
> unstated. In working with your customer and users, work deliberately
> to identify real requirements that they have not included. This will
> require a thorough understanding of the customer needs, attention to
> the system-level requirements, and thoughtful analysis. We never
> promised that the work of the RA would be simple or easy. One way
> to address this is evolution—seeing an early version or prototype or
> demonstration is a powerful aid to discovering unstated real require-
> ments. Models and mockups are inexpensive ways of eliciting
> unstated requirements. D. Leffingwell and D. Widrig [17] and Ellen
> Gottesdiener [5] offer other simple inexpensive techniques.

This is a good time to emphasize the importance of verification (does the
design solution meet the identified requirements?) and validation (are the
requirements implemented in the delivered system?) (V&V). See step 17
and Chapter 7 for further discussion and clarification.

Here are some other goals of good requirements practitioners as identified by Ivy Hooks in her requirements training:

> Identify incorrect assumptions;

> Ensure consistency;

> Increase compliance;

> Reduce misunderstandings between organizations and individuals;

> Improve the responsiveness of suppliers;

> ‣ Improve the satisfaction of all customers;

> ‣ Write good requirements.

It's worth noting that many stakeholders will be able to communicate requirements only in general terms. These will then need to be "translated" into usable design requirements by the team. My suggestion is to be tolerant early in the process in order to stimulate open communication and then to tighten up expectations as time and developing process insight allow.

12. *Provide requirements-related training sessions for project participants, including customers and users, and for RAs.*

Here is a challenge for you. Your peers on the project will in all probability resist this training. They will assert that they don't need it and that they are very busy with their own work. In reality, neither of these claims is valid, given overall project priorities and needs, because it is important that all stakeholders understand the value of investment in the requirements process and related information. *An important lesson we have all experienced, but unfortunately have not yet learned, is that technical work is initiated before the real requirements are identified, which results in a large amount of rework with its associated cost, schedule, quality, and customer satisfaction issues.* All project stakeholders need the benefit of understanding industry experience concerning requirements. See Table 5.4 for suggested topics. Visit my Web site for a sample "Early Project Requirements Briefing" [18].

Table 5.4 Suggested Topics for Early Project Requirements Briefing

Industry issues in requirements engineering;
The value of investing more in the requirements process;
The project and/or organization's requirements process;
Overview of the mechanisms, methods, techniques, and tools that will be used;
Types of requirements;
Gathering requirements;
Roles of the RA;
Criteria of a good requirement;
Types of requirements errors and how these can be reduced;
Why and how all members of the project team must recognize new and changed requirements during development and communicate this to the RA and PM;
Management support of effective requirements engineering;
Means for reducing rework on the project:
Identifying the real requirements;
Controlling changes to requirements and addition of new requirements;
Using peer reviews;
Providing inspections of all requirements-related documents.

Another important aspect is that the RAs who are supporting the project should be provided appropriate training. See Table 5.5 for a list of recommended topics. For example, it's important that all RAs be in agreement about how to write good requirements. They should be familiar with the types of requirements (see Chapter 4) and efforts to be made to reduce requirements errors. Particularly important is the approach that will be used to reduce rework on the project.

When training is vigorously resisted by the culture, it is often possible to accomplish the same goal through working sessions that apply the methods you want to communicate. An experienced RA shared his success in briefing management on the training that would be given to employees—he believed that it was the management team that most needed the insight!

13. *Rewrite the high-level system or software requirements as you proceed through the initial steps.*

A statement of the high-level customer needs, expectations, and requirements may already exist, at least in a preliminary form, in the historical

Table 5.5 Suggested Topics for Training for RAs

The importance of requirements to project success, based on industry experience;
The value of good requirements;
Roles, skills, and characteristics of an effective RA;
Having and using a requirements process;
The value of investing more in the requirements process (8% to 14% of total project costs);
The project's requirements process;
Overview of the mechanisms, methods, techniques, and tools that will be used:
Types of requirements;
The requirements repository (and its many components);
Gathering requirements—the techniques to be used;
Writing good requirements:
Ensuring that every requirement meets the criteria of a good requirement;
Documenting the rationale for each requirement;
Prioritizing requirements—all requirements are not equal;
Not inventing requirements independently;
Not making requirements decisions;
Not gold plating.
Types of requirements errors and how these can be reduced;
Using the project's automated requirements tool;
Ensuring that the identified requirements are used and do not become "shelf ware";
V&V on the project;
Management support of effective requirements engineering;
Reducing rework on the project:
Identifying the real requirements;
Controlling changes to requirements and the addition of new requirements;
Utilizing peer reviews.

information that you have already digested. By high-level, I mean the broad statements that describe the needed capabilities that customers seek. (On one project I supported, the customer provided an overly detailed requirements specification at the outset of our contract engagement—the customer had invested several person-years of effort over a two-year period to develop the specification. When we suggested revisiting the high-level requirements, the customer directed that we not do this, but rather proceed with the development effort using the detailed specification. One year later, after an investment of 40 person-years of effort, the customer decided to redo the high-level requirements.) Begin to rewrite the high-level requirements. This set should consist of 50 to 200 requirements, depending on the scope of the system. Focusing on the high-level requirements has important advantages:

▸ It will help you comprehend the scope of the system.

▸ It will keep you from being overwhelmed by the more detailed requirements.

▸ It will help you gain insights into the real requirements.

Manage the cultural expectations to prevent your first draft from becoming the "build-to" document.

T. Korson [19] emphasizes the importance of levels of abstraction in requirements gathering and believes there are critical principles of requirements gathering that must be observed. (He also believes that a use case–driven requirements approach often results in failure to identify the real requirements.) Table 5.6 shows how there are levels of abstraction associated with both the types of requirements and the development activities.

The following principles of requirements gathering expand on this:

▸ Start with high-level system requirements and work to more detailed levels (note that this is different from functional decomposition, which involves decomposing a particular function in the system).

▸ Keep business requirements separate from interface specifications. Korson believes that this is the way that most OO teams get into

Table 5.6 Using Levels of Abstraction Helps in Managing the Requirements Process

Types of Requirements (See Chapter 4)	Development Activity
Business	Domain analysis and modeling
Interfaces	Application analysis and modeling
Design	Architecture development
Detailed specifications	Source code development

difficulty—high-level requirements are put into detailed specifications that preclude clients from considering alternatives and that mislead designers.

‣ Facilitate users' gaining a deeper understanding of their real needs and requirements.

‣ Do not derive the design from use cases. Korson believes that use cases should stop at the system interface boundary. Others' experience is that system boundaries are set based on viewpoint, and use cases can often be excellent analytical aids at the subsystem level as well. You'll need to determine your own views based on your experience.

14. *Initiate development of the real requirements based on the stated requirements.*

Evolve and prioritize [20] the real requirements. You'll recall this suggestion from Chapter 1. *Don't fail to do it.* The "list of real requirements" is a work product that will evolve over a period of several weeks or months. Make sure that you use version control and change control on it, so that you always know precisely what the current work product actually is and exactly how it should read. If you aren't familiar with these CM techniques, look at the discussion of CM in Chapter 7. Also, find someone who is experienced with CM and learn from him or her. No pressure, but keep in mind that the whole project is totally dependent on a thorough, accurate, current statement of the real requirements. Without it, the project is out of control and in jeopardy. You may find yourself trying to catch up with designers who moved far down the life-cycle path while the requirements were being generated. This is a very common problem and an excellent motivation for the RA to get guiding documents out to the community as early as possible.

15. *Initiate documenting the rationale for each requirement.*

This is another requirements work product that will evolve over a period of weeks or months. Make sure that you track the source of any rationale that is accepted. This is an important component of the requirements repository, discussed below. Well-conducted trade studies provide not only a solid rationale for which path was chosen, but also contain the logic by which the choice was made and the assumptions that were used. This makes it much easier to defend the decision or to review it if assumptions change or are proven false.

16. *Establish a mechanism to control changes to requirements and new requirements.*

The second most important contribution you can make to the project (after establishing the joint team or similar mechanism to evolve the real requirements) is to establish a mechanism to control changes to requirements and new requirements. Industry experience verifies that without such a mechanism, most projects will soon get out of control and risk a high probability of failure. We refer to changes in requirements as "requirements volatility." Industry experience is that projects that exceed 2% requirements volatility incur cost and schedule risk. A target of 0.5% requirements volatility per month is recommended. "Whoa! You say, "That's not much!" Precisely. That is exactly why a mechanism is needed to control changes to requirements and the addition of new requirements.

An excellent mechanism you might consider for this is the joint team. It has a few empowered members who can speak for the customer and the project. Hopefully, the members have gotten to know one another during the process of evolving the real requirements and are working together as a high-performance team. If not, suggest a joint team workshop to consider the characteristics of a high-performance team (discussed in the section entitled "Teamwork" in Chapter 8). Select the characteristics that the members of your joint team want to use. This should help to create a TEAMWORKS environment.

Often we see projects with requirements volatility in excess of 24% per year. This suggests that we should not expect success.

We should proactively identify ways to mitigate risks[6] associated with new and changed requirements; for example:

- Use an incremental development approach.

- Provide subsequent releases or versions of work products.

- Increase the budget and schedule, recognizing that there is a geometric relationship between changes and cost/schedule. Recognize also that there are customer satisfaction and quality risks.

Capers Jones' company, Software Productivity Research (SPR) (www.spr.com), has documented that defect rates associated with new features added during development are about 50% greater than those of the artifacts associated with the original requirements [21]. Defect removal efficiency levels are depressed as well, sometimes by more than 15%. This combination means that a very significant percentage of delivered defects can be

---

6. RAs should get involved in project risk management activities. Visit the Web site for *Software Quality Management Magazine* (www.sqmmagazine.com). Subscribe. Review articles of interest and become proficient in risk identification, analysis, evaluation, planning, management, mitigation, and monitoring and control. Become a member of your project's risk management team. As noted by industry risk expert David C. Hall, "Despite increasing consensus on the value of risk management, effective implementation of risk-management processes in organizations and projects is far from common." (See www.sqmmagazine.com/issues/2002-04/maturity.html.) In my experience, even when a risk process exists on a project, and risk management is performed, risk management activities usually are not thorough. Project activities related to risk management are often an opportunity for continuous improvement, and these activities can have a potentially huge impact on the success or failure of the project. Rich Raphael is the Northrop Grumman IT DES process owner for risk and can provide expert counsel. Contact him at RRaphael@ngc.com.

traced back to creeping user requirements. In other words, by controlling the changes to requirements, the quality of products is increased significantly, and costs are reduced. To minimize harm from late requirements, formal change management procedures and state-of-the-art configuration-control tools are strongly recommended. Formal design and code inspections are also useful.[7]

Another valuable insight from Ivy Hooks' experience at NASA is that a one-third change in the requirements results in a *doubling* of the cost of the developed system. This helps explain the ire our customers feel as the costs of promised systems escalate. Customers and users need our help to understand that the constant changes they request have a huge impact on costs and the schedule. If we can help them understand this, and if we can gain their support in controlling changes and new requirements, we will have partnered for a more successful project outcome. An agreed-upon understanding of the system is critical to a successful project.

Requirements changes due to interpretation, scope creep, or other random factors should be suppressed to the greatest extent practical. Requirements changes that result from emerging insight must be embraced and managed. High levels of requirements volatility suggest that the underlying problem being solved by the system or software is not yet fully understood. In that case, moving further along the design cycle could well be the root cause of the problem, not the instability of requirements themselves. One experienced RA opined that many companies lie to themselves about design maturity solely to achieve internal metrics!

17. *Perform V&V planning.*

One of the criteria of a good requirement is that it is verifiable, that is, that the code that provides this capability can be tested to determine that the requirement is in fact met in the delivered system. The approach to be used to accomplish this should be provided early as an aspect of the requirements development effort and should be identified as an attribute of each requirement in the automated requirements tool. See the comments and references concerning V&V in Chapter 7 and Grady's book on this subject [22]. Hooks and Farry [23] encourage that V&V be addressed during requirements development, because this approach improves requirements quality, ensures that requirements support verification, provides a basis for estimating verification cost and schedule, and provides opportunities to control cost and risk. They identify words that flag unverifiable requirements and suggest possible substitutes you may be able to

---

7. See the discussion of creeping user requirements and software quality in Jones's *Software Quality: Analysis and Guidelines for Success* [21, pp. 134–137]. Note that many lessons really have been learned, but they haven't been applied. Major problems are that (1) we practitioners don't read enough, study lessons, take action to apply the lessons to our processes and procedures, and implement improved practices; and (2) management is content to allow us to muddle through and not continuously improve. In Watts Humphrey's context, we "don't practice what we preach." See www.sei.cmu.edu/publications/articles/practice-preach/practice-preach.html.

use. They provide examples of unverifiable and verifiable requirements and provide a checklist that summarizes verification-related questions that should be asked. Grady concurs: "Demanding that the same person who writes a product requirement also write the corresponding verification process requirement in approximately the same time frame reduces program risk more than any other activity" (personal e-mail message, April 2, 2000). This is a good time to reflect on the comments provided in step 11 concerning evolving the real requirements. There is a lot of confusion in our industry about the difference between validation and verification (see the clarification of these two terms provided in Chapter 7, topic 13).

18. *Select the practices, methods, and techniques that will be used to gather the requirements.*

There are a lot of practices, methods, and techniques available. Some are more useful and effective than others. Your project will enjoy a high ROI from taking some time to select those that are to be used. First, digest the related discussions about them in *Effective Requirements Practices* [2]. You will gain many insights from industry experience by doing this. Ensure that members of your project team have had successful experiences with all of the methods and techniques that are selected. A project—unless it's a research and development (R&D) project—is no time to try out a new method or technique. Your project should select only methods and techniques that are known, familiar to the developers, and proven. (An exception is that you might want to pilot a new or promising practice to determine its applicability to your project. By using an experienced mentor, the pilot could become a proof-of-applicability demonstration.) Extend your analysis to consideration of project best practices, based on identified risks for that project. Keep your manager and the PM involved and informed about these deliberations. Everyone involved in a particular project should use a common process, set of practices and mechanisms, techniques and methods, and automated tools. Have project team discussions, select and agree on a common set, and provide formal training as needed to ensure that the people who are expected to use them are empowered. It's counterproductive for individuals to go running off on their own, doing their own thing, not in coordination with the rest of the project team.

You may find that your project requires methods that are not familiar. This suggests that planning may be required for training or that the project may need to engage a consultant who has been successful in using an unfamiliar method, technique, or tool. Proceed cautiously and mitigate risks.

19. *Begin consideration and selection of an automated requirements tool, identification of the* attributes *that will be needed for each requirement, and the composition of the requirements repository.*

All three of these tasks are essential, and the RA will be expected to provide leadership and to take responsibility for their successful performance.

There are fewer than a dozen industry-strength automated requirements tools that provide the functionality needed by projects of various sizes (see Table 5.7).

All who have worked with systems and software for any period of time have had experiences with automated requirements tools (likely both good and bad); all will have their own biases and opinions about specific tools. Step back from all of this advice and feedback, assemble your analytical skills, and ask yourself the following questions:

- What is it that we are trying to do?

- What level of sophistication is required?

- How much formal tool training is needed and what can we afford?

- What work products do we need from the tool?

- How will we input data (e.g., the real requirements) into the tool? Does the tool provide an input approach that will support the project's needs?

- Who on the project has hands-on experience with which tools? Can that person be made available to help with initial tool-related activities?

- Who will be the primary, secondary, and backup tool users? How many licenses ("seats") do we need?

Table 5.7   Commercial Requirements Tools, Vendors, and Web Sites

Tool	Vendor	Web Site
Star Team System Requirements (formerly Caliber RM)	Starbase, Inc., Santa Ana, California	www.borland.com/caliber
C.A.R.E. 3.0	SOPHIST Group, Nuremberg, Germany	www.sophist.de/sophist.nsf/zStartEng l!OpenFrameSet
CORE 4.0	VITECH Corporation, Vienna, Virginia	www.vtcorp.com
DOORS 6.0	Telelogic, Malmo, Sweden, and Irvine, California	www.Telelogic.com/products
Rational Requisite Pro (ReqPro)	IBM Corporation, White Plains, New York	www.rational.com/products
RTM Requirements and Traceability Management	Integrated Chipware, Inc., Reston Virginia	www.Chipware.com
SLATE	Northrop Grumman Electronic Systems, Baltimore, Maryland	http://slate.md.essd.northgrum.com
SynergyRM	CMD Corporation, Addison, Texas	www.cmdcorp.com
Vital Link	Compliance Automation, Inc., Boerne, Texas	www.complianceautomation.com
Xtie-RT Requirements Tracer	Teledyne Brown Engineering, Los Angeles, California	www.tbe.com/products/xtie/xtie.asp

▸ How will customers and users communicate with the project team concerning requirements-related information, including requests for changes to the requirements, new requirements, and plans, ideas, and suggestions concerning later versions and releases of work products?

Think about other questions that need to be asked, based on your environment. The decision to select a particular automated requirements tool should be based on a thorough, objective analysis. This decision is important and should not be made quickly or based on biased or uninformed views. A trade study should be written (in CMMI® terminology, the trade study process is referred to as decision analysis resolution [DAR], an updated name from analyze candidate solutions [ACS] that was used in the SE-CMM® [24]). Review a sample automated requirements tools trade study on my Web site [25], and reuse it as a template for your analysis. See Insert 5.2 for important insights based on experience.[8] See also Wiegers's article, "Automating Requirements Management" [26], which compares four automated requirements tools: DOORS, RTM Workshop, Caliber RM (now "Star Team System Requirements"), and Requisite Pro.

As emphasized above, the selection of the specific automated requirements tool to support your project is an important decision. Get your manager and the PM involved early. I know of many projects that tried to work without an automated requirements tool. This is a recipe for disaster for a project of any size. Tiny projects (two to three people for three to six months) might get away with using MS Word or Excel as the automated requirements tool. A project of any larger size requires one of the tools listed in Figure 5.3. I'm aware of many projects where the complexity of the tool as compared with the needs for the tool became one of the reasons the project lost control. Make sure as the RA that you fulfill your role appropriately in this regard. Don't allow biased views and uninformed opinions to drive this decision.

Start identification of the attributes that will be needed for each requirement immediately upon assignment to the project as an (or the) RA. An *attribute* is a characteristic of a requirement that is useful in sorting, classifying, and managing requirements. This is one of those lists you should keep handy and be working on constantly, because as you are working, you'll identify attributes that are needed. It's likely that you'll wind up with a list of 20 to 40 attributes by the time you are ready to load your automated requirements tool. Give this consideration.

Also, start thinking immediately upon your assignment to a project as an RA about the composition of the project's requirements repository. Many people think of this as one automated database (in the requirements tool). This is a much less than adequate approach, in my opinion. Think of the requirements repository as some combination of the following:

---

8. With thanks to process and quality engineer Earl Hoovler for sharing his experiences and expertise.

Insert 5.2—Lessons Learned in Performing Trade Studies

Following a defined process on a system or software development project is usually a very good thing. However, one always needs to have an open mind when following a process—be alert to changes in the "real" process requirements. Be flexible and be ready to tailor the process as you go along so that you can meet those requirements. This case study of some lessons learned in performing evaluations of alternatives provides important insights.

While working on a proposal for a major COTS HR software implementation program, a senior analyst was responsible for reviewing automated CM tools and making a recommendation. Though he followed the organization's standard trade study process, after submitting his initial recommendation for a tool, he came upon information that the tool would not work in the environment it would serve. He realized that he needed to go back to the drawing board and revise his initial recommendation to reflect real-world requirements. The following lessons-learned from his experience may help you in performing evaluations of COTS products, regardless of the type of automated tool needed.

1. *Always keep in mind your customer's preferences, but don't make recommendations that merely cater to those preferences, when the trade study analysis does not support it.* Any customer deserves a balanced review of the options based upon selected criteria. The purpose of a trade study is to explore the facts and make recommendations based on those facts. It is good to be aware of a customer's preferences, but it should not be the major or only factor in your final recommendation, unless the facts support the customer's preference. This is very hard to accomplish, but it is a worthwhile goal. In my trade study experience, the customer had already invested in a tool suite and wanted a recommendation that supported that purchase. We needed to avoid the temptation to rubberstamp the customer's choice and tried to demonstrate exactly why their preferred tool would not work in their development environment. We were able to show that if we selected their preferred tool, the project would experience more effort and cost and create the need for mostly manual work-arounds (not an automated approach). Finally, we were able to convince the customer that its preferred tool was not acceptable because it could not accomplish needed identification and control functions.

2. *If you use previously defined selection criteria for your trade study, be sure to tailor the criteria to include appropriate factors and circumstances.* In our organization, our CM SMEs previously assembled the functions and other criteria they like to see supported through automated tools. Most teams will likely brainstorm

Insert 5.2—Lessons Learned in Performing Trade Studies (continued)

and list their own criteria. If they are using a set of criteria that they did not assemble themselves, the trade study team must review the criteria and tailor them to delete functions that are not needed, include additional requirements or functions, and reflect the expected work environment of the team. More specific criteria will provide the basic search criteria for the tools and save time in making initial selections for review.

3. *Continually talk to the customers and engineering teams who will be using the tool and involve them in the selection process.* Keeping customers and teams involved at all stages of the selection process is a key to success. Make sure they are included in demos, reviews of criteria, and peer reviews of draft trade study results. In my example, I did not include application specialists in the first iteration of the trade study and, thus, recommended a more mainstream CM tool, not one that addresses the specialized needs of the development environment. I also was not aware of the customer's tool preferences. In my second effort, I used the experience of development application engineers who were familiar with the issues of this unique environment. We worked together to come up with a solution that best served the customer and developers.

4. *Whenever possible, get a demonstration copy of the tools you are reviewing and pilot them in your environment.* Too often, vendors do not have a good understanding of your criteria or your customer's requirements. They often bring in a canned demo of their tool with limited capabilities that is not configured to work in your environment. They also work to convince you that the capabilities they demo will work in your environment, but they cannot show you exactly how it will work. This might seem like the best use of your time, and puts the burden on the vendor to prove they can perform, but often it forces decisions based on a feeling, rather than fact. The best remedy for this situation is to request the vendor to provide you with a time-limited version of their current tool, ask them for help configuring the tool, and review the performance of the tool using your criteria. Of course, you will need to include enough time in your trade study plan to conduct these in-plant demos. This will provide managers and customers with the facts they need to make their decisions.

5. *Be sure this is an iterative process.* It is usually the case that when you conduct a trade study, all of the information you need to make decisions is not available. When additional facts (e.g., requirements, tool capabilities) surface, you need to be

> **Insert 5.2**—Lessons Learned in Performing Trade Studies (continued)
>
> prepared to return to the drawing board, revise your criteria, update your analysis, and possibly change your recommendation. Of course, time is a major factor in doing this, but you should at least make mention of these changes to your customer when you make your recommendation and let the customer decide if these factors require another look.
>
> *Earl Hoovler*
> *Process Engineer*

- The project vision and scope document;
- The project glossary and project list of acronyms;
- The list of system-level requirements;
- Source documents concerning requirements (where the requirements came from);
- Notes of meetings with and interviews of customers and users;
- Requirements workshops notes and related documentation;
- Any documentation of the stated requirements;
- Minutes of meetings of the joint team;
- Lists of real requirements;
- The database in your automated requirements tool, including the RTM;
- Any requirements-related work products such as requirements specifications;
- Descriptions of related legacy (historical) systems, augmented with summaries of capabilities provided that are needed in the new capability or system;
- Known limitations of the planned capability, including functionality that can't or won't be provided;
- A description/vision of the growth path from initial release to the ultimate system through a set of staged releases or versions;
- Definition of exceptions to the normal situation and appropriate error conditions;
- Others.

20. *Select and acquire the automated requirements tool.*

Sounds easy, doesn't it? Sometimes the RA can gain access to the selected automated requirements tool from another project or a corporate engineering software environment (ESE).[9] Most often, however, the project will need to use the organization's procurement process. Depending on the situation, this might be quick and easy, but often this step turns out to be very time-consuming and complex. Don't allow your project to be jeopardized because of late availability of the appropriate automated requirements tool. Start early. Explain the importance to your procurement folks. Facilitate their becoming part of your requirements team. Follow up aggressively. Involve your manager, the PM, and the organization's senior management to ensure that you get the support you need to make things happen within reasonable time constraints.

21. *Load the initial real requirements into the selected requirements tool, label each requirement uniquely, and initiate assignment of appropriate attributes information to each requirement.*

We mentioned this task earlier in this chapter. You may find that this task turns out to be a lot more work than you anticipate. Some of the reasons for this are as follows:

- Documents providing source requirements do not always load automatically, or if they do, not all of the information is captured correctly or easily.

- There will be a learning curve associated with any automated tool. You'll find that it actually has capabilities that you don't realize initially, and you may need to do some rework.

- You'll need to decide on the unique numbering system or approach to be used.

- You'll need to think about bidirectional traceability for each requirement and how this should be achieved.

- The source, history, priority, status, author, assignment, and traceability of each requirement must be identified and included in the database. Many other attributes of each requirement will need to be tracked as well. For example, there are two kinds of attributes in DOORS, user-defined attributes and system-defined attributes. User-defined attributes may be built from specific attribute types such as text, integer, date, and so forth and are instantiated by users for their own needs. System-defined attributes, however, are predefined by DOORS and automatically record essential and highly useful information in the background. Attributes allow you to associate information with individual or related groups of requirements and often facilitate

---

9. Some organizations sponsor the availability of a set of automated tools that can be used by the organization's projects. In Northrop Grumman IT DES, we call this library of tools available for loan the engineering software environment, or ESE.

analysis of requirements data via filtering and sorting based on attribute values. System-defined attributes may also be used for filtering and sorting. Although they are, for the most part, read-only and are not user modifiable, they perform essential and automatic information gathering.

See Table 5.8 for examples of attributes you may want to include in an attributes matrix.

Avoid the temptation to use more attributes than really are required for the task at hand. A few well-chosen attributes that are actually entered and managed are much more useful than dozens that are poorly executed or easily confused.

Insert 5.3 provides some insights concerning the use of the system attributes based on information provided by Pete Carroll, formerly of Telelogic.

Table 5.8   Sample Requirements Attributes Matrix

Attribute	Requirement A	Requirement B, etc.
Unique ID	NFAK028	
Requirement text	The time required for the equipment to warm up prior to operation shall not exceed one (1) minute from a cold start at −20 degrees C.	
Source	System Requirements Specification	
Owner	Charles Smith	
Rationale	Verified	
Priority	Medium	
Status	Approved	
Cost	Low	
Difficulty	Medium	
Stability	Medium	
Assigned to	Bob Jones	
Location	NFA Annex K section C	
Author	Rick Chardon	
Revision	1.7	
Date	10 Jan 2003	
Reason	Marked trace to NFASSS289.	
Traced-from	NFARD125	
Traced-to	NFASSS289	
Root Tag#	208	
History	Original Requirement	
Verification	In Design xyz	
Validation	Delivered System	
Release	1.0	
Module	LDAP_Authenticate	
Etc.		

Insert 5.3—Some Insights into Using System Attributes in DOORS

Attributes in DOORS allow users to associate data with objects, table markers, table cells, modules, and projects. There are two kinds of attributes, user-defined and system-defined attributes. User-defined attributes may be built from specific attribute types such as text, integer, date, and the like, and instantiated by users for their own needs. System-defined attributes, however, are predefined by DOORS and automatically record a wealth of essential and highly useful information in the background.

Have you ever wondered how to make use of these system-defined attributes provided automatically by DOORS? Harnessing these "for free—out of the box" attributes can make your work in DOORS easier and more productive.

Attributes allow you to associate information with individual or related groups of requirements and often facilitate analysis of requirement data via filtering and sorting based on attribute values. System-defined attributes may also be used for filtering and sorting, and while they are for the most part read-only and not user-modifiable, they perform essential and automatic information gathering for us. The read-only system attributes, which exist automatically in all objects and modules, include the following:

Name	Name of formal, descriptive, or link module
Created By	Name of user who created object
Created On	Date object was created
Created Through	The manner in which an object was created (copying, manual input, extraction)
Last Modified By	Name of user who last modified the object
Last Modified On	Date object was last modified
Absolute Number	Unique number assigned upon object creation
Link Mapping	Rules for object linking (one-to-one, many-to-one, etc.)

Some system-defined attributes are not read-only and allow for some modification by the user. User modifiable object and module level system-defined attributes include the following:

Object Heading	The heading for the object
Object Text	The actual text of the object
Object Short Text	A short textual indication of the object used for graphical display
Description	Full descriptive name of the module

Insert 5.3—Some Insights into Using System Attributes in DOORS (continued)

Prefix	Optional prefix for the absolute number used to ensure unique object identification

All of the above system-defined attributes, modifiable or not, automatically record information and may be used just like user-defined attributes to display data essential to management of your requirements. Use system-defined attributes whenever you need to display information regarding who, what, where, and when, as well as crucial information on modifications to requirements.

In any DOORS module, insert a column and select from the Display Attribute list the system-defined Created By attribute to show who created a requirement. Insert a second column and use the system-defined Last Modified By attribute to show who made the latest change to a requirement. Insert a third column using the system-defined Last Modified On attribute to show when the last change was made. You now have a view that reflects the original creation and essential change information on your requirements! Better yet, select the Impact/Trace Wizard from the Tools-Impact/Trace menu, and in the second prompt window select to display any number of the available system-defined object and link attribute choices. This wizard, complete with system-defined attributes available for selection, quickly and easily builds impact and trace analysis views complete with essential information, such as object creation (Created By, Created On), dates of changes (Last Modified On), and other useful information, such as the link module name that links are recorded in (Link Module Name).

In summary, system-defined attributes provide solutions to some information tracking needs. Use system-defined attributes to your advantage to simplify requirements and change management.

Pete Carroll, formerly of Telelogic.

Ian Alexander cautions that while 20 to 40 attributes may be needed, often it's possible to manage with fewer. He has seen overachieving technical managers identify 20 or more attributes, fail to verify a need for them, and create a lot of unnecessary work. Just as we are responsible to identify the real requirements, we must ensure that work activities we recommend and use are really needed. Good planning and careful analysis of "why" work activities are "required" are important components of the RA's role.

22. *Perform requirements gathering.*

"Whoa!" You say, "we are already on step 22 in this chapter and we're only now going to talk about gathering the requirements?" Good point. Actually, we have been talking about related steps throughout this chapter. Each of the above steps is part of the requirements gathering process.

I suggest that you download the article "Recommended Requirements Gathering Practices" [27], from CrossTalk's Web site (click on the April 2002 issue concerning risky requirements). There, I provide detailed advice and discussion related to this step, recommend specific techniques, and suggest several appropriate references that will help you. (Don't feel that you have to read and digest every reference—just grab enough insights to get yourself working effectively on your current task. You can always go back and read more or again. In other words, try to use references to inform, motivate, and inspire yourself, rather than allow them to create a feeling of frustration about your lack of knowledge or be a barrier holding you back.)

Among over 40 requirements elicitation techniques that are available, the most effective techniques are the following:

- Interviews;

- Document analysis;

- Brainstorming;

- Requirements workshops (a modern day version of JAD);

- Prototyping;

- Use cases (when used correctly);

- Storyboards;

- Interfaces analysis;

- Modeling;

- Performance and capacity analysis;

- Scenarios.

Among the many books that include extensive treatments of requirements elicitation, be sure to have the following in your personal library:

- Alexander and Stevens, *Writing Better Requirements*

- Buede, *The Engineering Design of Systems: Models and Methods*

- Carr, et al., *Partnering in Construction: A Practical Guide to Project Success*

- Cockburn [pronounced co-burn], *Writing Effective Use Cases*

- Gottesdiener, *Requirements by Collaboration: Workshops for Defining Needs*

- Grady, *System Requirements Analysis*

- Grady, *System Validation and Verification*

- Harmon, Watson, *Understanding UML: The Developers Guide*

- Hooks, Farry, *Customer-Centered Products: Creating Successful Products through Smart Requirements Management*

- Humphrey, *Introduction to the Personal Software Process*

- Kotonya and Sommerville, *Requirements Engineering: Processes and Techniques*

- Leffingwell, and Widrig, *Managing Software Requirements*

- McConnell, *Software Project Survival Guide*

- Sommerville, and Sawyer, *Requirements Engineering: A Good Practice Guide*

- Wiegers, *Peer Reviews in Software*

- Wiegers, *Software Requirements*, 2nd ed.

- Wiley, *Essential System Requirements: A Practical Guide to Event-Driven Methods*

- Wood and Silver, *Joint Application Development*

- Young, *Effective Requirements Practices*

I strongly recommend that you develop a working knowledge of all of these books. It's not sufficient to have a cursory knowledge of a few requirements-related processes, practices, methods, techniques, and tools. In order to be effective in his or her role, the RA must be able to recommend a good, proven approach and to facilitate deploying, implementing, and institutionalizing it.

See Vitech's Web page (www.vtcorp.com) for information concerning the CORE requirements tool and a version that can be downloaded for evaluation. This tool provides behavioral modeling capabilities. Buede's *The Engineering Design of Systems: Models and Methods* [28] describes use of this tool for modeling and provides example problems to help familiarize you with using the tool. Rational Rose and BPwin are other tools that provide behavior modeling. At times, diagrams are extremely helpful to convey the essential system requirements, to view how a system fits into larger systems in its environment, and to understand how the components of a system fit together.

One of the techniques noted above is a scenario. Operational scenarios were mentioned early in this chapter as integral to the systems engineering approach of developing operational concepts. A method called Scenario-Based User Needs Analysis (SUNA) has been developed to facilitate clarifying and refining user needs. Insert 5.4 provides a description of this method.

Finally, read "A Quick, Accurate Way to Determine Customer Needs" by Cristina Afors and Marilyn Zuckerman [29]. The authors of this article believe customers tend to say one thing during requirements elicitation and then do something entirely differently. They recommend a technology called imprint analysis that takes human emotions into account. They believe imprint analysis can actually forecast human behavior.

23. *Involve system architects and designers in reviews of the requirements.*

One of the 10 effective requirements practices I recommend in my earlier book is "Iterate the requirements and architecture repeatedly." Industry experience has proven this to be valuable advice. I have previously recommended performing three or four iterations of requirements development (reference Ellen Gottesdiener's experience discussed in step 6). In a number of situations in my career, I have had the opportunity to work with a system architect or designer(s) to iterate the real requirements and the architecture or design envisioned for the planned system or software. My experience is that when we expended the time and effort to do this, we developed better requirements and a more robust architecture. The reason is that the requirements and the architecture depend on each other. When we iterate one with the other, both get better, stronger, more robust and flexible and are better able to accommodate future changes and new technologies (because we have a better understanding). Think about this. It makes sense and is a proven industry best practice.

Invite system architects and designers involved on your project to review the real requirements. Share the insight provided in *Effective Requirements Practices* [2, pp. 134–135] with them. Consider them part of the project requirements team and facilitate their gaining this same perspective. Remember, two heads are better than one (always).

24. *Develop the traceability strategy to be used.*

We mentioned this step earlier in this chapter. It turns out that bidirectional traceability (from customer and user real needs and requirements to products, and vice versa) of requirements is (1) critical to the success of the project, and (2) a complex and difficult task that requires considerable experience to perform well. Requirements traceability is the ability (1) to map the customer need to the requirement; (2) to trace (identify and track) the instantiation of each requirements to all work products from requirements specification to design, to system component development, through testing and system documentation; and (3) to map a parent requirement to a child requirement, and vice versa. This capability is absolutely critical for all systems. A key guideline here is to be consistent—use the same kind of traces for all of your source documents. An automated RTM in the automated requirements tool is the mechanism that should be utilized to provide this traceability. You should digest James D. Palmer's article "Traceability" [30] to strengthen your understanding and knowledge concerning this important RA skill. See also the discussion

Insert 5.4—Using Scenarios in Requirements Gathering

Well-known techniques such as document analysis, interviewing, observations, and workshops are all good ways to gather requirements, particularly where the job is to extend or evolve an existing system. However, on certain types of projects, it can be valuable to take an entirely different approach. When there is extensive human interaction, a limited number of legacy constraints, the scope and/or business requirements are not clear, or there is a mandate for innovation, collaborative scenario writing can be a useful tool. Used at the outset of the requirements gathering phase, and in conjunction with other gathering techniques, it can provide a good basis for a successful development.

The term *scenario* is widely used, particularly in the world of systems design and development, where it can mean anything from a set of storyboards to structured textual descriptions of user interactions with a computer system. In this context, the scenarios we refer to are stories—broad, descriptive, day-in-the-life-of narratives that are intended to engage the reader in an understanding of how the new development, product, or service will integrate with and affect the lives of different stakeholders. Rich narrative is a powerful tool because the act of creating it forces us to visualize situations and the logic of interactions in minute detail. In the context of visualizing software systems, it organizes our thoughts and enables human and business needs and potential technical solutions to be considered simultaneously. In a group setting, it helps people to think "outside the box" (i.e., beyond any preconceived constraints) and to synthesize their inspiration, knowledge, and experience into a logical whole. The resulting stories convey the vision in a way that can be readily understood by all the parties involved in the project.

Unbridled creative thinking, however, risks confusion, expanding scope, and spiraling costs. So it's important to ensure that the benefits of the envisioning process can be harnessed to generate cost effective innovative software solutions. The University of Essex in the United Kingdom has continued to develop SUNA, a process originally conceived by British Telecommunications (BT) in 1998 that provides a set of logical steps for this purpose. It is a nonprescriptive guide that supports a combined team of clients, users, RAs, designers, and developers through scenario generation to a process of distillation and, finally, integration with industry standard requirements gathering and software development methods. In relation to these methods, the purpose of SUNA is to refine the shape of the proposed development generated by the business requirements and to provide a starting point for the more detailed activity of gathering real requirements. It therefore overlaps with and feeds into the requirements capture activity or, alternatively, feeds directly into an iterative development cycle.

Insert 5.4—Using Scenarios in Requirements Gathering (continued)

A very brief outline of the process follows:

1. Set up a team of people who will represent the different aspects of the project.

2. Gather, analyze, and disseminate to the team documentation that relates to the scope and definition of the project and relevant research (technical, social, and market). This provides the starting point for the scenarios.

3. Call the team together for a workshop aiming to do the following:

    ‣ Identify all the stakeholders. Select three or four stakeholder groups on which to base the scenarios.

    ‣ Write several scenarios from different stakeholder perspectives. These are usually 1,000-word vignettes about how the proposed development fits into the stakeholders' and users' lives and the interactions that take place. Try to think beyond constraints.

    ‣ Analyze the scenarios and extract the common user needs (i.e., the requirements). Compile these into a uniquely numbered list that will form the basis of a requirements specification.

4. After the workshop, organize the user needs into a hierarchy using short summary descriptions (referred to as the needs hierarchy). This provides a first-cut logical structure for the proposed development and creates a valuable decision-making tool by allowing all the elements of the development to be viewed on a single page (or at least a small number of pages).

5. Sanity-check the scenarios with people who have an appropriate level of knowledge, but who are outside the project team.

6. Assess how highly the stakeholders value the different needs by sending out a questionnaire to a select group. Collate the results and reflect them on the needs hierarchy, for instance, by highlighting the needs in different colors reflecting the categories of high, medium, and low value.

7. Take all of this information into a second "scooping" workshop with the following aims:

    ‣ Presenting the needs hierarchy and using it to facilitate deciding on the scope of the development based on budgetary constraints, technical feasibility, and value to stakeholders. Mark the decisions on the hierarchy.

    ‣ Documenting the rationale for each requirement and indicating which needs are in scope and which are out of scope against the numbered user needs list.

Insert 5.4—Using Scenarios in Requirements Gathering (continued)

▸ Compiling the results and moving into the next stage of requirements gathering.

The key end products are (1) a number of scenarios that can be used to illustrate the development vision, (2) a numbered and annotated list of user needs and requirements, (3) a needs hierarchy showing both the broad vision and the scope of the proposed development, and (4) a document containing the details of the decision-making rationale.

SUNA was first developed in 1998 by BT as a by-product of a pan-European project that examined how we learn and whom we learn from. The outcome of the project was an innovative Web-based service prototype that influenced established learning product design. Positive relationships, created at the time, spurred subsequent SUNA-based collaborations.

SUNA has now been used extensively on small collaborative research projects in primarily commercial and some academic environments. It has been applied in fields ranging from learning and education to the technicalities of multiple device management, and overall has been found to help promote clarity, innovation, and good relationships. SUNA is not likely to be relevant to large complex systems and the benefits of the approach may be restricted where there is limited human interaction and numerous fixed constraints, but if there's flexibility and a desire for innovation, its worth consideration. For more information, see www.essex.ac.uk/chimera/consultancy.html.

Note: Scenario-based User Needs Analysis (SUNA) was first developed in 1998 by van Helvert and Fowler while they were working for British Telecommunications as a by-product of a pan-European project looking at how people learn. Used with permission.

Joy van Helvert and Chris Fowler (2003)
Chimera—Institute for Sociotechnical Innovation and Research
The University of Essex
Ipswich, Suffolk

---

in *Effective Requirements Practices* [2, pp. 208–210], including "Definitions and Guidelines for Requirements Traceability." Digest also Leffingwell and Widrig, *Managing Software Requirements* [17, pp. 333–346 and Chapters 32 and 33 concerning V&V].

25. *Identify the requirements that will be met in the first release or initial products (prioritize real requirements).*

Implicit in this statement is the concept of having more than one release, recognizing that rarely, if ever, are we able to meet all real requirements in one release! If you have worked well and collaboratively with your customers and users, they will have come to understand that the planned system can't be everything to every stakeholder, probably ever, but certainly not in its initial delivery, installation, conversion of related and needed databases, deployment, implementation, operation, documentation, and training efforts (please understand from this list that system delivery or turnover is a very complex set of activities—the project can easily get derailed because there are so many risks, many of which are not under the control of the project). Work hard with your customers and users to evolve and identify the real requirements that will be met in the first release or initial products. A requirements baseline is the set of requirements associated with a particular release of a product or system. Involve your manager, the PM, the customers, and the users in developing a requirements prioritization approach that has a high probability of success. Look carefully to identify, evaluate, and mitigate risks (hopefully, you are still a member of the project's risk management team, and the risk management process is well and active).

An experienced RA noted that in addition to being the correct way to approach the requirements and design process, prioritizing requirements also has the huge advantage of allowing the RA to accept questionable inputs from politically powerful individuals and defuse them by assigning the requirement to a subsequent release. Very often, either the individual or the questionable requirement go away before actual harm is done, and the RA lives to fight another day.

26. *Establish an approach for a proof of concept, prototype, or other approximation of work product.*

This step (and many others) falls into the common sense category. People often find it impossible to tell you what they want until they see something tangible they can react to. For minor design changes, the prior product version can perform this function quite well. When the design is a fundamentally new one, prototypes are essential to really understanding the requirements. If prototyping is omitted from the design process, the first release actually becomes the prototype, and all of its shortcomings are made visible to the market. We all are aware that getting customers and users to review prototypes and proofs of concept allows them to identify needs and issues early, prior to developers having developed final work products. This saves effort, time, and money in our goal of customer and user acceptance of work products. Industry experience shows that prototypes are effective in reducing requirements creep[10] and can be combined with other effective

---

10. The RA should have an in-depth understanding of requirements creep, requirements leakage, sources of unofficial requirements, and ways to control these problems. Study Chapter 10 in *Effective Requirements Practices* [2].

methods, such as requirements workshops and JAD [31]. Prototypes by themselves can reduce requirements creep by between 10% to 25% (read reduced cost and schedule). Prototyping should be considered both an elicitation technique and a part of the life cycle; it is an especially good way of approaching and validating the tacit needs and clarifying real requirements.

27. *Incorporate requirements best practices and garner management support for effective requirements engineering (including an integrated quality approach).*

Now, there is a tall order! We discuss requirements best practices in the next chapter. However, I believe that this topic is so important that I decided to write a whole book about it (in fact, two books). Study *Effective Requirements Practices* [2], giving thoughtful attention to Chapter 11. Discuss using those best practices you deem appropriate for your situation in your environment with your manager and the PM. Take action. Don't hold back. You'll find that you have done your project a valuable service. Note that it is a lot easier to *initiate* an action than it is to follow through and ensure that the best practice in fact has been *effectively deployed and implemented* on a project and *institutionalized* throughout an organization. Deployment, effective implementation, and institutionalization of any practice are challenging. One needs to convince others that spending the time and effort to perform the practices is worthwhile. Whenever possible, "manage by fact"; that is, collect data so that you can determine whether things have improved and, if so, by how much. Managing by fact (rather than by the seat of your pants or by intuition) is a valuable and useful habit to develop.

Study Chapter 8 of this volume. A reviewer of the draft table of contents for this book advised me that perhaps the topic of quality is outside the scope of this book. I struggled with this feedback, and I finally concluded that quality is inseparable from effective requirements work. Please read Chapter 8, and I hope that you will agree.

28. *Complete requirements gathering for the first release.*

Before completing requirements for release 1, satisfy yourself that a valid base or foundation exists to initiate the follow-on technical work, that is, the programming, development, or coding. *Be aware that industry experience is that after requirements are complete, downstream activities such as design inspections, code inspections, and testing are not very effective in removing requirements defects.* Indeed, once major defects are embedded in requirements, they tend to be immune to most standard forms of defect removal and are especially resistant to detection via testing. These lessons argue strongly for a major thesis of this book: more time and effort needs to be focused on the requirements process and on identifying the real requirements. I suggest that you familiarize yourself with the materials written by Capers Jones to become more aware of related issues [32–38].

Of course, the requirements gathering process continues after each release. It's valuable to incorporate the lessons we have learned to date in our subsequent activities. Too often, we don't spend the time and effort to do this. This is another enactment of PDCA—take the time at various milestones to assemble the team and assess what worked and what could have been done better and how. A team, a project, and an organization can learn an enormous amount of valuable information by simply asking its own members such questions. The hard part is following through to take action on the suggestions that result. You will need a mechanism to track this—an action plan, an action item list that is statused regularly, a calendar that is managed by responsible individuals—whatever works for you.

Summary

In this Chapter, I have suggested using a checklist of 28 steps that comprise a procedure for gathering requirements. This may seem like a lot of steps, perhaps suitable only for a large, mature project. Actually, projects of all sizes and all levels of maturity will need to address these steps! All projects will address these steps whether in an orderly or haphazard fashion. I have emphasized that when the requirements gathering approach is not effective, the stage is set for wasted technical effort during follow-on project activities (read: the rest of the project), creating the need for rework and jeopardizing the success of the project. I have another suggestion for you: read Wiegers's "Habits of Effective Analysts" [39]. In this article, another industry expert[11] shares his views. I think that you'll find a lot of correspondence between this chapter and Wiegers's advice. Visit his Web site and take advantage of his many suggestions, writings, ideas, prescriptions, and "goodies." Wiegers, Ian Alexander, Ivy Hooks, Jeff Grady (and I) provide effective requirements training and consulting.

Think broadly. Be flexible. Always foster teamwork and continuous improvement in everything that you do. Review Chapter 3 periodically (say over a weekend) and think about the things you should be doing or doing differently. Be a positive influence on others and the project. Ask your manager for feedback concerning how you are performing. Act on it. Have fun.

Case Study

Once the requirements were established and agreed upon, the project team committed to a delivery schedule and a method for controlling requirements. If a new requirement suddenly emerged, for whatever reason, the customer had to prioritize it. In order to do this, the customers demanded to know the impact it would have (e.g., person-weeks of effort). To provide this estimate, the key and most knowledgeable team leader had to spend

---

11. Strengthen your habit of utilizing materials and ideas developed by others, including industry experts. For example, Karl Wiegers, Ian Alexander, Ivy Hooks, Charles Markert, Tom Gilb, Jeff Grady, and others have helped me grow and learn. They have become friends, and their teachings are now a part of how I do my daily work.

time with the customer delving into the details of that particular requirement, fleshing out a number of derived requirements. The rate at which new requirements came in began to overwhelm the key people and a backlog of requirements analysis was created and continued to increase. To our customer, it looked like we could not evaluate a simple requirement; to the key RAs, the pressure built up to the boiling point as the scheduled delivery date loomed closer. Lesson-learned: we lost control of the project because we failed to manage requests for new and changed requirements effectively.

References

[1]   Porter-Roth, B., *Request for Proposal: A Guide to Effective RFP Development*, Boston, MA: Addison-Wesley, 2002.

[2]   Young, R. R., *Effective Requirements Practices*, Boston, MA: Addison-Wesley, 2001.

[3]   Alexander, I., and A. Farncombe, JBA, Stakeholder Analysis Template, Systems Engineering Foundation Course, 2003.

[4]   Sharp, H., et al., "Stakeholder Identification in the Requirements Engineering Process," *IEEE* (1999): 387–391.

[5]   Gottesdiener, E., *Requirements by Collaboration: Workshops for Defining Needs*, Boston, MA: Addison-Wesley, 2002.

[6]   Wiegers, K. E., *Software Requirements*, 2nd ed., Redmond, WA: Microsoft Press, 2003.

[7]   Weinberg, G. M., "Just Say No! Improving the Requirements Process," *American Programmer* (10) (1995): 19–23.

[8]   Young, R. R., Requirements Plan Template and Sample Requirements Plan, at www.ralphyoung.net.

[9]   Wiegers, K. E., *Peer Reviews in Software: A Practical Guide*, Boston, MA: Addison-Wesley, 2002.

[10] Waugh, P., "Peer Review Participant and Peer Review Moderator Training Materials." Northrop Grumman IT DES, 2003. Contact her at penny.waugh@ngc.com.

[11] Sorensen, R., *Comparison of Software Development Methodologies*, Software Technology Support Center, January 1995, at www.stsc.hill.af.mil/crosstalk.

[12] Boehm, B., "Spiral Model of Software Development and Enhancement," *IEEE Computer* (May 1988) (also published in Barry Boehm, *Software Risk Management*, IEEE Computer Society Press, 1989, 26).

[13] Boehm, B., and W. J. Hanse, "The Spiral Model As a Tool for Evolutionary Acquisition," a joint effort of the University of Southern California Center for Software Engineering and the SEI, *CrossTalk* (May 2001): 4–11.

[14] Wiegers, K. E., "10 Requirements Traps to Avoid," *Software Testing and Quality Engineering Magazine* (January/February 2000), at www.stqemagazine.com/featured.asp?id=8.

[15] Wiegers, K. E., "Do Your Inspections Work?" *StickyMinds.com* (June 24, 2002), at www.stickyminds.com.

[16] Wiegers, K. E., "Inspecting Requirements," *StickyMinds.com* (July 30, 2001), at www.stickyminds.com.

[17] Leffingwell, D., and D. Widrig, *Managing Software Requirements*, Reading, MA: Addison-Wesley, 2000.

[18] Young R. R., "Early Project Requirements Briefing," at www.ralphyoung.net.

[19] Korson, T., "The Misuse of Use Cases: Managing Requirements," at www.korson-mcgregor.com/publications/korson/Korson9803om.htm.

[20] Wiegers, K. E., "First Things First: Prioritizing Requirements," *Software Development Magazine* 7(9) (September 1999): 24–30.

[21] Jones, C., *Software Quality: Analysis and Guidelines for Success*, London: International Thomson Computer Press, 1997.

[22] Grady, J. O., *System Validation and Verification*, Boca Raton: CRC Press, 1997.

[23] Hooks, I. F., and K. A. Farry, Customer-Centered Products: Creating Successful Products through Smart Requirements Management, New York: AMACOM, 2001.

[24] EPIC, *A Systems Engineering Capability Maturity Model*, Version 1.1, November 1995. SEI, Carnegie-Mellon University, Pittsburgh, PA, at www.sei.cmu.edu/pub/documents/95.reports/pdf/mm003.95.pdf.

[25] Young, R. R., "Requirements Tools Trade Study," at www.ralphyoung.net.

[26] Wiegers, K. E., "Automating Requirements Management," *Software Development* (July 1999). Available at www.processimpact.com.

[27] Young, R. R., "Recommended Requirements Gathering Practices," *CrossTalk* 15(4) (April 2002): 9–12, at www.stsc.hill.af.mil/crosstalk/2002/index.html.

[28] Buede, D. M., *The Engineering Design of Systems: Models and Methods*, New York: John Wiley & Sons, Inc., 2000.

[29] Afors, C., and M. Z. Michaels, "A Quick Accurate Way to Determine Customer Needs," American Society for Quality, *Quality Progress* (July 2001): 82–87.

[30] Palmer, J. D., "Traceability," *Software Requirements Engineering*, R. H. Thayer and M. Dorfman, eds., Los Alamitos, CA: IEEE Computer Society Press, 1997, pp. 364–374.

[31] Wood, J., and D. Silver, *Joint Application Development*, New York: John Wiley & Sons, 1995.

[32] Jones, C., *Assessment and Control of Software Risks*, Englewood Cliffs, NJ: Prentice Hall, 1994.

[33] Jones, C., *Estimating Software Costs*, New York: McGraw Hill, 1998.

[34] Jones, C., "Positive and Negative Factors That Influence Software Productivity," Burlington: MA, Software Productivity Research, Inc., Version 2.0, October 15, 1998.

[35] Jones, C., *Software Assessments, Benchmarks, and Best Practices*, Reading, MA: Addison-Wesley, 2000.

[36] Jones, C., "Software Quality in 2000: What Works and What Doesn't," Burlington, MA: Software Productivity Research Inc., January 18, 2000.

[37] Jones, C., "Software Project Management in the 21st Century," *American Programmer* 11(2) (February 1998), at http://spr.com/news/articles.htm.

[38]   Jones C., " What It Means To Be 'Best in Class' for Software," Burlington, MA, Software Productivity Research, Inc., Version 5, February 10, 1998.

[39]   Wiegers, K. E., "Habits of Effective Analysts," *Software Development* (October 2000), at www.processimpact.com.

Best Practices for Requirements Development and Management

In earlier chapters I have suggested that you do certain things and not do other things. In this chapter, I share a set of best practices for requirements development and management. The phrase *"Best practices"* is used frequently in systems and software engineering (among many other professions). We hear and read a lot about best practices. Yet, we don't actually spend the time and effort to evaluate, analyze, pilot, deploy, implement, and institutionalize them. The reason for this is quite simple: it's a lot of work. It requires the following:

- Developing a thorough understanding of the practice;

- Communicating its value to coworkers and managers;

- Gaining commitment to trying the practice (piloting it);

- Providing some training about the practice so that others understand it and what we are attempting to achieve through its use;

- Deploying the new practice, changing from what we are doing now to doing something different;

- Implementing the new practice, ensuring that the new way is used;

- Sustaining the new practice, including gaining support for its use;

- Evaluating its impact, perhaps even designing a way to measure the results of using it;

- Declaring victory, acknowledging that the new way is better than the old way, perhaps even celebrating success;

- Institutionalizing use of the new practice throughout the project or organization.

109

Looked at from this perspective, it's easier to understand why best practices aren't implemented and institutionalized.

Table 6.1 provides a list of best practices for requirements development and management.

Some of these best practices have been discussed at some length elsewhere in this book, so I'll limit my comments about them in this chapter. My goal is to convince you that it's worth the effort at least to pilot each of these best practices on your project and make an earnest effort to evaluate the results of using each best practice.

Table 6.1 has been crafted carefully, and I'd like to explain its structure. First, requirements activities on a task or project are inextricably intertwined with project management activities as well as with other disciplines such as CM, systems engineering, and QA. The requirements approach that is used on a task or project is not developed and implemented in a vacuum by the RA. It is evolved through a set of decisions that of necessity involve other key people, including the customer, PM, system engineer, and others. *I recommend that you share Table 6.1 with the task or project leadership team (including the customer) and jointly select the best practices that you as a team determine should be used on your task or project.* This artifact is available for downloading at my Web site (www.ralphyoung.net).

Second, the best practices recommended in Table 6.1 are grouped into three categories:

1. Requirements development;
2. Requirements management;
3. Project management.

Within each category, they are organized approximately sequentially—one would do 1 first, then 2, and so forth. However, note that many of the project management-related best practices are overarching! For example, best practice 25 recommends that an agreed-upon goal, purpose, or mission for the task or project be established. Lacking an agreed-upon goal, purpose, or mission for the task or project will make it difficult to accomplish anything of value. All of the other best practices in the project-management category address areas that may be beyond the purview of the RA. They are proven industry best practices that can have a significant positive impact on the requirements development and management efforts. You will need the commitment of the task or project leadership team to implement these practices effectively. It's not enough for the RA just to allow practices to evolve willy-nilly. *Your responsibility is to provide this list to your task or project leadership team with the request that the practices to be used be selected collaboratively by the team.*

Third, the rightmost column in Table 6.1 provides a reference to the chapter in this book where the best practice is discussed so that you can get more information, guidance, and additional references about it. Each of the recommended best practices will be discussed in the order they are listed in Table 6.1.

Table 6.1   Best Practices for Requirements Development and Management

Number	Best Practice	Requirements Development	RM	Project Management	Chapter Reference
1	Develop a requirements plan.	X	X	X	1, 5
2	Write requirements that meet the criteria of a good requirement.	X			1, 6
3	Identify and involve all of the stakeholders in the task or project.	X			1, 5, 6
4	Ensure that the objectives of the task or project have been identified, documented, and agreed to by the stakeholders.	X			5
5	Use requirements workshops to achieve a shared vision, facilitate commitment, and gain the buy-in of all stakeholders.	X			5, 6
6	Provide requirements training for RAs, for members of the project staff, and for stakeholders.	X	X	X	5
7	Identify the real requirements. Collaborate with customers and users concerning the stated requirements to identify the real requirements. Look at the requirements from multiple viewpoints.	X			2, 5, 6
8	Document the rationale for each requirement, that is, why it is needed).	X			6
9	Use effective requirements gathering techniques.	X			5
10	Involve customers and users throughout the development effort.	X	X	X	6
11	Do not make requirements decisions.	X	X	X	6
12	Do not gold plate, that is, add features or capabilities).	X	X		6
13	Use a project glossary and a project acronyms list.	X	X	X	5
14	Iterate the requirements and the architecture repeatedly to evolve better requirements and a more robust architecture.	X			6
15	Utilize domain experts/SMEs who are knowledgeable and experienced in the functional areas being addressed by the technical effort.	X			5, 6
16	Quantify the ROI to select the requirements mechanisms, practices, methods, techniques, and tools to be used.	X		X	6
17	Identify the minimum requirements that meet real needs.	X	X		6
18	Prioritize requirements early and often.	X	X	X	6
19	Provide inspections of all requirements-related documents.	X	X		5, 7
20	Limit changes to requirements and the addition of new requirements consistently, with additional budget and schedule made available by the customer to complete the task, project, or system.		X		5, 6

Table 6.1   Best Practices for Requirements Development and Management (continued)

Number	Best Practice	Requirements Development	RM	Project Management	Chapter Reference
21	Use versions and releases of work products to accommodate new requirements, changed requirements, and lower-priority requirements.	X	X	X	5
22	Use an industrial-strength automated requirements tool. Provide and use attributes of requirements.	X	X	X	5, 6
23	Develop or tailor and use organizational and project requirements policies and a requirements process that is continuously improved on your task, project, or organization. Invest 8% to 14% of total project costs on the (system life cycle) requirements process.	X	X	X	5, 6
24	Use proven and familiar requirements mechanisms, approaches, practices, methods, techniques, and tools.	X	X	X	5, 6
25	Establish an agreed-on goal, purpose, or mission for the task or project. Write (and iterate) a task or project vision and scope document.		X		5
26	Develop, implement, and enforce meeting rules that describe how project staff members are to treat one another.		X		6
27	Develop and apply a set of guidelines for effective meetings and guidelines for effective e-mailing.		X		6
28	Perform a risk assessment of new and changing requirements.	X	X	X	3, 7
29	Learn how to manage teams effectively.	X	X	X	7, 9
30	Establish a quality improvement and process improvement climate.	X	X	X	8

1. *Develop a requirements plan.*

The reasons for performing planning regarding requirements-related activities and the suggested contents of an requirements plan are discussed in Chapters 1 and 5.

2. *Write requirements that meet the criteria of a good requirement provided in Table 1.1.*

If you don't do this step, stop here. Table 1.1 provides a list of suggested criteria of a good requirement. There is a lot of information about this topic available—several authors have provided various versions with very similar criteria. Amazingly, the criteria are infrequently applied in practice. This is a flagrant example of a situation where we know how to do better, but we choose not to use our knowledge and experience. Here is an opportunity for you to make a valuable contribution to the projects you support. Consider including these criteria as a checklist in your automated requirements tool. You will find that much time and money will be saved as a result of applying the criteria.

3.   *Identify and involve all of the stakeholders of the task or project.*

Ensure that all parties are identified and involved in the requirements development process. Too frequently, we don't identify all of the stakeholders that we should. Omitting a stakeholder group can result in a flare-up later in the development work. Stakeholders include the customer, users, program management and control organizations, development and architecture teams, legal staff, testing groups, interface customers, and so forth. Suggestions and approaches for how to accomplish this are provided in Chapter 5.

4.   *Ensure that the objectives of the task or project have been identified, documented, and agreed to by the stakeholders.*

This should be done early and can be accomplished by writing a "vision and scope document" [1]. The availability of defined, agreed-on project goals helps the development team maintain focus and provides a common basis for identifying the real requirements and evaluating their priorities. It helps ensure that everyone is looking at the needed system or software capabilities from the same perspective and also helps those who are providing the funding understand what is to be done and how it supports the organization.

5.   *Use requirements workshops to achieve a shared vision, facilitate commitment, and gain buy-in of all stakeholders.*

Of all of the requirements gathering methods and techniques, requirements workshops seem to be the most effective. Ellen Gottesdiener's definition of a requirements workshop provides insights into why it is so effective [2, p. 9]:

> A requirements workshop is a structured meeting in which a carefully selected group of stakeholders and content experts works together to define, create, refine, and reach closure on deliverables (such as models and documents) that represent user requirements. The benefit of the workshop process is that it nurtures team communication, decision making, and mutual understanding. Workshops are also an effective way to bring together customers, users, and software suppliers to improve the quality of products without sacrificing time to delivery. These sessions tend to commit users to the requirements definition process and promote their sense of ownership of the deliverables and, ultimately, of the system.

6. *Provide requirements training for RAs, for members of the project staff, and for stakeholders.*

It should be apparent from the material presented so far that it is advantageous to provide requirements training for three distinct groups: RAs, members of the project staff, and stakeholders. The reason is that industry experience has a lot to offer to each group to improve the approach. The subject matter differs for each of the groups, as noted in Chapter 5. Of particular benefit is the realization that communication among all groups is improved when all share the same insights and understanding.

7. *Identify the real requirements. Collaborate with customers and users concerning the stated requirements to identify the real requirements. Look at the requirements from multiple viewpoints* [3].

I trust that by now you understand the difference between stated requirements and real requirements. *Your foremost responsibility is to collaborate with customers and users concerning the stated requirements to identify the real requirements.* This is Role 1 in the context of the roles defined in Chapter 2—serving as the requirements facilitator to work collaboratively with customers, users, and system architects and designers to identify the real requirements. Your first step will be to convince your PM, customer, and users that it is essential and worthwhile to invest added time and effort in the requirements process, in this case, *to review the stated requirements and evolve the real requirements using a joint team concept or mechanism.* Don't skip this critical step—it is the most important industry problem in requirements engineering and one that is almost always paid insufficient attention. Apply effective requirements gathering techniques such as those described in Chapter 5. Collaborating with your customer and users, tailor the checklist provided in Table 5.1 to the needs of your project in your environment. Review the real requirements from a variety of perspectives, namely those of all of the project stakeholders.

8. *Document the rationale for each requirement, that is, why it is needed.*

Rationale is an attribute that you should include in your automated requirements tool. Industry experience shows that by taking the one step of documenting the rationale for each requirement, up to half of the stated requirements can be eliminated. The savings in terms of not having to do follow-on technical work to meet the eliminated requirements are obviously huge. Moreover, this effort will clarify and tighten the requirements you choose to keep. Ivy Hooks's experience is that recording the rationale for each requirement reduces the total number of requirements, exposes bad assumptions, removes unintended implementation, improves communication between team members, shortens the review cycle, maintains corporate knowledge, reduces risk in defining a derivative product, and supports maintenance and operations costs [4].

9. *Use effective requirements gathering techniques.*

This was the subject of Chapter 5. Some requirements gathering techniques are more effective than others. Ensure that someone on your task or project has previously used the selected techniques successfully.

10. *Involve customers and users throughout the development effort.*

Recognize that industry experience shows that projects that involve customers and users throughout the development process are successful— design and use mechanisms to keep the project's customers and users involved, such as the joint team, collaborative requirements gathering techniques, and a joint configuration control board (CCB) to manage the project.

11. *Do not make requirements decisions.*

By requirements decisions, I mean decisions about what a requirement is or should be, including how it is worded. One of the ways that we RAs create problems for our projects is by making requirements decisions. Set a personal policy to not make requirements decisions. Requirements decisions are the responsibility of the customer and user within the joint team mechanism. While it may be quicker and easier just to decide something rather than to get clarification, resist this temptation because it is dangerous. Reflect on how difficult it is to communicate effectively and how differently individuals interpret the things they hear, read, and see. You have a high risk of making an incorrect decision. Moreover, your decision could have a major negative impact on the project, however unintended.

The approach of not making requirements decisions needs to be communicated throughout the development team, to ensure that developers don't make requirements decisions either. This should be clarified in the requirements-related training provided to the project team.

12. *Do not gold plate, that is, add features or capabilities.*

Do not decide that you have an idea that you know the customer and users will just love! They may indeed love it, and it may add to cost and schedule, as well as to the technical work that has already been completed (read: cause rework). Meet minimum real requirements. Do not gold plate.

13. *Use a project glossary and a project acronyms list.*

I have previously made this suggestion and provided the rationale for doing this. See Chapter 5, step 8.

14. *Iterate the requirements and the architecture repeatedly to evolve better requirements and a more robust architecture.*

The point here is that the requirements and the architecture impact each other. As we modify the architecture to address meeting the real requirements better, we learn more about the requirements and find that the architecture changes cause us to want to change the requirements, and around we go. Iterating the requirements and the architecture repeatedly results in better real requirements and a more robust architecture. This work can be accomplished in connection with the three or four iterations of the requirements development process previously recommended.

15. *Utilize domain experts/SMEs who are knowledgeable and experienced in the functional areas being addressed by the technical effort.*

I mentioned earlier some advantages brought to a project by a newly assigned RA, such as having a new perspective, unfettered by the constraints and history of the legacy system and procedures. The other side of this is the value of involving people who have extensive experience and knowledge in the functional areas being addressed by the system. They have a deep understanding of why things are done in certain ways and look at the customer needs with a seasoned perspective that may include aspects unimaginable by those less knowledgeable or less experienced. Involve such people in requirements gathering activities, for example, requirements workshops, or use them as advisors.

16. *Quantify the ROI to select requirements mechanisms, practices, methods, techniques, and tools to be used.*

I provide detailed information concerning this best practice in *Effective Requirements Practices* [5, pp. 50–52]. Making decisions based on data rather than by the seat of our pants or via intuition is a good practice—in our company, we refer to this habit as "managing by fact." Your PM should expect data to be provided when decisions are requested. Providing data concerning the ROI in improved requirements practices is one way you can earn support for your suggestions and recommendations. It's really not difficult to develop ROI information. Use the template provided in my earlier book.

17. *Identify the minimum requirements that meet real needs.*

Some people have difficulty with the concept of identifying minimum requirements. They interpret this as not doing everything possible to satisfy customers. The point is that we need to be in partnership with our customer, committed to project success, and the requirements development process should result in *a set of requirements that are the minimum required to meet real needs.* Any added requirements and features that go beyond real needs complicate the development process, make it more expensive, take additional time, jeopardize the quality of the work product, and potentially jeopardize project success (defined as an effective system, completed on time, within budget, using a win-win partnership relationship throughout the system life cycle). The system and software development process is complicated and difficult. Both partners should constantly strive to meet minimum real requirements in the interest of project success. If you're having difficulty understanding or accepting this concept, read "Meet Minimum Requirements: Anything More is Too Much," by Neal Whitten [6]. Determining what are the appropriately prioritized minimum requirements should involve members of the development team, user community, and the project CCB—this triad should work in concert to recommend prioritization and funding of requirements.

18. *Prioritize requirements early and often.*

It is equally important to prioritize real requirements early and often. Realize (and help your customer and users understand) that there is never enough time and money to do everything and that all requirements are not of equal priority. Use your joint team or a similar mechanism to agree jointly on requirements priorities. There are articles and tools available to help.[1] Take the time to read them and use them. Don't put off advocating and applying mechanisms, practices, methods, techniques, and tools that will improve the chances of your project being successful.

Once the real requirements are identified and prioritized, the development team can estimate the effort required to provide additional features, and the customer can evaluate the cost of providing them and decide if they are worth the additional money and time. The key is to ensure that the developed work products will be acceptable to the customer and users and to get the agreement of all stakeholders up front.

19. *Provide inspections of all requirements-related documents.*

The rationale for providing inspections of all requirements-related documents is provided in Chapter 7, topic 11.

20. *Limit changes to requirements and the addition of new requirements consistently with additional budget and schedule made available by the customer to complete the task, project, or system.*

This is the second most important thing an RA can do to support a project (after establishing a joint collaborative mechanism and approach to identify the real requirements). Requirements changes and new requirements are the second major reason that projects get out of control. Your responsibility in this area is to familiarize your project team, your customer, and the users with industry experience and to gain commitment to controlling changes and new requirements. For example, consider the approach of having subsequent versions and releases of work products, rather than pretending that the project can accommodate changes while it is in development.

---

1. See, for example, Karl E. Wiegers' "First Things First: Prioritizing Requirements," *Software Development Magazine* 7(9) (September 1999): 24–30. Wiegers provides an easy-to-use spreadsheet tool downloadable from his Web site, at www.processimpact.com (see the "goodies" button). See also Wiegers' *Software Requirements*, [1].

Of course, you'll need to satisfy yourself that any request for a change represents a real need and is therefore a real requirement. As before, determine the rationale for the request—why is it needed? Careful analysis will enable elimination of up to half of the requests. Most importantly, the development team needs to learn to say no. It's in neither the interest of the customer nor the developer to allow the project to get out of control. Create and maintain a partnership with the main objective of successful completion of the project. Partnering is about commitment to success and being flexible to achieve the desired outcome. Set objectives for different situations, for example, 0.5% requirements change per month for validated requirements, and seek verification of the technical team that any proposed change will not jeopardize project success. Requirements changes after the requirements baseline is set jeopardize project results and success, unless they serve to clarify the intent of a requirement instead of changing functionality. Some believe that a limit of 0.5% requirements volatility is too strict, unrealistic, and unachievable. Nevertheless, it provides a good goal. An interesting guideline from industry experience is that a one-third change in the requirements (33% per year or 2.75% per month) will result in a *doubling* of project costs. Track your requirements volatility metric within the joint team mechanism. Ensure that the customer is willing to provide additional schedule and budget in proportion to the percentage of requirements volatility; otherwise, do not accept changes to requirements or the addition of new requirements. Learn to say no.

21. *Use versions and releases of work products to accommodate new requirements, changed requirements, and lower-priority requirements.*

The importance of using versions and releases of work products is discussed in Chapter 5.

22. *Use an industrial-strength automated requirements tool. Provide and use attributes of requirements.*

Select your industrial-strength automated requirements tool early and carefully. Ensure that the selected tool supports your process. Selecting the tool without first having the requirements process in place can cause the project to force-fit its process to the tool—a major risk. The wrong tool or a tool that is overly complex for the work can retard project efforts. Ensure that you use a proven automated requirements tool—you can't afford to invest the time and effort required to write software that performs functions such as traceability. Given the commercial tools that are available, it's not cost-effective to develop your own automated requirements tool capabilities. Provide formal training for those who will use the tool most frequently—this is a valuable investment and should not be overlooked. Determine the requirements attributes that are needed—see the discussion of attributes in Chapter 5. Too often, the choice of the automated requirements tool to be used on a project is dictated by factors beyond the control of the project. For example, one RA's experience concerning the selection of the automated requirements tool to support five different projects he supported was as follows:

- On one project, we developed our own requirements database using Informix because we already had Informix and plenty of expertise in using it.

- On another, we proposed an OO approach using the Rational Unified Process (RUP) and the Rational Tool Suite—RequisitePro was the default tool simply because it was part of our overall toolset.

- On a third project, Rational was selected based on the fact that the technical director taught a class in use cases at a local university and was already familiar with the Rational Suite.

- On still another project, the customer specified Rational RequisitePro in the SOW.

- And on another, the project used DOORS because the customer used DOORS.

So, of five projects, this RA's experience was that the automated requirements tool was selected based on arbitrary criteria in all five situations—because of budgetary constraints, because it was preordained, or because someone had a personal preference. There was no instance in which an automated requirements tool was selected because it was the best choice for that specific project! The approach in selecting the project's requirements tool was in contrast with that applied for CM and testing tools, where more logical thought processes and specific criteria were used. The RA should recommend that a requirements tools trade study [7] be written to ensure that the criteria for selecting the automated requirements tool are consistent with the needs of the project.

23. *Develop or tailor and use organizational and project requirements policies and a requirements process that is continuously improved on your task, project, or organization. Invest 8% to 14% of total project costs on the (system life cycle) requirements process.*

It's helpful to have (and use) an *organizational policy* concerning requirements. We are all familiar with projects and organizations that *have* policies, but don't *use* them in practice. I'm talking about a different situation: I recommend that organizations and projects have policies and use them! Development of the organizational policy should involve senior management and include their direction that requirements will be used as the basis for engineering and management activities. The organizational policies concerning requirements can be as simple as those suggested by the two requirements-related process areas of the CMMI® [8], requirements development and RM:

- *Concerning requirements development:* "In order to identify and satisfy customer needs, projects will: (a) Collect stakeholder needs, (b) Formulate product and product component requirements, and (c) Analyze and validate these requirements."

- *Concerning RM:* "In order to ensure that customer needs are satisfied, projects will: (a) Manage requirements and requirements changes, and (b) Identify inconsistencies between project work and requirements."

Because requirements-related activities that are performed on projects are critical to the success of projects, I advocate a more detailed project requirements policy, such as that provided in *Effective Requirements Practices* [5, pp. 119–122] and also available on my Web site (www.ralphyoung.net). This artifact serves as a template that you should tailor (modify) to the needs of your project in its environment. An alternative to having a project requirements policy is to incorporate needed components into the project's requirements process.

Develop or tailor and use a documented requirements process. See Chapter 8 of this book for guidance on how to design a process. It's not difficult (or at least, it doesn't *have* to be difficult) to design or tailor a process. If you're not familiar with designing and using processes, you may want to engage the help of someone who is very familiar with doing this to serve as a facilitator for your stakeholders. It's important for the members of the project team to have a good understanding of the processes the team is using. Take time to brief everyone concerning the processes, and ensure that there is consensus and that the process approach is accepted—members of the team may be able to offer improvements, based on their experiences.

The data provided in Figure 4.1 of *Effective Requirements Practices* [5] provide a compelling case to invest 8% to 14% of project costs on the project's requirements process. It should be apparent from the discussion thus far that providing improved requirements practices is a good investment that yields leverage in controlling costs, for example, of rework (40% to 50% of the total costs of the average project). Encouraging investment in the project's requirements process and using effective requirements practices provide opportunities for the RA to have a major positive impact on project success.

24. *Use proven and familiar requirements mechanisms, approaches, methods, techniques, and tools.*

Commit to using proven and familiar mechanisms, approaches, methods, techniques, and tools. You should be familiar with examples of these from earlier portions of the book, but I'll mention a few examples in each category to keep them foremost in your mind:

- *Mechanisms:* the joint team (or whatever you choose to call this collaborative mechanism); a set of rules of conduct on your task, project, or organization to describe how members will treat each other; PDCA to determine how meetings went or how we are doing at a point in time, for example, upon completion of a milestone; a Purpose, Agenda, and Limit (PAL) provided in advance of meetings so that people can prepare for the meeting and know how much time to plan for the meeting;

- *Approaches:* partnering; use of peer reviews and defect prevention (DP) techniques throughout the task or project; project planning and tracking; training; CM; QA; using techniques to facilitate project communication; measurement; and so forth;

- *Methods:* requirements gathering methods such as interviews, document analysis, requirements workshops, prototyping, storyboards, scenarios, and modeling;

- *Techniques:* project risk management, peer reviews, DP, "brown bags";

- *Tools:* ReqPro, DOORS, other automated requirements tools noted in Table 5.7; automated risk management tools; brickcharts; a project notebook.

You may find it worthwhile to learn about and use a new method or technique; recognize, however, that time and effort will be required for people to learn new methods and techniques to utilize them effectively and that there is risk in using a method or technique that is not proven and familiar. Make decisions concerning using new methods and techniques with your eyes wide open.

25. *Establish an agreed-on goal, purpose, or mission for the task or project. Write (and iterate) a task or project vision and scope document.*

As noted at the beginning of this chapter, lacking an agreed-on goal, purpose, or mission for a task or project makes it difficult to accomplish anything of value. One needs to be able to articulate the goal and to garner support from stakeholders to achieve it. Writing and iterating a task or project vision and scope document provides a common basis for identifying and prioritizing more specific objectives and identifying the real requirements.

26. *Develop, implement, and enforce meeting rules that describe how project staff members are to treat one another.*

This entails two key elements: establishing and following an agenda (PAL) and following rules of conduct. Each of these elements is a key component of meetings designed to elicit and adopt new requirements or changes to existing requirements. The person requesting a meeting provides a PAL in advance of the meeting so that everyone knows what is to be discussed, each person can prepare appropriately, and all know when the meeting will end.

It's been my experience that I enjoy work and feel most effective when my coworkers appreciate and support my contribution to the overall effort. I have found that having a set of rules of conduct for the work efforts that I'm involved in has been an effective way to facilitate an attitude of supporting each other in our work environment. Examples of rules of conduct that I value include the following:

- Respect each person;
- Share responsibility;
- Criticize ideas, not people;
- Keep an open mind;
- Question and participate;
- Arrive on time;
- Keep interruptions to a minimum;
- Manage by fact.

These rules are posted in conference rooms at our company. People are called to task when they violate one of these rules. I feel empowered to contribute my best efforts. I know that my coworkers will respect me, even when my ideas seem unusual. We try to support each other in every way possible. Everyone shows up for meetings on time, and we start on time. Side-talk is not permitted. Focus is expected. We save incredible amounts of time. But more importantly, we respect each other and we are there for each other.

27. *Develop and apply a set of guidelines for effective meetings and guidelines for effective e-mailing.*

We spend a lot of time in meetings and reading and writing e-mail. It's logical that a set of guidelines for these time-eaters will save time and effort. I have previously recommended a set of guidelines for each: see *Effective Requirements Practices* [5, pp. 165–167 and pp. 167–172, respectively]. The specific guidelines are less important than (1) being committed to using guidelines for these purposes, and (2) people on projects and in organizations taking the time to develop guidelines that they will honor and use.

28. *Perform a risk assessment of new and changing requirements.*

Guidance for how to perform requirements-related risk assessments is provided in Chapter 7, topic 18.

29. *Learn how to manage teams effectively.*

We have seen throughout the book how important it is to work collaboratively, to gain consensus, to get buy-in of stakeholders, and to achieve results working in teams. The RA should develop the skill of managing teams effectively. There are training sessions and workshops one can attend to learn and practice the needed skills and techniques. One of the better books concerning managing teams is Scholtes et al.'s *The Team Handbook* [9].

30. *Establish a quality improvement and process improvement climate.*

Guidance for how to accomplish this is provided in Chapter 8.

Summary

This chapter presents 30 best practices for requirements development and management for your consideration. One can't do everything, at least not at one time. Dust off your requirements plan. Develop a reasonable approach to deploy, implement, and institutionalize those best practices that you deem appropriate for your project in its environment over a reasonable period of time. Collaborate with the task or project team to prioritize the value of the best practices that you decide to implement. Write an action plan that will enable the project to implement them. For each best practice, define the actions and schedule required to implement it. Do this in collaboration with your project team and your customer. Gain their buy-in and support for the selected best practices. Communicate what you are doing by means of project staff meetings or brown-bags. Involve your project team and customer in the decision-making process to gain the buy-in and support of others. The main thing is to ensure that the project team is moving together in concert with your customer, not to have the largest number of best practices. Remember, commitment is needed to achieve anything of value.

Case Study

Several years ago, I was asked to assist attorneys working on a legal case between a systems integration contractor and the U.S. government. The government had terminated the contract for default and then reprocured the system from another contractor. The system built by the new contractor blew up when it was subjected to actual data volumes. The few hours of consulting assistance originally requested grew into years of litigation support as the case unfolded, before it went to settlement five years later.

What caused this massive disconnect? The short answer is a lack of understanding of roles and responsibilities for managing requirements.

The government recognized that it needed requirements and had contracted years earlier for a feasibility study that included data requirements and functional requirements. Then, when it was clear that it needed to move forward quickly and no longer had time to complete the contract to build the system, it tasked the development contractor through a series of task orders. The first two tasks were to (1) "Evaluate the hardware and software specifications and perform a requirements analysis for the Head-quarters Local Area Network (LAN)," and (2) "Review and validate the (prior) study, versus current requirements."

The first task, "evaluate the hardware and software specifications and perform a requirements analysis for the Headquarters LAN," was taken as a low-risk task to recommend office automation personal computers (PC) hardware and software for workstations and servers. It was undertaken quickly, using end-of-year funding, and was intended to deliver equipment to users in the field. The contractor considered this task "achievable."

The second task, "review and validate the prior work," resulted in a document that described areas where current functional requirements had changed and identified areas where additional requirements work was necessary. The contractor was more concerned about being able to accomplish this work effectively, because of the requirements-related issues.

A third task was issued by the government to design an electronic transmission capability for the system. The SOW for this task was extremely detailed and called for the design of numerous interfaces. This suggested a major change in the architecture. The original study had assumed that the system would be a centralized mainframe-based system. Suddenly, it became clear that the client had a different approach in mind—a client-server architecture. By expressing how the requirements would be implemented, the government was imposing detailed constraints on the solution. The contractor began having anxiety because there were many unknowns, such as the design of the rest of the system beyond its transmission capability. Work continued without effective communication between the government and the contractor. The open issues were not resolved.

At a major design review, the contractor and certain government personnel met for the first time, and the light began to dawn. The lead designer of the electronic transmission capability declared, "Now I know what you want!" Everyone declared the meeting a success. One action item was to prepare a plan for when the transmission capability would be completed.

When the plan was delivered, it indicated that the projected system completion date would be a year beyond the desired date. This prompted the government to terminate the contract. The government waited until the other design deliverables were complete, turned them over to a new contractor, and got work underway to quickly build the system.

At system acceptance testing, the system blew up with massive data corruption, and it was clear that it just would not work. What was the problem?

Some of the requirements-related issues were as follows:

1. The hardware and software specifications evaluated under task 1 were not properly done because the selected components could not accommodate the data volume. Were those specifications simply system requirements for purchasing commodity PCs, or were those PCs purchased with the intent that they would be part of the solution for the overall system? This nuance would later prove significant,

because the government claimed that the evaluation of the PCs was for their suitability to support the agencywide system. The performance requirements for such a system had not been defined, because nobody on the contractor's side realized that the architecture was no longer centralized.

2. No overall, unified requirements document or repository was developed. Requirements were to be found in numerous sources of varying age and validity (for instance, handwritten notes by government personnel on deliverables they reviewed). In some cases, requirements were contradictory or lacking. Areas identified in the review and validation of prior requirements documents as needing further requirements definition were left that way because no tasking was received to explore them. There was no CM of the requirements.

3. The specification of detailed requirements by the government for the transmissions capability, while not communicating the overall architecture for the system or allowing the contractor to design the architecture, was an overspecification of design requirements and a constraint on the system—one that (as it turned out) would not work.

4. Data volumes identified in the data requirements done by the prior contractor grew in a few key places without any reassessment of the overall impact on the architecture—until the delivered system would not work.

5. The design of the system by the contractor was considered by the government to be so poor that the contract was terminated, yet the fact that the government directed the follow-on contractor to use those same design deliverables to build the system implies acceptance of that design. They were, in fact, a set of system requirements for the new contractor.

The major lesson to be learned from this case study concerns the roles and leadership of the requirements tasks. Because the government defined through its tasking which portions of the requirements it would require the contractor to take responsibility for and which portions the government would specify in detail, there was no overall RM strategy or process. Some of the end results of this scenario were (1) the user requirements were not met as intended by both the government and the contractors, (2) the original contract was terminated, (3) the system developed by the second contractor did not work, (4) a lot of money and time were wasted, (5) some people lost their jobs because of issues that developed, (6) some families were impacted negatively because of various interpersonal issues that developed, (7) years were spent in expensive litigation, (8) significant negative information concerning systems and software engineering and the problems of both parties was put forward in various communications, including the newspapers, and (9) a lot of finger pointing occurred. In my experience, this scenario is not unique—related scenarios have been repeated in various ways over the past two dozen years, and they continue even today.

Name withheld by request, requirements-engineering consultant

References

[1] Wiegers, K. E., *Software Requirements,* 2nd ed., Redmond, WA: Microsoft Press, 2003, 77–93.

[2] Gottesdiener, E., *Requirements by Collaboration: Workshops for Defining Needs.* Boston, MA: Addison-Wesley, 2002.

[3] Sommerville, I., P. Sawyer, and S. Viller, "Viewpoints for Requirements Elicitation: A Practical Approach." *Proceedings of the 1998 International Conference on Requirements Engineering* (ICRE'98), April 6–10, 1998, Colorado Springs, CO, New York: IEEE Computer Society, 1998, 74–81. See http://computer.org/proceedings/icre/8356/8356toc.htm. See also Chapter 13 of I. Sommerville and P. Sawyer's *Requirements Engineering: A Good Practice Guide,* New York: John Wiley & Sons, 1997, and G. Kotonya and I. Sommerville's *Requirements Engineering: Processes and Techniques,* Chichester, UK: John Wiley & Sons, 1998.

[4] Hooks, I. F., and K. A. Farry, *Customer-Centered Products: Creating Successful Products through Smart Requirements Management,* New York: AMACOM, 2001, 120–133.

[5] Young, R. R., *Effective Requirements Practices,* Boston, MA: Addison-Wesley, 2001.

[6] Whitten, N., "Meet Minimum Requirements: Anything More Is Too Much," *PM Network,* September 1998, p. 19.

[7] Young, R. R., "Requirements Tools Trade Study," at www.ralphyoung.net/publications/Requirements_Tools_Trade_Study1.doc.

[8] CMMI Web site, at www.sei.cmu.edu/cmmi.

[9] Scholtes, P. R., et al., *The Team Handbook,* 2nd ed., Madison, WI: Oriel, Inc., 2001.

CHAPTER 7

The RA's Specialty Skills

The topics in this chapter cover a set of specialty skills that will help you perform your responsibilities. Some skills recommended in Table 3.1, RA's Skills Matrix, have been mentioned, but not yet discussed in detail. Also, there are areas concerning the work of the RA that deserve further elaboration. Table 7.1 provides a list of these topics. You may find that you don't need all of these at a particular point in your career or on a specific project. However, it's likely that you will need to know about most of these topics at some point in your work. Use this book as a desk guide when the need arises. I will also suggest other useful references that provide more information to help answer the questions listed in Table 7.1.

Each of these topics will be discussed in turn.

1. *Why are requirements errors so devastating and how can RAs help address the problem?*

Industry experience is that errors associated with requirements are not only the most common type of error in developing systems and software, but also the most expensive to find and fix. Industry experts continue to express concern that both the number of requirements errors and the cost to fix them increase geometrically the further into the life cycle the error is discovered. Table 7.2 provides some data points that illustrate why requirements errors are so devastating.

What do we mean by a requirements error? Table 7.3 provides information concerning the types of requirements errors and their relative frequency, provided by industry expert and author Ivy Hooks in *Customer-Centered Products: Creating Successful Products through Smart Requirements Management* [1].

It's not surprising that the two largest categories are incorrect facts and omission of requirements. By following the

Table 7.1   RA Specialty Skills Topics

Topic	Question	Page Number
1	Why are requirements errors so devastating and how can RAs help address the problem?	127
2	What does the RA need to know about CM?	129
3	What does the RA need to know about the Unified Modeling Language?	135
4	What if I'm supporting a small project? Does any of this stuff still apply? How can I convince the PM and my coworkers to incorporate a degree of discipline and process into our approach?	139
5	What is the difference between a requirements specification and specifying the requirements?	141
6	I notice "impact estimation" on the requirements skills matrix—what is it, and how can I learn more about it?	142
7	You seem to suggest that the RA should be a leader on the project. Why do I need to be a leader? How can I be a leader? What should I lead?	143
8	You have stressed the role of the RA in facilitating discussions, presentations, meetings, training sessions, and workshops. What can I do to become a better facilitator?	144
9	You have emphasized that having a defect prevention (DP) process is advisable for all projects, perhaps necessary. Can you provide a DP process that I can implement easily?	145
10	You indicate that estimation is an important skill. What aspects of estimation are critical for the RA?	149
11	You advise doing inspections for all requirements-related documents. Why shouldn't we be satisfied with doing peer reviews of them? How are inspections different from peer reviews, and why go to the extra trouble? What type of inspection is best?	150
12	You have placed a lot of emphasis on quality. How can the RA help apply quality principles on systems and software development projects?	152
13	There seems to be a lot of confusion in our industry concerning the terms *verification* and *validation*. Can you explain why this is so and also clarify suggested uses of the two terms?	153
14	The "agilists" advocate that agile development methodologies promise higher customer satisfaction, lower defect rates, faster development times, and a solution to rapidly changing requirements. Should I recommend that we consider agile development methods on my project?	154
15	What is the value of practical knowledge?	154
16	What if my PM, our organization's management team, or our customer does not support the concept of process improvement?	154
17	How should the work breakdown structure be applied?	156
18	What is a good approach for considering requirements risks?	159

recommended approach to work collaboratively with your customer and users to identify the real requirements, using the requirements gathering checklist provided in Table 5.1, you will have reduced the risk of these types of errors. What else can RAs do to reduce requirements errors?

Table 7.2 Industry Experience Concerning Requirements Errors

Capers Jones:

"Errors that originate in requirements tend to be the most expensive and troublesome to eliminate later. Prevention is more effective than defect removal."

TRW Experience:

"Most errors were found after unit testing, and over 80% were requirements and design errors."

Tom DeMarco:

"More than half of all defects can be traced to requirements errors."

U.S. Air Force:

"41% of all errors discovered were requirements errors."

Table 7.3 Types of Requirements Errors and Their Relative Frequencies

Requirements Error	Relative Frequency (%)
Incorrect fact	49
Omission	31
Inconsistency	13
Ambiguity	5
Misplaced requirement	2
Total	100

From: Hooks and Farry [1].

Table 7.4 provides suggestions contributed by practitioners.[1] Note that several of these activities can mitigate the risk of errors in multiple categories. Performing these types of activities has a high return on the time invested; they are "highly leveraged" activities.

2.   *What does the RA need to know about CM?*

CM is a key discipline on a project of any size. Lacking effective CM, the project is not in control because the status of its work products is not in control. Configuration control is one of the critical functions on a task or project that an RA must be knowledgeable about since it is vital to the overall integrity of the evolving requirements and other engineering work products. RAs must take an active role in managing the requirements baseline from its inception and ensure that changes to the baseline are identified, documented, reviewed, approved, and tracked through implementation. These requirements controls and processes are very similar to the CM processes

---

1. With special thanks to RA Pat Little who contributed several of these ideas.

Table 7.4 Suggested Actions to Reduce Requirements Errors

Assumptions:

Approximately 8% to 14% of total project costs will be invested in the requirements process.

Formal training will be provided to RAs to explain how to write good requirements and how to address the various types of typical requirements errors.

The customer will be involved throughout the development process.

A project glossary will be established and used to ensure that the definitions are agreed upon and that words are used consistently in all project activities.

Types of Requirements Errors and Suggestions for Addressing Them

Incorrect facts:

Provide an attribute in the requirements tool for verification of the factual basis for each requirement, and perform research to validate facts. For example:

V = verified;

N = not yet researched;

Q = questionable.

Provide stakeholder reviews of requirements work products.

Require a link to an authoritative source (mission statement, policy document, formal guidance, etc.). If no authoritative source can be found, write a detailed rationale for the requirement. The reference to an authoritative source is similar to, but more formal than, the idea of requiring a rationale for each requirement.

Provide a mechanism (such as a Web page or broadcast e-mail) or multiple mechanisms for wide review of the requirements and feedback by users, customers, stakeholders, and so forth.

Build a logical data model (LDM) from an enterprise perspective.

Omission:

Solicit user needs from a variety of different viewpoints.

Perform requirements modeling.

Use a structured methodology such as use case modeling or a comparable technique.

Develop an OCD or CONOPS before drilling down into specific requirements statements.

If the business process that the system will support is documented, use the process documentation to lead users through the requirements elicitation process. If the business process is not documented, consider working with the user to create this documentation. It may exceed traditional boundaries of requirements analysis, but in the end you will have a better understanding of the requirements and the user may have mitigated one or more risks of system failure (even if the system met all the documented requirements).

Inconsistency:

Conduct inspections of requirements-related work products by members of the project team.

Examine and analyze the RTM for consistency and proper placement of requirements.

Require a link to an authoritative source (mission statement, policy document, formal guidance, etc.). If no authoritative source can be found, write a detailed rationale for the requirement.

Define all terms and ensure their use in requirements statements is consistent with the formally recognized definition.

Build an LDM from an enterprise perspective.

Ambiguity:

Conduct inspections of requirements-related work products by members of the project team.

Require a link to an authoritative source (mission statement, policy document, formal guidance, etc.). If no authoritative source can be found, write a detailed rationale for the requirement.

Define all terms, and ensure their use in requirements statements is consistent with the formally recognized definition.

Misplaced requirement:

Examine and analyze the RTM for consistency and proper placement of requirements.

Source: Contributions from requirements analysts who participated in the author's tutorials and workshops.

used by other project teams to control their evolving work products. At all times, the RA will need to work with the current and correct versions under CM control and be able to account for each change and version of that work product. Thus, the RA needs to have knowledge of and experience with the following CM practices.

CM Planning   CM planning must include considerations regarding the following: contract requirements, overall scope, customer CM, processes, tools, and resources. From a requirements perspective, an RA would need to work with CM planners to ensure that CM and RM processes are coordinated and that configuration items include identified requirements, documents, and other items. Integration of CM policies, processes, procedures, and practices with the requirements and other engineering policies, processes, and methods will ensure a cohesive, team-centered approach. Forming a close working relationship with all project groups and with the customer fosters strong, mutually supportive working relationships. Communications, process, and effective tools will help assure overall integrity of delivered work products.

CM Tools   The requirements team needs to ensure that the selected requirements tool is not only adequate for control purposes, but that it is also well integrated with CM tools. Some commercial CM tools have automated interfaces with requirements tools and other engineering tools. They in turn must work in concert with and in support of the overall project process, including requirements and CM. Figure 7.1 describes the relationships between an RM tool and a CM tool on a sample project. Note the identification of several documents and activities in the requirements tool, that data is submitted directly from the requirements tool to the CM tool, that requirements are mapped to software packages, and how each of the tools assists with critical project activities.

Engineering Baselines   In engineering projects, CM works early in the project life cycle with the other project groups to identify work products (identified as configuration items) and to incorporate them into controlled baselines. Engineering teams (including the RAs) manage these baselines as they move through an established engineering life cycle. These baselines will likely have unique identifications (as do individual configuration items) so that managers, customers, requirements, design, test engineers, QA, and CM all have the same understanding with regard to baseline status and content, configuration item status, versions, and the approved changes incorporated.

Operations Baselines   Operations and maintenance (O&M) projects find it critical to maintain a steady state of an operational system or group of systems. Baselines are also important here as well, since they include controlled hardware, software (developed and integrated COTS), and standard operational procedures (SOPs).

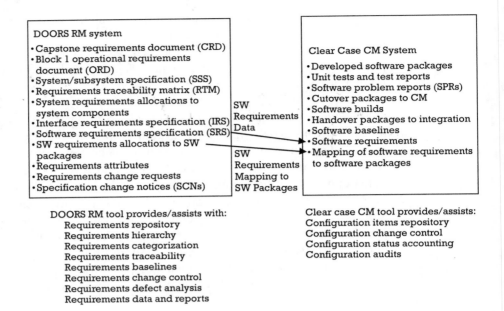

Figure 7.1 Relationships between a project's requirements tool and its CM tool. (*Source:* Michael Davis. Used with permission.)

Configuration Control   Control provides a wide spectrum of activities and methods that ensure that configurations are adequately managed and that they have the highest integrity possible. These activities include tools and repositories in which work is performed in a managed manner and management of changes to those work products. In terms of the RA's tasks, the use of a requirements tool in the management and control of project requirements is most important. The RA must work with CM to ensure their requirements and other work products (e.g., requirements documents) are in a controlled environment (in a tool or other controlled space), that they are available for work purposes, and are properly backed up or archived and available for re-creation if needed. Within the tool or repository, the requirements team needs to ensure that individual requirements are traceable (which is in itself a necessary CM need in order to show overall status accounting). Requirements must have backward traceability to previous versions of the same requirement, or be traceable back to their source. The selected tool must also provide forward traceability to show allocations of the requirements to program components (e.g., hardware, software) and the tests to be performed, and it must be able to identify and recover previous versions of the requirements, based upon approved changes. The requirements tool must also be able to show change indicators [e.g., change requests (CRs) and engineering change proposals (ECPs)] that propose changes to requirements. This is required later in the life cycle when CM performs configuration audits to verify that requirements have been satisfied (tested) through the delivered work products. Figure 7.2 provides a

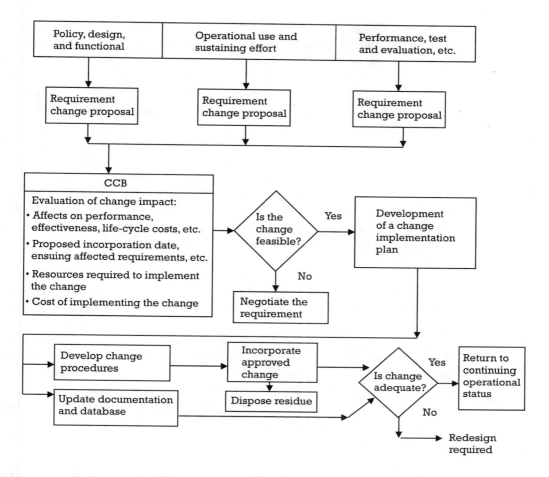

Figure 7.2 Requirement change control procedure. (*Source:* Michael Davis. Used with permission.)

high-level view of some of the interrelationships between the CM and requirements activities on a project, in this case concerning requirement change proposals.[2]

Configuration Control Board (CCB)   As noted in Figure 7.2, the RA often will be called upon to participate in CCB meetings and provide not only status, but also expert engineering advice and analysis of the impacts of requested changes. The CCB evaluates whether the change is feasible to ensure that requirements changes are either (1) disapproved, or (2) approved, coordinated, and implemented in a coordinated manner. This ensures that all interested parties understand the change and are able to perform the necessary work, as well as the integrity of the evolving work products. This approach of maintaining configuration control is essential to project success.

---

2. With thanks to RA Michael Davis for lending his project experiences as documented in Figures 7.1 and 7.2.

Operational Change Management   All of the items noted above concerning the operational baselines undergo frequent change. These changes also undergo a change process using a CCB to review and approve the change and an implementation process that oversees the implementation of the change. In regard to these changes and overall operational effectiveness, an operations staff must also be aware of their requirements. These are no less important than those found in the engineering environment. They must maintain a level of support or service to the customer through documented service-level agreements (SLAs). They must be implemented through the operation of the deployed and fully implemented system and must be monitored constantly. These SLAs are managed, much as requirements are in an engineering project, through collection of operational data (metrics) that are analyzed, tracked, and reported against. Changes to the SLAs are managed through change requests and may involve engineering changes as user needs change.

Configuration Status Accounting   Those involved in managing requirements and requirements work products must understand their responsibilities with regard to recording status for their activities. For example, if changes to requirements are proposed (following the change process), the RA must document or record the change, record their impact analysis, and follow through on the implementation of the change, recording the status of its implementation when complete. For the RA, this would involve updates to the requirements tool and affected requirements work products. If reports are needed, CM and the RA need to coordinate the information needed and how best to collect, format, and deliver the information.

Configuration Audits   Because their work is integral to the delivery of work products that meet stated customer requirements, the RAs must participate in both informal and formal CM audits to help verify that the requirements used are correct, current (reflecting all approved changes), and were made available to the design, development, and test teams for their work.

CM Metrics   Often the CM office may be given responsibility for managing program metrics, or at least providing input to the project metrics program. Some metrics may involve requirements directly (as in measuring requirements volatility or change), or they may have input into the metrics gathered for overall changes.

The wise and proactive RA will form a strong and mutually supportive relationship with the CM team. I suggest that if you are not already quite familiar with CM, find someone who is and ask for his or her support in familiarizing you with CM activities. In addition, study a good CM book such as Frank B. Watts's *Engineering Documentation Control Handbook: Configuration Management for Industry* [2]. Watts focuses on a simplified, fast CM system that exceeds U.S. Department of Defense (DoD) standards. Case studies are provided. Also, a book that is considered a must-read by many software CM practitioners is Alexis Leon's *A Guide to Software Configuration*

Management [3]. An example of a good CM plan is available at www.air-time.co.uk/users/wysywig/cmp.htm. This link also provides another link to a brief description of principles of change management. A more detailed discussion of technical management is available at sparc.airtime.co.uk/users/wysywig/techman.htm.

See also EIA Standard 649, "National Consensus Standard for Configuration Management" [4].

3. *What does the RA need to know about the UML?*

The short answer is either not very much or a whole lot, depending upon whether your project is using an OO approach. The Unified Modeling Language (UML) is a general-purpose notation developed in the 1990s that describes the static and dynamic behavior of a system. It is a visual modeling language and is not intended to be a visual programming language in the sense of having all the necessary visual and semantic support to replace programming languages. For example, complex branches and joins are best expressed in a textual programming language. The UML provides a complete, formal model to document a system. It's a graphical language for visualizing, specifying, constructing, and documenting the artifacts of a software intensive system. Grady Booch, Ivar Jacobson, and Jim Rumbaugh of Rational Corporation started the UML and were its original chief methodologists. See Fowler's *UML Distilled: Applying The Standard Object Modeling Language* [5] for a good reference. Later products were a team effort of many partners under the sponsorship of the Object Management Group (OMG), an international organization that includes information systems vendors, software developers, and users. An "Introduction to OMG's UML" can be downloaded from the Web [6]. The current version of the UML is also downloadable from the Web [7]. The UML has become a vendor-independent standard for expressing the design of software systems. The UML incorporates use cases as the standard means of capturing and representing requirements. Use cases are essentially functional and used extensively by RAs for both OO and non-OO approaches. Some industry experts, including Karl Wiegers, believe that use cases are among the most effective techniques for capturing requirements; others feel that use cases alone don't provide adequate information for developers to know what to build. The following are concerns in using use cases: (1) a lot of experience with them is required to gain familiarity; (2) it's difficult to know when you are finished expressing the requirements—one can continue to do a lot of analysis without getting done; (3) information may be provided in the use cases at the wrong level of abstraction; (4) use cases are typically too detailed and almost always have to be redone; and (5) use cases are often full of errors. See Gottesdiener [8] who believes she has encountered most every type of error people can make in writing use cases. It is interesting to note that roles in use cases fit well with the notion of viewpoints as a vehicle for requirements elicitation. If a requirements development group has had a lot of experience using use cases, the team might want to consider using them to help capture the requirements. If not, use a requirements-specification approach to help represent the requirements. System engineers may want to use IEEE Standard 1233, "IEEE Guide for Developing System Requirements Specifications" [9], while software engineers may prefer IEEE Standard 830, "IEEE Recommended Practice for Software Requirements Specifications" [10]. Another detailed requirements specification template, the Volere Requirements Specification Template [11], is available on-line at www.atlsysguild.com/GuildSite/Robs/Template.html. Several examples of requirements are provided.

Those choosing to use the UML will need to familiarize themselves with the Object Management Architecture (OMA), which provides the conceptual infrastructure upon which all OMG specifications are based, with UML Semantics, the UML Notation Guide, and UML Standard Profiles. It should be apparent from this discussion that a lot of study and experience is needed to utilize the UML effectively. On the other hand, it is essential to develop a model for an industrial-strength software system. Good models are needed to facilitate communication throughout the project team to ensure that the system architecture is sound. The importance of using good modeling techniques increases with system complexity. The creators of the UML believe that prior to the UML, there was no clear leading modeling language. The cost of using and supporting modeling languages with minor differences motivated the efforts of representatives of more than two dozen companies to partner to develop the UML. The UML is not a process. The experience of the UML developers is that the UML must be applied in the context of a process, but different organizations and problem domains require different processes. The UML developers recognized the value of a use case-driven, architecturecentric, iterative, and incremental process.

Kulak and Guiney explain the diagrams used in the UML in *Use Cases: Requirements in Context* [12]. Be sure to digest their considered list of problems related to using use cases [12, pp. 154–165] before making a decision to rely on use cases to represent your requirements. Other good references are Cockburn's (pronounced "co-burn") *Writing Effective Use Cases* [13] and Korson's *The Misuse of Use Cases* [14]. I believe that Korson's counsel is wise: "before considering use cases, ensure that a well understood and managed requirements process is in place and that you have high-quality requirements."[3] As suggested earlier in this book, investing in these areas first is a prerequisite for a good requirements approach.

A colleague experienced in using OO technologies advocates using the UML in requirements-related work. He provided an analysis, based on his experience—see Insert 7.1.[4] This vignette provides insights and suggestions.

---

3. "The Misuse of Use Cases" and "Constructing Useful Use Cases" are available at www.korson-mcgregor.com. Korson also provides a template that lists and describes a set of fields needed for a well-written use case. Korson believes that the major problems in systems development are not technical but rather have to do with requirements—"getting the right requirements and getting the requirements right."

4. With thanks to Wayne O'Brien of Raytheon Corporation who graciously agreed to lend his experience.

Insert 7.1—Experience in Using the UML and Use Cases

Use cases, with the automated tools available to support UML, provide an active semantic link from the most detailed view of a system (e.g., software code or hardware logic, to the top-level requirements, which are captured in the use cases). This active link means that there is information for understanding the system that is current and accessible at all times to all stakeholders.

User stakeholders include not just operators, but managers, investors, auditors, and others. Developer stakeholders include whatever disciplines are required for the system under consideration, both temporally and functionally. Temporally, the active semantic link supports the developer disciplines for the full life cycle of a system, including RAs, designers, and testers. The active link also supports functional developer disciplines, including hardware, software, communications, and human factors engineers.

This broad support for stakeholders that is provided by use cases depends on the features of UML, as well as the tools that support UML. Giving diverse stakeholders access to accurate information about the system of interest to them takes advantage of the multiple view aspect of UML (a best practice described by IEEE Standard 1471). The concept of a use case within UML captures the semantics of a system in a way that is readily communicated to people with a wide range of interests and expertise, rather than just ability in a single field. It is precise enough to be useful for building systems and yet readily understood by people who don't build systems for a living. This same communications characteristic of use cases underlies the temporal and functional cross-discipline support for the developers, who do make their livings building systems.

Wayne O'Brien
Raytheon Corporation
January 2003

I had the opportunity to hear Grady Booch (as noted above, one of the three chief methodologists of the UML) speak at a session sponsored by Rational Corporation in Northern Virginia on November 22, 2002. Among the insights offered by Booch are the following:

- Customers don't know what they want until it's delivered. This argues for an incremental approach, the value of iteration, and the approach of showing work products and plans to users on an incremental basis. An incremental approach allows us to make mid-course corrections.

- There is a big gap between where we are and where we need to be. A good approach is to look at "where things hurt" and attack the points of pain.

- The primary barrier that we face today is the ability to develop software.

- Invest in the process of software development, because software is the life-blood. Software development is still very labor-intensive, and this won't change. The best processes become invisible—it's simply "the way we do business."

- Most companies are at CMM® "level 1½." The CMM® is orthogonal to project success. It is not sufficiently agile for economic success.

- There are common failure modes at opposite ends of the process spectrum: at the one end, we have overengineering and overdesigning of systems; at the other end, we have agility. (Maintaining the magic of a gifted group is difficult because developers do not want to maintain or to build another release. Magic happens when there is synergy between executives and developers.)

- Architecture is important and will become more important, for example, portals that cross information silos and barriers. There is no perfect design. "Perfect" is the enemy of "good enough."

- The Universal Business Language (UBL) is coming; it enables another level of abstraction.

- There are several global trends concerning the future of software:

1. Inceasing growth and complexity.

2. Rise of platforms. We need patterns. Read *Design Patterns* [15] to familiarize yourself with the vocabulary. We can build systems rapidly by using patterns and frameworks—this is where companies get their competitive advantage.

3. Growth of Web services.

4. Rise in open source software (Linux is not a good model for developing systems).

5. Growth of model-driven development (MDD). This will provide the ability to debug at a higher level.

6. Aspect-oriented programming (looking at a system from one stakeholder aspect). This is three to five years away. A tool (Aspect J) is used to weave the aspects together.

7. Security. This is an increasing and emerging area and an overarching issue. Processes and technologies are needed to help with security.

8. Collaborative development environments and use of the Web for virtual project space (the embodiment of tribal memory).

9. Component-based development.[5]

---

5. The requirements process for component-based development (based on development with reuse) is different for systems developed from scratch.

Booch's summary was a testimony to the magnitude of the man:

> There are only fourteen million programmers in the world. Look at what we have done! We have changed the world. What a privilege it is to be part of the community that has made a big difference. What a responsibility this is to do a better job all the time. You are the people who are doing the heavy lifting.

UML is, to be sure, an excellent methodology by which to derive requirements. However, at the time of this writing, it is a relative newcomer to the field of requirements development. A methodology that has been extant for over fifteen years is Integration Definition for Function Modeling (IDEF). This started with the initial IDEF0 method and continues through IDEF5. Insert 7.2 contains real-world experience comparing UML with IDEF0. These experiences were provided by an RA with over twenty years of experience in software development and requirements engineering. The RA may want to familiarize him- or herself with IDEF0 as an alternative to the UML. Excellent references concerning IDEF0 are FIPS PUB 183 [16], the IEEE Standard for Functional Modeling Language [17], and Feldmann's *The Practical Guide to Business Process Reengineering Using IDEF0* [18]. There are also some IDEF workflow simulator tools that can be useful in deriving requirements, for example Business Modeling Workbench.

4. *What if I'm supporting a small project? Does any of this stuff still apply? How can I convince the PM and my coworkers to incorporate a degree of discipline and process into our approach?*

Good questions! I've been challenged with these questions many times, and there is information in the literature about them, too. First, let's start with a definition of a small project. Understanding there is no agreement on the definition of a small project, my arbitrary definition is one to six professionals working on a single task for as long as three to six months.

Some analysts and engineers may feel that the CMM® (and the more recent CMMI®) are applicable only for medium to huge projects. My experience suggests that the CMM® and CMMI® are scalable to a project of any size—one needs to do project planning, project tracking, requirements development and management, CM, QA, and other processes such as DP on all projects!

My advice is to urge members of small projects to scale down the approach and tailor it. Try not to allow such projects to use smallness as an excuse for not using processes, mechanisms, methods, techniques, and tools that will enable them to be successful. There are several good publications that provide advice for how to implement processes on small projects. See Paulk's *Using the Software CMM with Judgment: Small Projects & Small Organizations* [19] for elaboration on this theme and Rita Hadden's *"How Scaleable Are CMM Key Practices?"* [20]. Hadden's view based on observations and experience with more than 50 small projects is that professional judgment should

Insert 7.2—Some Experiences from the Real World Concerning the IDEF

I think as far as requirements analysis is concerned, the customer's preference and level of sophistication should play a big part in selecting which modeling methodology to use. The UML is just the currently used favorite approach in the overall topic of modeling. An analyst with the same level of understanding of IDEF0/IDEF1X as he or she has of UML would be just about as effective with either. They both provide insight into the problem space, help the analyst know what questions to ask, and provide a picture of the functionality of the system to support the requirements text. (I think function point analysis (FPA) also gets you there by different and less graphical means.)

IDEF is easier to comprehend than UML. On two large projects that I supported, we started out by creating requirements in UML. In both cases someone got cold feet at the end and decided that some important stakeholder group on the customer side would never understand the UML presentation of the requirements, and we reverted to presenting requirements as plain text. Ironically, in both cases the customers were generally familiar with IDEF models already.

This was clearly our fault. If you are going to use modeling of any kind, make sure customers have an adequate understanding of the modeling approach. If they don't, then it is your obligation to teach them, and the earlier the better.

In the DoD world this problem has been mostly solved with IDEF, assuming the approach outlined in Appendix C of FIPS 183 is followed. The joint team consists of customers (who are generally IDEF readers) and contractors (who are generally IDEF writers). The kits (IDEF review packages) are reviewed early and often. By the time the model nears completion, nobody is surprised by what it looks like or what it describes.

As much as I like modeling as a tool, I can't emphasize enough that the modeling methodology has to be understood by everyone, not just a few specialists, to be successful. I believe this is the root cause of all failed modeling efforts, regardless of the methodology. After all, each of us has spent years communicating through a common spoken language—yet we still fail to understand each other much of the time. Why do we expect someone who has little or no previous experience communicating in models to understand them?

Terry L. Bartholomew
RA

be used to scale down and apply key practices to support small projects. Brodman and Johnson's *LOGOS Tailored CMM for Small Businesses, Small Organizations, and Small Projects* [21] may also be helpful.

So my answer is yes, this stuff does apply to small projects—tailor the processes, mechanisms, methods, techniques, and tools as needed for the small project in its environment. Convincing your PM and coworkers to incorporate a degree of discipline and process may turn out to be a difficult or impossible task if they are set in their opinions. My suggestion here is to avoid arguments; rather, (1) address a "point of pain" on the project—an area where the project is experiencing difficulty—and (2) use data to support your position. Starting small on a small task can have immediate benefits to customers and serve as a way to convince management and staff of the usefulness of a process-centered approach. This area might well be requirements elicitation—the project may be experiencing some issues in identifying real requirements. Customers and users may not differentiate between stated requirements and real requirements. This is a great place to start, because with some effort in understanding and analyzing the stated requirements, you will very likely be able to identify ways to help—for example, by applying the criteria of a good requirement to the stated requirements; researching and identifying the rationale for each requirement; collaborating with the customer and users to prioritize the requirements in a requirements workshop environment, facilitated by an experienced outsider; creating a joint team to discuss requirements and make shared decisions about them; providing some requirements-related training based on the topics suggested in Table 5.5; suggesting use of an automated requirements tool such as Requisite Pro (ReqPro) to assign attributes to each requirement (e.g., priority) and perform requirements traceability to ensure that each requirement is addressed throughout the system—the possibilities are endless because the opportunities for continuous improvement abound! Try to position yourself as a trusted advisor. Use data to prove your point, and identify other points of pain. Review the roles of the RA discussed in Chapter 2. Consider which of those roles seem most appropriate to you for the particular situation. Be a positive influence on the project. Find ways to help, and contribute more than your share. You will be successful and become a valued member of the team.

5. *What is the difference between a requirements specification and specifying the requirements?*

Great question! This is a cause of a lot of confusion, and it's important for the RA to be able to clarify this and other areas—not with a know-it-all attitude, but rather with humility and understanding that it's human nature for people to have different views and definitions of things and varying opinions. I mentioned the requirements specification earlier in this chapter and provided two good references concerning it. A requirements specification is a document that contains requirements. You'll recall from Chapter 5 that I recommend that you view the requirements repository as consisting of several items—the requirements specification (or specifications if you are developing a large system) is one important item. Some people will use the verbiage "specifying the system requirements" to mean something else—namely, determining what the requirements of the system should be. I encourage that the phrase "specifying the requirements" be avoided to reduce confusion. A better description would be defining or documenting the system requirements.

6.   *I notice "impact estimation" on the requirements skills matrix. What is it, and how can I learn more about it?*

Impact estimation (IE) is an analytical technique advocated by industry expert and consultant Tom Gilb. Gilb devotes Chapter 11 to it in his book *Principles of Software Engineering Management* [22]. Gilb believes that the IE technique provides a better way to evaluate the design process than any other technique. As shown in Figure 7.3, IE provides an analytical tool to quantify requirements.

This enables RAs to evaluate requirements quantitatively rather than only subjectively. The technique estimates the impact of selected strategies on specified goals. IE tables enable analysis of technical or organizational ideas in relation to requirements and costs. Gilb advises [23] that he has used IE to do the following:

‣ Compare alternative design ideas;

‣ Estimate the state of the overall design architecture;

Requirements \ Solutions	Planned level	Tag=Exper.Co Selfmetric	User Simplicity	Robustness Stab., Surv.	Open-end Re-eval	File description	Command. Interface and manager dialect	Total %	Deviation	
Profitability	20% ROI	5	10	10	10	20	20	75	−25	Under design
Usability	30 min.	30	60	25	20	20	40	195	95	Over design
Connectivity	5 min.	10	40	0	40	40	40	170	70	Over design
Availability	99.98%	30	20	30	10	20	20	130	30	Over design
Integrity	99.99%	10	10	20	5	20	−10	55	−45	Under design
Performance	>12 Tr/S	30	5	20	5	5	5	70	−30	Under design
Marketability	12 languages	40	40	40	20	30	40	210	110	Over design
Adaptability	10 yr.	30	30	10	10	30	30	140	40	Over design
Dev. resources	$12 million	20	30	30	10	30	30	150	50	Over budget
Marketing costs	$1 million/yr.	5	10	20	10	5	15	65	−35	Under budget
Value/cost ratio		1.85	1.34	0.78	1.5	1.32	1.03			
Decision		Best solution	Not best	Not best	Not best	Not best	Not best			

Figure 7.3 An example of use of the IE technique to evaluate requirements. (*Source:* Tom Gilb. Reprinted with permission.)

‣ Plan and control project delivery steps;

‣ Analyze risks.

Gilb acknowledges that IE is "filled with possibilities for errors" (because the analyst provides the estimates based on a best-estimate approach). He believes these errors are unavoidable, and that the IE technique should be used to calculate the "approximately correct order of magnitude" [22, p. 184]. If you have a need to use this technique, I suggest that you study Chapter 11 of Gilb's book and read more about the technique at Gilb's Web site, www.gilb.com.

7. *You seem to suggest that the RA should be a leader on the project. Why do I need to be a leader? How can I be a leader? What should I lead?*

Although the role of being a leader was not specifically identified in Chapter 2, the tone of this book does suggest that the RA should take the opportunity to provide leadership on the projects you support. Change is endemic in today's working environments, and leaders are needed to help manage the changes and to facilitate adapting to them. You may feel that demonstrating leader qualities is "above your pay grade"—the purpose of this discussion is to convince you that the RA can and should help lead the project. Table 7.5 suggests some of the ways that the RA can help lead.

Table 7.5   Some of the Ways That RAs Can Help Lead

Urge identification of the real requirements;
Urge implementation of a mechanism to control changes to requirements and new requirements;
Suggest use of a set of rules of conduct on your project;
Suggest development of a set of guidelines for effective meetings for use on your project;
Recommend using peer reviews of all work products and inspections of requirements-related work products;
Suggest implementing and using a DP process;
Provide requirements training for RAs, the project staff, and customers and users, including explanations of the requirements-related industry problems and their causes;
Urge proactive steps to improve project communication, such as regular brown-bag presentations by each work group (for all others on the project) concerning current work activities;
Urge tailoring of the requirements gathering approach for your project;
Recommend use of an industry-strength automated requirements tool on the project and formal training for those who use the tool most frequently;
Evaluate your requirements against the criteria of a good requirement and the rationale for each requirement; share the results of this exercise with your customer/users.

These are just a few of the ways that an RA can help lead—the possibilities are endless. Opportunities come up every day for each of us to lead. Set the example and help nurture winning ways on your project.

Some people feel that not everyone is cut out to be a leader and that the RA need not be a leader, but rather a good team player, willing to share his knowledge and problem-solving skills.

8. *You have stressed the role of the RA in facilitating discussions, presentations, meetings, training sessions, and workshops. What can I do to become a better facilitator?*

My advice to you concerning this is "just do it." I have found that the more presentations I make during my career, the easier making them gets. I still get nervous prior to a presentation, but that's okay. I use that nervous energy to prepare for the presentation and to be a bit animated during the presentation. None of us is happiest during a dull presentation. Being upbeat, enthusiastic, moving about the audience, inviting participation, acknowledging good comments and contributions—these all have the effect of involving participants and in my experience result in presentations that are received well. When you really stop to think about making a presentation, what is there to be afraid of? What is the worst thing that can happen? Some people in the audience may not think highly of your remarks, but this is the case even when experienced speakers take the podium—not everyone will relate to every speaker's views and presentation. I have given hundreds of presentations, and there has never been one where at least one person in the audience did not come up afterward with some kind remarks and expression of interest.

There are some steps you can take to help:

- Attend presentations by others and discern what you like (and don't like) about them.

- Team with someone you consider more proficient and experienced in making presentations or facilitating workshops to get yourself in front of an audience and improve your skills and confidence.

- Arrange to have yourself videotaped when you are making a presentation. View the tape. You may be surprised by what you see. My experience, having done this several times, is that I'm quite different than I thought I would be.

- Seek opportunities to give talks. For example, local chapters of professional associations are always looking for speakers for luncheon meetings, evening meetings, and Saturday tutorials. Also, consider making a presentation at annual meetings and conferences. I think that you'll find that the more you make presentations, the easier it becomes to do it. You could even organize brown-bag sessions at your office and give some of the talks yourself.

▸ Attend training sessions about giving presentations or join a group, such as Toastmasters, that provides support, opportunities, and encouragement. Don't take the attitude, "I can't do that!" As in other areas of life, each of us can do much more than we think we can. We are limited only by our own willingness to get out there and do things. Go for it!

9. *You have emphasized that having a DP process is advisable for all projects, perhaps necessary. Can you provide a DP process that I can implement easily?*

DP is concerned with learning from the defects found in work products and implementing ways to improve processes to prevent defects from recurring. It is a valuable process because it can reduce the number of errors that are made early in the development process, thus saving rework (time and money). Of course, DP can be used at any time in any project to improve the results from our work activities. A DP process is easily tailored and documented, taught, learned, and applied. Unfortunately, most organizations don't make an effort to implement a DP process. I think one reason that DP processes are not deployed and used more frequently is that people have so many other things going on that they don't want to take on yet another process and activity. Another reason is that many people don't appreciate the power and value of DP activities.[6] Keep in mind that the main thing is for the project to be successful. Our criteria for success include, among others, completing the project within budget and on time. DP can make a valuable contribution to achieving these goals.

A DP Process   Figure 7.4 provides a straightforward DP process that you can begin with and then add additional features to as you deem necessary, for example, metrics to evaluate the effectiveness of the process, a DP plan, a DP repository, and so fourth. [Note that DP has been given another name in the CMMI®: "Causal Analysis and Resolution" (CAR).]

The purpose of DP is to identify root causes of defects and other problems and take action to prevent them from occurring in the future.

The first step is to identify a work product or process that is creating issues. Where is the project experiencing problems ("points of pain")? For example, you might decide that the project is experiencing some problems because of issues concerning the requirements. Therefore, perhaps a good improvement activity might be to evaluate the project's requirements process. If it's documented, great, let the project's documented

---

6. DP is a high maturity process in the CMM®. This suggests to the casual observer that we shouldn't worry about it until we have already addressed all of the processes at Levels 1 to 4 of the CMM®/CMMI® models. My experience is that DP should be used by most projects, no matter what the maturity level. The reason is the same as for my earlier suggestion to use peer reviews on all projects: these activities identify problems and defects earlier in the development process than would be the case if we didn't use these techniques. As a result, time and money are saved, and the quality of work products is better than it would have been if we didn't use them.

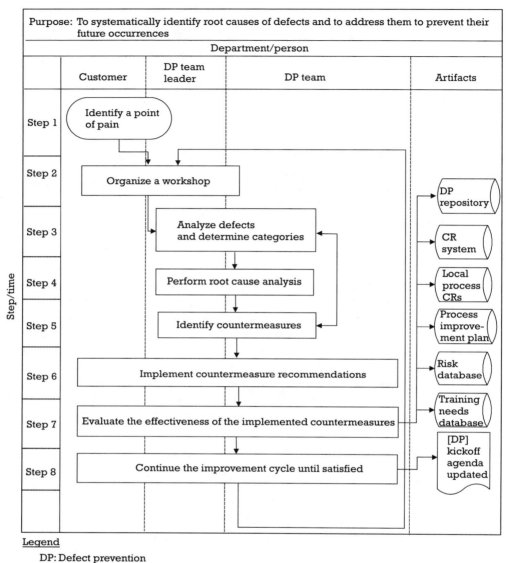

Figure 7.4 DP process.

requirements process be the topic of a "DP workshop." If the process is not documented, gather a few interested and motivated stakeholders in a room for an hour or two and document it using the procedure described in Chapter 8 for design of a process. The documentation of the process does not have to be "perfect" in order to allow DP analysis. Don't get bogged down making work products perfect. (Observing me manicure our yard one day, our younger son remarked: "Dad, it will never be perfect." He was right!) Refer to Table 7.6 for ideas about possible improvements to the requirements process.

Table 7.6 Some Ideas Concerning Improving a Requirements Process

1. Evolve a project glossary (and possibly a project acronyms list).
2. Provide a mechanism to increase understanding and communication between developers and users.
3. Define and document the requirements elicitation process.
4. Select a few metrics to track progress and provide regular visible reporting.
5. Develop an action plan (AP) for implementation of the requirements engineering process.
6. Improve reporting to management.
7. Take actions to have better meetings where we actually accomplish things and get things done.
8. Implement an action tracking system that is characterized by closure criteria for the action items.
9. Take proactive steps to achieve better communication.
10. Ensure that decisions are disseminated.
11. Provide training concerning project processes.
12. Evolve strategies for increasing "buy-in" from stakeholders.
13. Provide and ensure customer involvement in the requirements process.
14. Figure out how to identify the "real" requirements.
15. Select a development method that is appropriate for the level of understanding of the customer's requirements.
16. Do prototyping.
17. Define a requirements process.
18. Take some steps to foster and nurture additional visible and vocal senior management support. Couple this with a cost-reduction initiative.
19. Provide the appropriate level of detail concerning requirements for different stakeholder groups, for example, a higher level of detail for customers that captures the essence of what they need, and a much more defined and detailed level for developers who are charged with actually coding the requirement.
20. Through discussions, evolve an agreed-on set of practices, approaches, methods, and tools that will be used on the project.
21. Foster *commitment to follow* the set of practices, approaches, methods, and tools that have been agreed on.
22. Provide traceability of requirements from the customer need to definition of the requirement and to all steps in the development process (e.g., to the design, to the code, to the test case and verification that the requirement has been met, to inclusion in user documentation).
23. Improve the training that is provided.
24. Record requirements so that there is a common understanding, and resolve discrepancies in the understanding of each requirement.
25. Meet with users to achieve a common meaning of the user requirements.
26. Clarify interpretations of formal documents, such as laws and policies.
27. Solicit "buy-in" from management concerning process.
28. Gain consensus concerning the requirements development process among all stakeholders.
29. Involve all stakeholders throughout the system development life cycle.
30. Select, train, and implement a requirements tool early.
31. Acknowledge people for their contributions and efforts.
32. Celebrate progress.
33. Provide periodic reviews of the requirements.
34. Ensure greater awareness about the requirements within all project groups.
35. Provide feedback mechanisms.
36. Ensure flowdown.

Table 7.6 Some Ideas Concerning Improving an Requirements Process (continued)

37. Document the things that have been done on the project.
38. Ensure communication of understandings.
39. Document the rationale for each requirement (why is it needed?).
40. Capture the costs of requirements volatility for discussions with the customer.

Note: This list was developed based on a discussion of effective practices with inputs from 35 practitioners in a requirements workshop. The list is not prioritized and not all items are directly related to requirements.

Table 7.6 is intended to serve two purposes: first, to offer some ideas concerning how your project might improve its requirements process, and second, to provide topics that might be considered in your workshop—for example, workshop participants could multivote to select from these ideas some areas that might warrant countermeasures in your environment.

Step 2 is to organize a DP workshop. In a DP workshop, the objective (Step 3) is to analyze defects or problems to identify the *categories* of problems or defects that exist. It's best if you have some data and can divide up the defects to determine distinct categories of problems. But even if you don't have data, people who are familiar with the process will be able to identify what they believe the major causes of the problems are. Once we have identified the categories of problems, we should arrange them in descending order with the category that causes the most problems first, followed by the category with the next largest number, and so forth. This is called *Pareto analysis*, and it is a powerful quality improvement technique. Figure 7.5 provides an example of a Pareto chart.

Step 4 is to perform root cause analysis to identify the root causes of the categories of problems or defects. A root cause can be defined as the *major reason* that results in a condition. We want to be careful to look deeper than the symptoms of the problem or characteristics about it. The reason for this is that when we find the root cause of a problem, then identify (Step 5) and

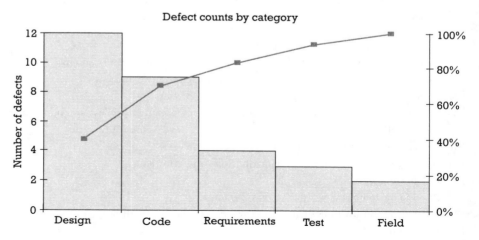

Figure 7.5 Example of a Pareto chart.

implement (Step 6) *countermeasures* (actions or steps that eliminate the root causes of problems) that effectively resolve the root cause, we now have a process that produces better results (*the capability of the process* has been strengthened or improved).

Step 7 is to evaluate the effectiveness of the implemented countermeasures. After a reasonable period of time, gather the same group of stakeholders that participated in Step 2, and discuss whether things have improved. Again, having data is best—one of your countermeasures that you may have identified in Step 5 could have been to collect data so that we can improve our ability to *manage by fact* rather than by intuition. After completing all of the steps of the DP process, it's likely that you will want to undertake another "improvement cycle"—that is, to go through the entire DP process again. This approach embodies the desired continuous improvement ethic or value and provides an opportunity to further strengthen and improve upon the point of pain.

Alternatively, the group may decide that it simply wants to keep the defined countermeasures in place, perhaps making some minor adjustments ("tweaks") based on feedback and observation by stakeholders. It's important to continue emphasis on process improvement activities to ensure they are not only deployed, but also effectively implemented and institutionalized. We want the improvements to become "the way we do business," rather than something that requires a special effort. My experience is that process improvements must be nurtured and supported, or they go away. In fact, process improvements go away much more quickly than they come—my experience about this is that they go away ten times faster than they come. It may not be quite that quickly, but it is fast! Make efforts to reinforce improvements, such as developing and using checklists and procedures, providing training, tracking results, and ensuring management sponsorship and support. (An important aspect of management sponsorship is vocal expression that the process improvements are helping the organization to achieve its business objectives. Lacking active executive sponsorship and support, any process or quality improvement effort will wane and eventually die.)

10. *You indicate that estimation is an important skill. What aspects of estimation are critical for the RA?*

Accurately planning and estimating software projects is an extremely difficult software management function. Few organizations have established formal estimation processes, despite evidence that suggests organizations without formal estimation are four times more likely to experience delayed or canceled projects. One valuable resource, should you become involved in your project's efforts to improve estimation, is Software Productivity Research (SPR), Inc. Digest the information at the SPR Web site [24], and do extensive reading and research. There is a lot of information available. Perhaps 20% of it is really helpful. Before making suggestions, ensure that you have digested industry experience.

There are tools, methods, and techniques that can be applied to support the development of estimates, such as MS Project, estimation models such as Constructive Cost Model (COCOMO) and SLIM that use lines of code, and Knowledge PLAN and COCOMO II that use function points (FPs). A lot of effort can be expended on estimation. The point is that the basis of the estimates (BOE) should be as valid as possible, or else all of the work applied to the estimation process is wasted. *Industry experience is that higher-quality requirements at the start of a project contribute significantly to estimation.*

Capers Jones's company, SPR, has been collecting data concerning software development since 1984. Jones strongly recommends using FPs and emphasizes the value of utilizing FPs in connection with requirements—see Insert 7.3 for insights and sources of additional information.

As suggested at the beginning of this chapter, consider reading and studying two books that provide insight into estimation: *Introduction to the Personal Software Process* [28] and *Introduction to the Team Software Process* [29], both by Watts Humphrey. He provides experience-based insights into estimation and what makes teams work effectively. These books offer approaches that any project and every PM should consider.

11. *You advise doing "inspections" for all requirements-related documents. Why shouldn't we be satisfied with doing peer reviews of them? How are inspections different from peer reviews, and why go to the extra trouble? What type of inspection is best?*

First, some background concerning inspections: Inspections add the *defect detection* process to the *DP process* discussed earlier in this chapter. The *defect detection* process is concerned with document quality, particularly identifying and measuring defects in documentation and using this information to decide how best to proceed as a result. A *major defect* is one that will likely have an order of magnitude or larger cost impact if it is not discovered at the requirements or design stage of a development effort. According to Tom Gilb's data [30], on the average, the find-and-fix cost for major defects is one work hour upstream, but nine hours downstream! These are powerful data! *They (and perhaps some further reading and study) should convince you to recommend use of inspections for all requirements-related documents on your project.* Gilb's experience is that, given management support, an organization can improve from 20 or more major defects per page to between zero and two major defects per page within one year [30].[7] He believes that the ROI from incorporating the inspection process into a development effort is 10:1. (These are more powerful data to help convince you to recommend that inspections be used on your project!) Other benefits include reduced rework

---

7. The book is really about inspections of any work product, not just software. The authors' approach is very rigorous and, therefore, requires more training and is more expensive to conduct than other types of inspections. Gilb now advocates another form that he calls "extreme inspection." See his Web site for more information.

Insert 7.3—FPs and Requirements (With thanks to Capers Jones for the data provided below)

An FP is a measure of the complexity of software development.

FP metrics have been used to study requirements sizes, costs, defects, and rates of change. Capers Jones believes it is helpful for RAs to understand results expressed in terms of FPs, but they don't need to know the actual details of counting. For example, requirements specifications for many projects average around 0.5 pages per FP. Testing is not efficient in finding requirements problems, but formal inspections of requirements average about 65% success in finding them. By measuring the FP totals after the requirements are first assembled, and then again at the end of the project, industry experience shows that the average rate at which new requirements surface during design and coding phases is 2% per month. The maximum rate has topped at 5% per month. With such information, it is possible to plan ahead for effective change management approaches. Some of the methods that have been found useful in deducing requirements changes are JAD requirements gathering (requirements workshops), prototypes, and requirements review boards.

Several outsource vendors are using FPs as the basis for contracts. Some use a sliding scale, such as initial requirements cost $500 per FP; changes during the first three months after the initial requirements are completed cost $600 per FP; and later changes cost $1,000 per FP. This sliding scale encourages early and complete requirements analysis and solves some difficult areas in outsource contracts.

Sources for additional information:

> Garmus, David, and David Herron, *Function Point Analysis: Measurement Practices for Successful Software Projects* [25].

> The International Function Point Users Group (IFPUG) Web site, at www.ifpug.org [26].

> Jones, Capers, *Software Assessments, Benchmarks, and Best Practices* [27].

From: Capers Jones. Used with permission.

---

costs, improved predictability, increased productivity, and better document quality.[8] Industry experts have different views of how the inspection process should be performed and the amount of training that is required to implement an effective inspections program. Rob Sabourin offers an economical

---

8. Gilb, Tom, "Planning to Get the Most Out of Inspection," in Daughtrey's *Fundamental Concepts for the Software Quality Engineer,* [31, p. 178}.

inspections training and implementation approach. Contact him at rsa-bourin@amibug.com [32].

12. *You have placed a lot of emphasis on quality. How can the RA help apply quality principles on systems and software development projects?*

The astute RA will study quality principles and constantly strive to achieve high quality. Taz Daughtrey provides a good summary of ways to do this in *Fundamental Concepts for the Software Quality Engineer* [31], a collection of works gathered from 32 authors with a wealth of experience in quality. The works are experienced-based reports of practices that have proven effective in a variety of industries, applications, and organizations. Study of these articles will provide insights, professional growth, and improvement in your skills. Several of them offer further insights concerning topics addressed in this book:

- Risk management;
- Customer satisfaction;
- Use of an evolutionary approach;
- Defect reduction;
- Justifying process improvement to managers (see topic 16, below);
- Human elements in system development;
- Utilizing statistical process control (SPC) to measure process capability;
- Managing with metrics;
- Selecting tools;
- Evaluating software products;
- Applying quantitative methods.

Strive to ensure that you have proactive QA on your project. By proactive QA, I mean quality assurance specialists that participate in developing and applying processes and defect prevention efforts that build quality into the work products. Experience has shown us that it's not possible to remove poor quality from work products. For example, although testing is important, industry experience shows that testing finds less than 50% of the defects in a software product.[9] One must have quality software going into the test process in order to have even better quality result

---

9. Watts Humphrey, PSP tutorial at Northrop Grumman IT DES on February 20, 2003. Humphrey emphasized that the current software development practice in use in industry today is preoccupied with removing defects. His experience is that many organizations spend 40% of project effort and costs on testing, whereas more process-mature organizations are able to reduce testing costs to 10%.

from the testing activities. QA specialists can and should have an enormous positive impact on a system or software development project. They (like the rest of us) must be empowered by management to make a valued contribution [33].

I would like to discuss one additional method before leaving this topic: Quality Function Deployment (QFD). QFD began in the mid 1960s in Japan as a quality system focused on developing products and services that satisfy customers. Jones provides a description of QFD and a status report on its use in his book *Software Quality: Analysis and Guidelines for Success* [34]. He notes that QFD is a structured group activity that involves clients and product development personnel. QFD is sometimes called "the house of quality" because one of the main kinds of planning matrixes resembles the peaked roof of a house. In *Developing Products in Half the Time*, 2nd ed., Smith and Reinertsen discuss "Blitz QFD" [35, pp. 102–103]. Bicknell and Bicknell's *The Road Map to Repeatable Success: Using QFD to Implement Change* [36] provides a comprehensive review of QFD and shows how it can be used at all levels of an organization. Ramaswami of Global Technology Operations in India has utilized QFD in several projects (see their Web site at www.gemedicalsystems.com). Mark Paulk reports that nine organizations in the SEI's database of level 4 and 5 organizations use QFD, five in India and four in the United States.

Zultner advises that the use of software QFD is growing. Zultner has made presentations on software QFD at the QAI conference in Bangalore, at the European Organization for Quality conference in Budapest, and at the Second World Congress for Software Quality in Yokohama. He reports that some U.S. companies (such as Andersen Consulting) have been using software QFD on a global basis for years. He advises that the best way to start with QFD for software is Blitz QFD. Zultner believes no other tool, technique, or method even comes close to QFD for dealing with the "fuzzy front end of requirements definition." Capers Jones's experience is that QFD works best in companies that have fairly sophisticated QA departments. In summary, concerning QFD, from my perspective, the bottom line is that one must first discover and evolve the real requirements in order for the method to be effective.

13. *There seems to be a lot of confusion in our industry concerning the terms verification and validation. Can you explain why this is so and also clarify suggested uses of the two terms?*

Yes. As Jeff Grady points out in his training materials, books, and presentations, software people and systems engineering people tend to use the two words inversely, and this causes tremendous confusion [37]. *The most important thing in this regard is to clarify how the two words will be used on your project.* Here are the definitions I suggest:

> ‣ *Verification:* a process for ensuring that the design solution satisfies the requirements;

▸ *Validation:* a process for confirming that the real requirements are implemented in the delivered system.

You should clarify these two words to help your project avoid endless frustrating discussions of what these words "really mean" and who is "right."

14. *The "agilists" advocate that agile development methodologies promise higher customer satisfaction, lower defect rates, faster development times, and a solution to rapidly changing requirements. Should I recommend that we consider agile development methods on my project?*

I believe that there is something to be said for both disciplined and agile approaches. I'm concerned when I read and hear views that come down strongly on one side or the other, especially when one is critical of the other. Both approaches have shortcomings that, if left alone, can lead to project failure. Each approach has a "home ground" where it is preferable to the other—see Table 7.7.

My suggestion here is that you read and digest "Observations on Balancing Discipline and Agility," [38] by Barry Boehm and Richard Turner. They believe that strategies are emerging for integrating the two approaches in a way that will take advantage of their strengths and avoid their weaknesses.

15. *What is the value of practical knowledge?*

During the course of writing this book, industry requirements-engineering expert and consultant Ian Alexander [39] was a valued advisor and, as a result, has become a good friend. Ian shared an insight concerning practical knowledge with me:[10]

> The overemphasis on intellectual knowledge as compared to practical skill goes right back to Aristotle: the creative "Fire" and communicative "Air" were male elements, whereas heavy fertile "Earth" and emotional "Water" were female. Practical earthiness was despised. But we might argue the opposite today: practical skill that integrates emotional intelligence (cf. Daniel Goleman) and appropriate amounts of creativity and intellect is what makes projects work. (For instance: Do academics know better than the people who actually do the work?)

16. *What if my PM, and/or our organization's management team, or our customer does not support the concept of process improvement?*

My experience in making improvement suggestions on projects and in organizations for over 30 years is that perhaps one-third of all managers are open to process improvement. The majority of managers in my experience are not very supportive of process improvement, especially when it is

---

10. Personal e-mail communication with the author, January 25, 2003.

Table 7.7 Home Grounds for the Agile and Disciplined Approaches

Characteristic	Agile	Disciplined
Application:		
Primary goals	Rapid value; responding to change	Predictability, stability, high assurance
Size	Smaller teams and projects	Larger teams and projects
Environment	Turbulent; high change; project-focused	Stable; low change; project/organization focused
Management:		
Customer relations	Dedicated on-site customers; focused on prioritized increments	As-needed customer interactions; focused on contract provisions
Planning and control	Internalized plans; qualitative control	Documented plans, quantitative control
Communications	Tacit interpersonal knowledge	Explicit documented knowledge
Technical:		
Requirements	Prioritized informal stories and test cases; undergoing unforseeable change	Formalized project, capability, interface, quality, forseeable evolution requirements
Development	Simple design; short increment; refactoring assumed inexpensive	Extensive design; longer increments; refactoring assumed expensive
Test	Executable test cases define requirements, testing	Documented test plans and procedures
Personnel:		
Customers	Dedicated, collocated CRACK* performers	CRACK* performers, not always collocated
Developers	At least 30% full-time Cockburn level 2 and 3 experts; no Level 0 or −1 personnel	50% Cockburn Level 3s early; 10% throughout; 30% Level 0s workable; no Level −1s**
Culture:	Comfort and empowerment via many degrees of freedom	Comfort and empowerment via framework of policies and procedures

* Collaborative, representative, authorized, committed, knowledgable.

** These numbers will particularly vary with the complexity of the application.

From: Barry Boehm. Reprinted with permission.

presented to them using those words. The root causes of this behavior are a mystery to me. One simple possible cause is that PMs are just too busy to give improvement opportunities serious consideration. Another possibility is that their beliefs are set against the idea. A third possible explanation is that PMs may be reluctant to recommend initiatives unless they are suggested, or at least supported, by the customer, and many customers are not aware of the power and value of process improvement. Another possibility is that the project's organizational culture is not committed to continuous improvement. Still another possible explanation is that managers have not had a way to determine how much improvement is due to process versus other factors. The bottom line from the RA's perspective is that you probably can have far more impact by aligning yourself in an environment that supports continuous process improvement. My belief is that you will also enjoy far more job satisfaction and have more fun at work by doing this. See Bradford Clark's "Effects of Process Maturity on Development Effort" [40] for valuable insights. His study, using a 112-project sample, concluded that a change in one level of process maturity using the CMM® framework resulted in a reduction of development effort of 10 to 32 percent. This is phenomenal and deserves the attention of every project. See also (1)Brodman and Johnson's study of ROI from SPI as measured by U.S. industry [41]; (2) Butler's "The Economic Benefits of SPI" [42]; (3) Dion, "Process Improvement and the Corporate Balance Sheet" [43]; (4) Herbsleb et al.'s "Benefits of CMM-Based SPI: Initial Results" [44]; (5) Humphrey et al.'s "SPI at Hughes Aircraft [45]; (6) McGibbon's "A Business Case for Software Process Improvement Revised: Measuring Return on Investment from Software Engineering and Management." [46]; and (7) DACS Technical Reports [47]. I do not agree with Grady Booch that "CMM is orthogonal to project success and not sufficiently agile for economic success." This is contrary to my personal experience. I asked Booch to explain his perspective on this—he clarified that in his experience, some "process-mature" projects are not successful because the project team is so engrossed in process that they neglect the importance of being nimble in the marketplace.[11] Booch was clarifying that the CMM® measures process maturity, whereas success in business is measured by ROI.

So, in answer to the question, I advise that, first, you try to encourage your manager, your project, and your organization to embrace process improvement. If you find that you are running up against a brick wall (no one will support process improvement initiatives), change your environment (move to a different project or organization that does support process improvement). Life is too short, and we spend too much time at work to not be fulfilled by what we do. Our attitude about our work impacts our families and our lives. Take action if necessary. Our Lord provides.

17. *How should the work breakdown structure be applied?*

The work breakdown structure (WBS) is a planning tool that decomposes the activities of a project into categories of work tasks from which costs and effort can be allocated and tracked. The development of a WBS depends on the organization's culture, the project management style, customer preference, and other project-specific factors. A typical approach is to decompose the work into subsystems, components, functions, organizational units, and life-cycle phases. My experience is that the structure of a project's WBS is often arbitrary, and the use of WBSs is flawed because they are prematurely structured around the product design and are defined in either too much or too little detail. An alternative approach is to organize the planning elements around the process framework. Insert 7.4 offers an approach that relates the requirements to the work products.

---

11. Personal e-mail communication with the author, March 12, 2003.

Insert 7.4—Product Breakdown Structure

Most guidance on project management suggests that planning a project is a relatively straightforward sequence of events. First, you define the requirements and then identify the final work products that will be delivered to the customer. Next, you identify intermediate work products needed to develop the final work products and then develop a WBS, which tells you what work has to be done. With the WBS, it should be a straightforward process to estimate the effort needed to do the work and assign the available resources to develop a schedule. With a schedule in hand, all is well. Your project is planned, and success is ensured. You can even use sophisticated and inexpensive project-planning tools to print out very large and impressive looking bar charts that detail down to the last day exactly when all the work will be done.

Unfortunately, the real world of project management is sometimes not that simple. One major difficulty can be the leap from requirements to the WBS through those stepping-stones called "work products." Sure, the major work products you will deliver to the customer at the end of the project should be relatively straightforward to determine. After all, that is what the requirements effort should be spelling out in sufficient detail that you know what your customer wants. But it's those pesky intermediate work products and other potentially hidden deliverables that don't make themselves obvious during the early stages of project planning that can cause the path to be slippery, if not downright dangerous. If the project involves any sort of innovation, from something you or your team has never done before to something no one else has ever done before, then these intermediate work products might not be at all obvious.

Then there's the challenge of the WBS itself. The standard defined in the Program Management Body of Knowledge is that a WBS is a "family tree of activities that organizes, defines and graphically displays the total work to be accomplished in order to achieve the final objectives of a project." [48] Standard guidance is that the WBS should be product based, meaning that it's hierarchy should be driven by the major final work products. But almost anyone who has worked on an IT project knows that many WBSs are organized by phase at the top levels, with something akin to Define Requirements, Design, Build and Unit Test, Integration Test, and Product Delivery representing the top levels of the hierarchy. These are not product-related at all, but instead represent a workflow that will hopefully result in the desired outcome. Unfortunately, many PMs leap to this standard structure very early in the project, without really knowing what subcomponents need to be built or what intermediate steps need to be taken. It can provide the false assurance that we know what we are doing, when in fact there are still significant unknowns in what the final or intermediate work

Insert 7.4—Product Breakdown Structure (continued)

products will be and what tasks will be required to build them. Then there is the problem that once the WBS is organized, there is great reluctance to change it. As Noel Harroff has pointed out, "once the WBS is cast, it can be a "dog of a job to undo" [49].

Unfortunately, many projects fail because they are working to a schedule, based on a WBS that does not provide a realistic roadmap to accomplish the work. What looked good on paper is not at all doable in the real world. Is there anything that can help?

The PRINCE2 project management methodology developed for the British government offers some ideas that can help. Product-based planning is a key feature of PRINCE2. It focuses on the products to be delivered and their quality. A key step in project planning is the development of a product breakdown structure (PBS). In the PRINCE2 method, planning is done in three steps: (1) develop a PBS, (2) document product descriptions, and (3) produce a product flow diagram that results in a work activity network. Max Wideman [50] provides an excellent comparison of PRINCE2 and the PMBOK approaches to project management. The PRINCE2 methodology also views planning as a continuous activity that occurs throughout the life cycle of the project. That way, as new information is gained about the requirements or the potential solution, the project has a process for reincorporating this information into the project plan.

It is not necessary to change over to the entire PRINCE2 methodology to benefit from some of its concepts, especially the idea of a PBS. A key advantage of developing a PBS is that it can focus attention on the deliverables at the smallest practical level, on what is needed to define the end products. This process will necessarily identify subcomponents and intermediate components needed to produce the final product. This focus on product rather than the work needed to produce the product can help clear the path and identify areas that are poorly understood and need clarification. This can result in recognition of areas needing feasibility studies or further research.

At what point does the PBS stop and the work, identified in a work activity network or a WBS, begin? For instance, a common approach in IT projects is to develop a system as a series of builds. Using the PBS approach, each build would be a deliverable to the customer, and the resulting workflow would reflect this at the top level of the hierarchy. However, at the beginning of project planning, the concept of separate builds might not even be considered. The distinction between product and work is not as critical as the recognition that planning is a creative process of discovering the components, activities, and relationships between them. What starts out as the initial PBS, which will necessarily focus strictly on the immediate deliverables to the customer, will evolve as planning identifies risk reduction activities, which might be

---

Insert 7.4—Product Breakdown Structure (continued)

manifested as separate builds, to ultimately deliver the product. The key point is that a PBS can serve as another tool in project planning that will minimize slipping up on those ill-defined work products or intermediate work products that could cause delay or disaster.

John E. Moore
Project management engineer

---

18. *What is a good approach for considering requirements risks?*

Some organizations use the SEI's Taxonomy-Based Questionnaire (TBQ) as a tool for risk identification. A number of the TBQ questions were designed to elicit requirements-related risks—these are provided in Table 7.8. Those described in Section A.1 relate to the quality of the requirements themselves. Those described in Section A.2 are requirements-related risks associated with the design, and those described in Section A.4 are associated with integration and test. Those described in Section A.5 are risks associated with the engineering specialties. Those described in Section B relate to the development process. These questions provide a good basis for evaluating requirements-related risks associated with your task or project.

Ian Sommerville provides a good overview of the risk management process and risk sources, probabilities, and effects in *Software Engineering*, 6th ed. [52, pp. 84–90]. Barry Boehm provides pioneering insights *Software Engineering Economics* [53, pp. 279–288, 297–300, and 588–590].

Summary

This chapter provides a discussion of additional skills and information useful to the RA. It's likely that you won't need the information concerning all of these topics either immediately or at any one particular time. It's also likely that you will need to know about most of these areas at some point in your work. You might consider trying out techniques such as DP and inspections if (1) you haven't used them, or (2) your project is not currently applying them. The approaches and techniques discussed in many of these topics should be used continuously on all projects, for example, reducing requirements errors, CM, understanding V&V, and inspections of requirements-related work products. Others are more in the "nice to have but very important" category, such as estimation, improving and refining your facilitation skills, being a leader on your project, and pursuing continuous improvement. Still others, such as IE and use of FPs are applicable to special situations. For example, consider using IE when there is a need to estimate requirements quantitatively to make design decisions. FPs may help when measuring FP totals at different points in the project will assist in planning

Table 7.8   Analysis of Requirements-Related Risks

A.1	Requirements: Are there risks that may arise from requirements being placed on the product?
A.1.a	Requirements—Stability
	Are requirements changing even as the product is being produced?
[1]	Are the requirements stable?
[1.a]	If NO: What is the effect on the system?
	Quality/Functionality/Schedule/Integration/Design Testing
[2]	Are the external interfaces changing?
A.1.b	Requirements—Completeness
	Are requirements missing or incompletely specified?
[3]	Are there any TBDs in the specifications?
[4]	Are there requirements you know should be in the specification, but aren't?
[4.a]	If YES: Will you be able to get these requirements into the system?
[5]	Does the customer have unwritten requirements or expectations?
[5.a]	If YES: Is there a way to capture these requirements?
[6]	Are the external interfaces completely defined?
A.1.c	Requirements—Clarity
	Are requirements unclear or in need of interpretation?
[7]	Are you able to understand the requirements as written?
[7.a]	If NO: Are the ambiguities being resolved satisfactorily?
[7.b]	If YES: There are no ambiguities or problems of interpretation?
A.1.d	Requirements—Validity
	Will the requirements lead to the product the customer has in mind?
[8]	Are there any requirements that may not specify what the customer really wants?
[8.a]	If YES: How are you resolving this?
[9]	Do you and the customer understand the same thing by the requirements?
[9.a]	If YES: Is there a process by which to determine this?
[10]	How do you validate the requirements?
	Prototyping/Analysis/Simulations
A.1.e	Requirements—Feasibility
	Are requirements infeasible from an analytical point of view?
[11]	Are there any requirements that are technically difficult to implement?
[11.a]	If YES: What are they?
[11.b]	If YES: Why are they difficult to implement?
[11.c]	If NO: Were feasibility studies done for these requirements?
[11.c.1]	If YES: How confident are you in the assumptions made in the studies?
A.1.f	Requirements—Precedent
	Do requirements specify something never done before or something that your company has not done before?
[12]	Are there any state-of-the-art requirements?
	Technologies/Methods/Languages/Hardware
[12.a]	If NO: Are any of these new to you?
[12.b]	If YES: Does the program have sufficient knowledge in these areas?
[12.b.1]	If NO: Is there a plan for acquiring knowledge in these areas?

Table 7.8 Analysis of Requirements-Related Risks (continued)

A.1.g	Requirements—Scale
	Do requirements specify a product larger, more complex, or requiring a larger organization than in the experience of the company?
[13]	Is the system size and complexity a concern?
[13.a]	If NO: Have you done something of this size and complexity before?
[14]	Does the size require a larger organization than is usual for your company?
A.2	Design: Are there risks that may arise from the design that the project has chosen to meet its requirements?
A.2.a	Design—Functionality
	Are there any potential problems in meeting functionality requirements?
[15]	Are there any specified algorithms, which may not satisfy the requirements?
[15.a]	If NO: Are any of the algorithms or designs marginal with respect to meeting requirements?
[16]	How do you determine the feasibility of algorithms and designs?
	Prototyping/Modeling/Analysis/Simulations
[18]	Are there any requirements or functions that are difficult to design?
[18.a]	If NO: Do you have solutions for all the requirements?
[18.b]	If YES: What are the requirements? Why are they difficult?
A.2.d	Design—Performance
	Are there stringent response time or throughput requirements?
[22]	Are there any problems with performance?
	Throughput
	Real-time response
	Database response, contention, or access
[23]	Has a performance analysis been done?
[23.a]	If YES: What is your level of confidence in the performance analysis?
[23.b]	If YES: Do you have a model to track performance through design and implementation?
A.2.e	Design—Testability
	Is the product difficult or impossible to test?
[26]	Do the testers get involved in analyzing requirements?
A.2.f	Design—Hardware constraints
	Are there tight constraints on the target hardware?
[27]	Does the hardware limit your ability to meet any requirements?

Under [22] right column: Scheduling asynchronous real-time events / Response time / Recovery timelines

Under [27]:

Architecture	Throughput	Response time	Database performance
Reliability	Memory capacity	Real-time response	Recovery timelines
Functionality			Availability

A.4	Integration and test: Are there risks that may arise from the way the project is choosing to bring the pieces together and prove that they work as a whole?
A.4.a	Integration and test—Environment
	Is the integration and test environment adequate?
[48]	Does hardware and software instrumentation facilitate testing?
[48.a]	If YES: Is it sufficient for all testing?
A.4.b	Integration and test—Product
	Is the interface definition inadequate? Are facilities inadequate? Is time insufficient?

Table 7.8 Analysis of Requirements-Related Risks (continued)

[50]	Have acceptance criteria been agreed to for all requirements?
[50.a]	If YES: Is there a formal agreement?
[55]	COTS: Will vendor data be accepted in verification of requirements allocated to COTS products?
[55.a]	If YES: Is the contract clear on that?
A.5	Engineering specialties: Are there risks that may arise from special attributes of the product?
A.5.b	Engineering Specialties—Reliability
	Are the reliability or availability requirements difficult to meet?
[64]	Are reliability requirements allocated to the software?
[65]	Are availability requirements allocated to the software?
[65.a]	If YES: Are recovery timelines any problem?
A.5.c	Engineering Specialties—Safety
	Are the safety requirements infeasible and not demonstrable?
[66]	Are safety requirements allocated to the software?
[66.a]	If YES: Do you see any difficulty in meeting the safety requirements?
[67]	Will it be difficult to verify satisfaction of safety requirements?
A.5.d	Engineering Specialties—Security
	Are the security requirements more stringent than the current state-of-the-practice or program experience?
[68]	Are there unprecedented or state-of-the art security requirements?
A.5.f	Engineering Specialties—Specifications
	Is the documentation adequate to design, implement, and test the system?
[72]	Is the software requirements specification adequate to design the system?
[74]	Are the external interface requirements well specified?
B.1	Development process: Are there risks that may arise from the process that the project has chosen to develop the product?
B.1.a	Development process—Formality
	Will the implementation be difficult to understand or maintain?
[78]	Are there formal, controlled plans for all development activities?
	Requirements analysis Installation Design QA Code CM Integration and test
[78.a]	If YES: Do the plans specify the process well?
[78.b]	If YES: Are developers familiar with the plans?
B.1.e	Development process—Product control
	Are there mechanisms for controlling changes in the product?
[85]	Is there a requirements traceability mechanism that tracks requirements from the source specification through test cases?
[86]	Is the traceability mechanism used in evaluating requirement change impact analysis?
[87]	Is there a formal change control process?
[87.a]	If YES: Does it cover all changes to baselined requirements, design, code, and documentation?
[89]	Is there adequate analysis when new requirements are added to the system?

Table 7.8   Analysis of Requirements-Related Risks (continued)

B.2	Development system: Are there risks that may arise from the hardware and software tools the project has chosen for controlling and facilitating its development process?
B.2.b	Development system—Suitability
	Does the development system support all phases, activities, and functions?
[94]	Does the development system support all aspects of the program?

Requirements analysis	Performance analysis	CM
Design	Coding	Requirements traceability
Test	Documentation	Management tracking

Modeled on the SEI TBQ [51].

ahead for effective change management approaches (to anticipate and control requirements changes) or when using FPs can facilitate costing work or understanding and reducing the complexity of code. Some industry requirements engineering experts remain skeptical concerning the general applicability of IE and FPs.

It's worth reiterating that small projects should avoid using smallness as an excuse for not using discipline and processes. Most of the things that need to be done on medium and large projects also need to be done on small projects—it's a question of scale.

The most important thing is for you to be fulfilled in your work as an RA. I trust that the discussion in this chapter will help you.

Case Study

An article in the Washington *Post*[12] reported on a situation involving systems developers and integrators. A federal board fired the contractor it hired in 1997 to create a new computer system to keep track of $100 billion in retirement savings, citing repeated delays and software that contained many defects. The board stated that the contractor was "incapable of fulfilling commitments" and filed suit for $350 million in damages. The lawsuit alleged that the system required 40 hours to post transactions, rather than the requirement of 11 hours, and that it could not tell the difference between a participant who lived in Delaware and one who lived in Germany, which would require all correspondence to be addressed manually, rather than by the computer.

The termination of the contract and the lawsuit "stunned contractor officials," who explained that its customer repeatedly asked for design changes, making timetables for delivery of the new system a moving target. "After more than three years, the board still has not determined what its systems

---

12. Washington *Post,* July 18, 2001, pp. B1 and B5.

needs are. We have developed more than 1.2 million lines of software code—five times the original estimate—and more than 70 percent of the software has been completed and fully tested."

The new computer system was originally scheduled to be in operation by May 2000. The delivery date was postponed several times.

Another contractor was hired to take over the project, but it was unclear when the new system might go on-line.

This example of requirements gone wrong jeopardized the reputation of the contractor company, wasted millions of dollars, adversely affected the mission and operations of the customer, and negatively impacted the lives of many people and families who were involved on both sides of the contract.

What could have been done to avoid this disaster? Most fundamentally, a partnership relationship needed to be created, developed, and maintained that set project success as the objective. The customer and the development contractor should have put in place at the beginning of the contract a set of mechanisms to keep the train on the tracks rather than risk allowing things to go wrong. Specifically, the following could be done to avoid a similar disaster:

- Through the use of a partnering workshop facilitated by an outside expert, a joint vision of project success should be defined, documented and signed. The document should include a set of mutually agreed upon objectives that define the high-level requirements for the contract. Most importantly, commitment of both parties to support each other should be established at the outset.

- The commitment noted here should include a commitment to resolve problems and issues as soon as they come up. An "issue resolution ladder" should be created in the initial partnering workshop and the commitment of the individuals involved on both sides of the contract gained to use this mechanism to keep the train on the tracks while work proceeds.

- A set of guiding principles for how the parties will treat each other during the contract should be collaboratively developed. Some examples of these guiding principles are honesty, open communication, proactive leadership, prompt completion of assigned action items and reviews of documents, mutual support of each other, and establishing a set of "rules of conduct" for meetings, e-mail communications, and how people are to treat each other.

References

[1] Hooks, I. F., and K. A. Farry, *Customer-Centered Products: Creating Successful Products through Smart Requirements Management*, New York: AMACOM, 2001, p. 6.

[2] Watts, F. B., *Engineering Document Control Handbook: Configuration Management in Industry*, 2nd ed., Park Ridge, NJ: Noyes Publications, 2000.

[3] Leon, A. A., *Guide to Software Configuration Management*, Norwood, MA: Artech House, 2000.

[4] EIA Standard 649, "National Consensus Standard for Configuration Management."

[5] Fowler, M., *UML Distilled: Applying The Standard Object Modeling Language*. Reading, MA: Addison-Wesley, 1997.

[6] Object Management Group (OMG), "Introduction to the UML," at www.omg. org/gettingstarted/what_is_uml.htm.

[7] OMG, "OMG Unified Modeling Language Specification," Version 1.4, September 2001, at www.omg.org/technology/documents/formal/mof.htm.

[8] Gottesdiener, E., "Top Ten Ways Project Teams Misuse Use Cases—And How to Correct Them," at www.therationaledge.com/content/jun_02/t_ misuseUseCases_eg.jsp.

[9] IEEE Software Engineering Standards Committee, IEEE Standard 1233a-1998, "IEEE Guide for Developing System Requirements Specifications," IEEE Computer Society, December 8, 1998.

[10] IEEE Software Engineering Standards Committee, IEEE Standard 830, "IEEE Recommended Practice for Software Requirements Specifications," IEEE Computer Society, December 2, 1993.

[11] Robertson, S., and J. Robertson, *Mastering the Requirements Process*, Harlow, UK: Addison-Wesley, 1999.

[12] Kulak, D., and E. Guiney, *Use Cases: Requirements in Context*, New York: ACM Press, 2000.

[13] Cockburn, A., *Writing Effective Use Cases*, Boston, MA: Addison-Wesley, 2001.

[14] Korson, T., "The Misuse of Use Cases: Managing Requirements," white paper, copyright Korson-McGregor, 2000, at www.korson-mcgregor.com/ publications/korson/Korson9803om.htm.

[15] Gamma, E., et al., *Design Patterns*, Reading, MA: Addison-Wesley, 1995.

[16] Federal Information Processing Standards Publications (FIPS PUBS) 183, "Integration Definition for Function Modeling (IDEF0)." This standard describes the IDEF0 modeling language (semantics and syntax) and associated rules and techniques for developing structured graphical representations of a system or enterprise. Use of this standard permits the construction of models comprising system functions (activities, actions, processes, operations), functional relationships, and data (information or objects) that support systems integration. Available from www.itl.nist.gov/fipspubs/idef02.doc.

[17] IEEE, IEEE 1320.1. "IEEE Standard for Functional Modeling Language—Syntax and Semantics for IDEF0." IEEE Computer Society, 1998.

[18] Feldmann, C. G., *The Practical Guide to Business Process Reengineering Using IDEF0*, New York: Dorset House, 1998.

[19] Paulk, M. C., "Using the Software CMM with Good Judgment," *Software Quality Professional* 1(3) (1999), at www.sei.cmu.edu/publications/articles/ paulk/judgment.html.

[20] Hadden, R., "How Scalable Are CMM Key Practices?" *CrossTalk* (April 1998): 18–23. See also www.ppc.com.

[21] Brodman, J. G., and D. L. Johnson, *The LOGOS Tailored CMM for Small Businesses, Small Organizations, and Small Projects*, LOGOS International, Inc., at www.tiac.net/users/johnsond.

[22] Gilb, T., *Principles of Software Engineering Management*, Harlow, UK: Addison-Wesley, 1988.

[23] Gilb, T., "Impact Estimation Tables: Understanding Complex Technology Quantitatively," white paper, November 1997, at www.gilb.com.

[24] SPR, Web site, at www.spr.com.

[25] Garmus, D., and D. Herron, *Function Point Analysis: Measurement Practices for Successful Software Projects.* Boston, MA: Addison-Wesley, 2001.

[26] IFPUG, Web site, at www.ifpug.org.

[27] Jones, C., *Software Assessments, Benchmarks, and Best Practices.* Boston, MA: Addison-Wesley, 2000.

[28] Humphrey, W. S., *Introduction to the Personal Software Process*, Reading, MA: Addison-Wesley, 1997.

[29] Humphrey, W. S., *Introduction to the Team Software Process*, Reading, MA: Addison-Wesley, 2000.

[30] Gilb, T., and D. Graham, *Software Inspection*, Boston, MA: Addison-Wesley, 1993.

[31] Daughtrey, T. (ed.), *Fundamental Concepts for the Software Quality Engineer*, Milwaukee, WI: ASQ Quality Press, 2002.

[32] Sabourin, R., Web site, at www.amibug.com/index.shtm.

[33] Walton, M., *The Deming Management Method*, New York: The Putnam Publishing Group, 1986.

[34] Jones, C., *Software Quality: Analysis and Guidelines for Success*, London: International Thomson Computer Press, 1997.

[35] Smith, P. G., and D. G. Reinertsen, *Developing Products in Half the Time*, 2nd ed., New York: John Wiley & Sons, Inc., 1998.

[36] Bicknell, B. A., and K. D. Bicknell, *The Road Map to Repeatable Success: Using QFD to Implement Change*, Boca Raton: CRC Press, 1995.

[37] Grady, J. O., *System Validation and Verification*, Boca Raton: CRC Press, 1997.

[38] Boehm, B., and R. Turner, "Observations on Balancing Discipline and Agility," in from *Balancing Agility and Discipline: A Guide to the Perplexed*, Boston, MA: Addison-Wesley, 2003.

[39] Alexander, I., Web site, at easyweb.easynet.co.uk/~iany/index.htm.

[40] Clark, B. K., "Effects of Process Maturity on Development Effort," at www.ralphyoung.net/goodarticles.

[41] Brodman, J. G., and D. L. Johnson,. "Return on Investment (ROI) from Software Process Improvement As Measured by U.S. Industry," *Software Process Improvement and Practice.* Sussex, UK: John Wiley & Sons Ltd., 1995, 35–47.

[42] Butler, K., "The Economic Benefits of Software Process Improvement," *CrossTalk* (1995): 28–35.

[43] Dion, R., "Process Improvement and the Corporate Balance Sheet," *IEEE Software* (October 1993): 28–35.

[44] Herbsleb, J., et al., *Benefits of CMM-Based Software Process Improvement: Initial Results*. Technical Report CMU/SEI-94-TR-013. Pittsburgh, PA: Software Engineering Institute, August 1994.

[45] Humphrey, W. S., et al., "Software Process Improvement at Hughes Aircraft," *IEEE Software* (August 1991): 11–23.

[46] McGibbon, T., "A Business Case for Software Process Improvement Revised: Measuring Return on Investment from Software Engineering and Management," Contract Number SP0700-98-4000, Data & Analysis Center for Software (DACS), ITT Industries, Advanced Engineering and Sciences Division, Rome, N.Y., September 30, 1999, at www.dacs.dtic.mil/techs/roispi2.

[47] DACS, DACS Technical Reports, at www.dacs.dtic.mil/techs/tr.shtml.

[48] Project Management Institute, *A Guide to the Project Management Body of Knowledge (PMBOK)*, 1996.

[49] Harroff, Noel, "Work Breakdown Structure (WBS)," at www.nnh.com/ev/wbs2.html.

[50] Wideman, Max, "Comparing PRINCE with PMBOK," AEW Services, Vancouver BC, Canada, at www.pmforum.org/library/papers/Prince2vsGuide3.htm, 2002.

[51] SEI, "Taxonomy-Based Risk Identification," Technical Report CMU/SEI-93-TR-6. Pittsburgh, PA: SEI, June 1993, at www.sei.cmu.edu/pub/documents/93.reports/pdf/tr06.93.pdf.

[52] Sommerville, I., *Software Engineering,* 6th ed., Reading, MA: Addison-Wesley, 2001.

[53] Boehm, B. W., *Software Engineering Economics,* Englewood Cliffs, NJ: Prentice Hall, 1981.

An Integrated Quality Approach

Many "quality approaches" have been put forward over the years, such as Total Quality Management (TQM), the Malcolm Baldrige Award Criteria, Six Sigma, Quality Is Free, Zero Defects, the Balanced Scorecard, standards developed by the International Standards Organization (ISO), and others. One of the problems in deploying quality programs has been convincing management and the organization that they are worthwhile. Another problem is that, often, quality initiatives are difficult to sustain.

From my experience, quality in an organization or on a project is more a way of life than a separate program, and the choice of the quality model to be used is less important than focusing on meeting customers' real needs. Quality is the way we work, not a separate function. This chapter is important to the RA because there is a direct connection between meeting customers' real requirements and a quality approach. There is a set of business drivers (high-level customer needs and expectations) that are really high-level customer requirements, which RAs must address. Management has a critical role relative to quality. If management does not value quality, quality won't happen. There is a set of principles in any organization that serves to provide guiding values for the work that is performed in the organization. This requires a set of quality improvement techniques (described below). Individuals are responsible for the quality of their products and services. This chapter explains an integrated quality approach that facilitates and supports the work of the RA. It will show that an effective requirements process is necessary in order to have an integrated quality approach and that an integrated quality approach is required for the process to work best. By an integrated quality approach, I mean the use of quality improvement techniques that are incorporated into the daily work performed on a project and in an organization with the goal of achieving customer satisfaction. This is easier when there is a supporting infrastructure and an expectation of management (through its stated values and principles) that supports the work of the analyst. A caution is that no matter how committed people or teams are to quality and to the effective use of quality improvement techniques, they may not be successful if other teams, members of their own team, and management do not share that commitment.

Business Drivers for Quality

A set of drivers exists that may be considered high-level customer requirements, but that often are not expressed. These include the following:

- Continued business success;
- High-quality products or services;
- Meeting customer requirements;
- Cost reduction;
- Customer and employee loyalty;
- Improved performance;
- Defect removal;
- Efficiency;
- Reduced cycle time;
- Innovative solutions.

It's important for projects and organizations to consider these customer needs.

Management's Role

In high-performing organizations, strategic goals and business drivers are linked to process improvement goals and activities. Values and guiding principles are documented and communicated, and senior management sets its expectation that all levels of the organization will abide by these principles in their daily work habits. Relative to quality and process improvement, management's role is to do the following:

- Define strategic goals, such as revenue, profit, customer satisfaction, and employee retention;
- Enable process improvement (PI):
  - Act as sponsor and advocate of PI;
  - Verbalize the value and results of PI;
  - Provide resources for PI;

> • Establish an improvement cycle.
> • Establish values, such as the following:
>> • Focus on fixing the process, not the people;
>> • Measure and periodically update the processes in use;
>> • Promote continuous improvement as essential to maintain and grow the organization;
>> • Promote the view that the organization's people are its most important resource.
> • Make timely decisions;
> • Determine areas that (a) matter most to customers, and (b) need improvement, such as the following:
>> • Providing competitive solutions;
>> • Taking ownership of projects;
>> • Being flexible concerning working arrangements;
>> • Responding well to changes;
>> • Being responsive;
>> • Employing high-quality people;
>> • Providing good value;
>> • Meeting commitments;
>> • Listening well and understand needs;
>> • Being competent.

Guiding Principles

In any organization, a set of guiding principles establishes values for how things are to be done. These principles may or may not be articulated. In some organizations, the guiding value is that just getting along is okay. In others, there exists a set of values that serve to provide high and effective standards for how things are to be done, for example:

> • Customer satisfaction is imperative for our continued existence.
> • We will manage by fact (using data) rather than by intuition or by the seat of our pants.
> • We have a set of rules of conduct used by the people in our organization that reflect respect for people.
> • Continuous improvement is essential for all of our processes.

In my experience, having a set of guiding principles that is both practiced and valued by management and the people in the organization creates a sense of purpose for employees and emphasizes that employees are key stakeholders in the success of the enterprise. As a result, people feel valued and are motivated to contribute their best efforts.

Priority Management

The process used by management to decide what it wants to achieve is depicted in Figure 8.1. Note that the process utilizes QI teams to address priority activities or problems and develop plans and recommendations for review and approval by responsible executives. This approach capitalizes on the experience, expertise, and commitment of the employees.

The Components of an Integrated Quality Approach

The components of an integrated quality approach may be described as management, customers, projects and tasks, QI teams, and QA. Figure 8.2 describes how these components work together. Note the following:

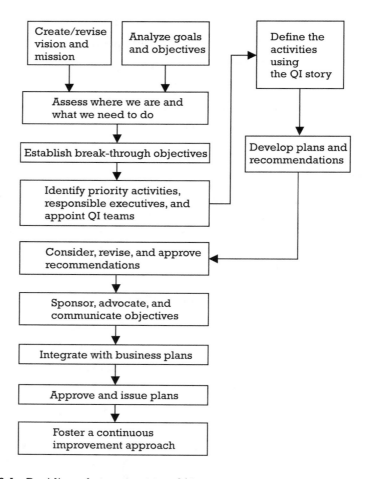

Figure 8.1 Deciding what we want to achieve.

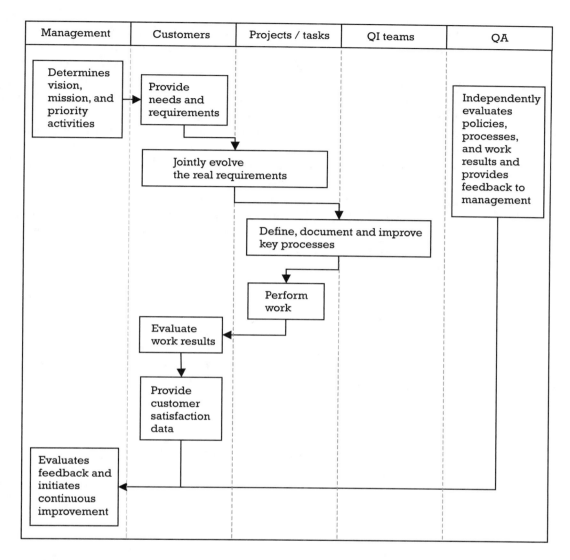

Figure 8.2 How the components of an integrated quality approach work together.

- A critical aspect is the use of the joint team to evolve the real requirements, as discussed in Chapter 1.

- Employee satisfaction data are another form of feedback provided to management that helps guide the organization.

- Standards such as the CMM® may be used to measure organizational effectiveness.

Quality Improvement Techniques

Regardless of the size of their projects, good PMs can make improvements on local projects under their own initiative using one or more of the quality improvement techniques described below. But, if a business wants to improve the quality of its products and services, the most effective approach is do it from the top and implement these techniques across all projects. The best way to manage quality improvement is to establish a quality management board (QMB) as a management team that can implement these ideas at the top and, thus, lead the company down the road to quality by example. In the QMB, managers can determine appropriate organizational policies and quality and PI objectives. To accomplish their goals, they implement plans for improvement and provide needed resources and skills. They track the status of improvements, reward teams and individuals for successes, and identify ways to transfer lessons learned and improvements to other parts of the organization. Regardless of the size of the organization, the QMB sets its agenda through easy-to-understand quality goals and provides direction regarding the implementation of the following quality improvement techniques:

▸ *Quality improvement and process improvement models:* Consider adopting a framework (such as the CMM® or CMMI®) as a standard for systems or software engineering and conducting annual evaluations of the current situation against the standard (see Figure 8.3). Experience has shown that CMMs, in use since 1987, enable a systems or software engineering project or organization to perceive how it stacks up

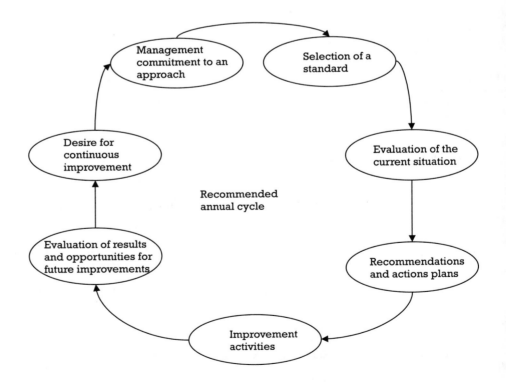

Figure 8.3 The quality improvement cycle.

against what industry considers a best practice and whether or not improvements it has implemented are having the desired effect. Use the results to identify priority areas for improvement activities and initiate continuous improvement initiatives, including QI teams where appropriate. Though it can take some planning, resources, and time to determine how the organization fits with the chosen process model, this investment will provide valuable information that can help steer improvements. It might be easier for larger organizations to absorb the expense of evaluations and improvements, but smaller organizations can look at their improvement program in strategic terms and look for other ways to implement improvements. For example, they may want to partner with other contractors or customers to accomplish their goals.

▸ *Training:* Regular and appropriate training is always a valuable investment for any size company. Customers demand that workers have the latest technology skills, and employees want to improve their professional development and performance. If organizations expect to continue to meet their customers' evolving needs and their employees' desire for personal and career growth, then management must take responsibility to ensure this happens. Smaller or medium-size organizations might have difficulty (through lack of resources) establishing an organizational training program. Partnering with local colleges or universities for lower rates may be an option they could explore.

▸ *QI teams using the QI story:* Though always conscious of the bottom line, large companies have more leeway in terms of resources to staff and fund QI teams. Because they have less staff and smaller budgets, small and medium-size projects or companies need to be judicious in the establishment of teams. At the same time, because they must operate their businesses and respond to customer demands and deal with chronic quality problems, they should establish QI teams to attack only what senior managers feel are the most critical company problems. In other words, smaller organizations should establish teams to deal with those problems that hamper their ability to do business or meet customer demands. (See below for more information about the QI story process that can be used by QI teams to foster continuous improvement.)

▸ *Customer satisfaction surveys* (e.g., by phone): Consider providing a mechanism to deal immediately with customer dissatisfaction, such as "red alert procedures" to escalate concerns, deal with them, and provide feedback to the customer. Large projects or companies have established mechanisms and tools to track and manage customer satisfaction issues. Managers can take advantage of existing resources to collect and analyze the information and use it to improve or to win new business. Even though they may not have the advantage of a corporate approach or infrastructure, smaller companies also have an advantage. Because they may work with a smaller group of customers, it is easier to take the personal approach and discuss issues one on one with customers and to develop immediate corrective actions. Regardless of the size of organization, if managers do not follow up or track their customer satisfaction issues, they will pay they price in reduced funding, canceled contracts, or awards to competitors.

▸ *Employee satisfaction surveys:* Learning about employee concerns through objective data and acting on the results builds employee loyalty and improves retention. As with the customer satisfaction surveys, larger companies use considerable resources to address employee issues and to retain their workforce. They know that these resources have feet and can leave at any time to find better a work environment or opportunities for advancement. This is true for smaller companies as well, but it may be more critical to their business if a few skilled workers who are the core of their expertise in any given area leave to join the competition. Small business managers would do well to develop a short, 20-question survey to find out what is on the minds of their staff, to determine what works well in the company and what does not, and to identify areas for improvement. Such a survey does not need to be scientific, but to serve as a basis for management decisions.

▸ *QA:* In most large companies, having an independent objective view concerning policy and process compliance and use in the organization provides valuable feedback on quality improvement and process improvement efforts or points to other problems that might not have their immediate attention. This makes it possible to have a trained QA staff available to support any size project or team as a matrixed function. Smaller organizations may not have the trained personnel or budget to support a full-time QA staff or a matrixed organization from which they can assign QA. In those cases, it is recommended that the entire project team adopt a quality team strategy, where all the members of the team are responsible for the quality of the work they perform and the products and services they provide. In this environment, each staff member must perform reviews or audits on another team member's work product or service and on the process used. This approach requires that each team member be trained for his or her QA role and that a corrective action system be in place that tracks the status of problems found in QA reviews and keeps management informed. Managers must take special care to ensure that reviewers can prove their objectivity in their role as QA (a main requirement of the CMMI®) and that they are not directly involved in the process or product they are reviewing.

▸ *Process design, management, and improvement:* A process is a set of activities that results in the accomplishment of a task or the achievement of an outcome. Any size organization should use process as one of the fundamental building blocks in its work. Larger and more complex projects require more detail in their documented processes and show the roles and responsibilities of all groups who are involved in the process. For obvious reasons, getting large groups of people to work together to meet shared goals can be more of a challenge. On the other hand, smaller project teams have an advantage since they may be able to rely on less detail in their documented process. For example, they can use checklists or simple process flowcharts. Having fewer people on the project team makes it easier to determine what the desired outcome of the process is, what inputs and outputs are required, and the specific process steps that need to be followed. Having small teams also makes it easier to train and to make desired changes.

> If you can't describe what you are doing as a process, you don't know what you're doing.
> —William Edwards Deming, management consultant, 1900–1993.

▸ *Monitoring performance through metrics:* Managers need to make decisions based upon data. Sometimes this data can be qualitative or quantitative. For any size organization to improve, it must have quantitative data on which to base its improvements. It is an unwise manager who decides to expend resources to implement a quality improvement when he or she does not know if such an improvement is needed. For quality improvements and process improvements, managers need to set reasonable objectives (that they have a good shot at making) and identify measures they can use to determine whether or not they have met that goal. Examples of potentially useful metrics include business win rates, customer satisfaction ratings, and a customer loyalty index. The latter can be generated as simply as by asking three questions: (1) How do you rate our quality? (2) What is the likelihood of your continued business? (3) What is the likelihood of your recommending us to a new customer?

▸ *QI techniques:* QI techniques such as brainstorming, multivoting, Pareto analysis, barriers and aids analysis, action plans, cause-and-effect analysis, checklists, the QI story, and PDCA (discussed below) are easy to learn and invaluable in a forward-looking organization.[1] These techniques can work well in any size project or organization, as long as the group is trained to use the technique and the results of the exercise.

▸ *QI story:* The QI story, developed by Qualtec Quality Services (now part of Six Sigma Qualtec), provides a structure for tackling priority activities and problems. As mentioned above, because they have fewer

---

1. An excellent, inexpensive guide for using these techniques is Six Sigma Qualtec's *QI Story: Tools and Techniques, A Guidebook to Problem Solving,* [1]. Another resource for organizational improvement materials is GOAL/QPC, available from goalqpc.com or by calling (800) 643-4316.

resources, smaller projects or companies should be judicious in the use of the QI story to solve problems; they should identify problems that will be the most cost-effective to solve. A modified set of steps is as follows:

1. Identify the reason for improvement.
   - Determine the nature of the problem.
   - Collect data.
   - Identify key processes.
   - Develop a plan and schedule.
2. Analyze the current situation.
   - Identify customers' real requirements.
   - Set a target for improvement.
3. Conduct analysis.
   - Identify probable root causes of the problem.
   - Select root causes that seem to have the most impact.
   - Verify the selected root causes with data.
4. Select countermeasures that attack the verified root causes.
   - Evaluate whether the countermeasures will do the following:
     - Address the verified root causes;
     - Impact the customers' requirements;
     - Prove to be cost beneficial.
5. Develop an action plan to implement the selected countermeasures.
   - Obtain management approval.
   - Coordinate with stakeholders to garner support and cooperation.
6. Implement the countermeasures.
7. Measure the results.
   - Did the countermeasures work?
   - Are things improving?
   - Are root causes being impacted?
   - Evaluate the results compared to the target for improvement.
   - Implement additional countermeasures if needed.
8. Standardize an approach based on the results.
   - What can be changed to ensure the problem does not recur (e.g., a new or revised policy, procedure, work process, standard, training)?
9. Consider what lessons have been learned from performing the quality improvement effort.

▸ Should related problems be addressed?

▸ Should the approach for performing the QI story be revised?

The PDCA Cycle

A popular and useful paradigm utilized for quality improvement is the PDCA cycle [2] mentioned in Chapter 3 in connection with assessing the value and usefulness of meetings. The idea is to plan the approach, implement ("do") it, check on how things are working, act on the results of that checking, and continue the cycle. The PDCA cycle is shown in Figure 8.4.

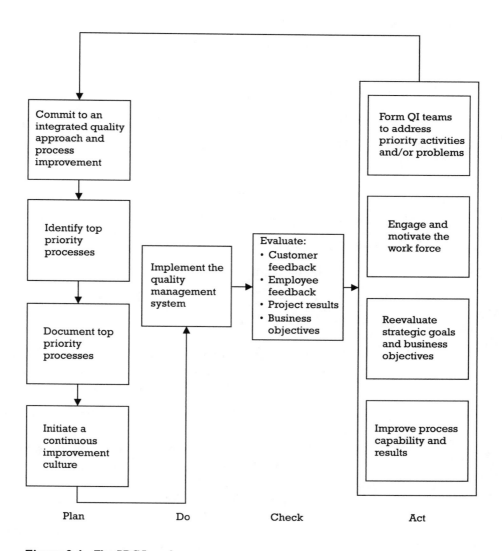

Figure 8.4 The PDCA cycle.

How to Design a Process

A critical skill needed by the RA is the ability to design and to improve processes—more specifically, to facilitate process design and improvement sessions. Recall that we defined a process as a set of activities that results in the accomplishment of a task or the achievement of an outcome. For example, in this book we have referred to the requirements process, a full system life-cycle set of activities that includes the following:

- Identifying requirements;
- Understanding customer needs and expectations;
- Clarifying and restating the requirements (evolving the real requirements);
- Analyzing the requirements;
- Defining the requirements;
- Specifying the requirements;
- Prioritizing the requirements;
- Deriving requirements;
- Partitioning requirements;
- Allocating requirements;
- Tracking requirements;
- Managing requirements;
- Testing and verifying requirements;
- Validating requirements.

Process design and process improvement are activities that do the following:

- They involve stakeholders (those who have an interest) in deciding how things should be done, thus gaining their buy-in to the implementation, use, and continuous improvement of the process.
- They enable a project or organization to become increasingly proficient. Once a process is documented, everyone can understand it, and it can be done repeatedly in the same way with the same results. Also, improvements can be suggested, discussed, and incorporated.

Designing a process is straightforward. Gather a few smart people in a room who are familiar with the process to be documented. It's best if all of the stakeholder groups are represented. Using a whiteboard or large piece of paper, create the template provided in Figure 8.5.

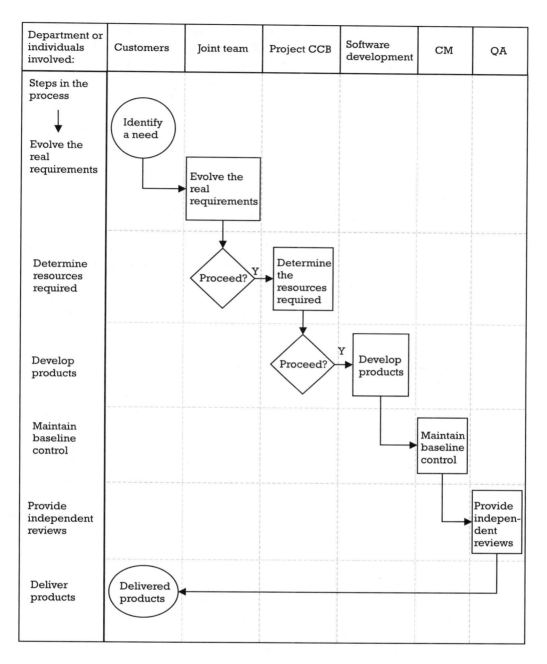

Figure 8.5   Process design flowchart template with simplified product development process.

Across the top, list the departments, organizations, or individuals involved in the process. Along the vertical axis, list the steps in the process (number or describe each step). Using small sticky sheets, ask people to describe what should be done to accomplish the tasks in the process on the sticky sheets and place them in the appropriate places on the template. An alternative approach is to document what is actually done in the current process as a starting point for improvement. Once most of the activities have been identified, make a final check to ensure that they are assembled in the order in which the activities should be performed and are assigned to the organization or person that should do them. Later, use standard flowchart symbols to connect them. I have provided a simplified product development process in the template to help you grasp the concept. You'll find that some of the activities of the process will require more detailed definition—in this case, consider designing subprocesses to capture and document more detailed understandings of the "should be" approach.

As emphasized in Chapter 3, the RA should be proficient in designing and developing a process. Take the opportunity now, while you are thinking about it, to design a process. Select an important activity related to your current work responsibilities that is not yet documented. Invite three to six coworkers who are very knowledgeable about the activity or who are stakeholders to participate with you in a process design workshop. Transcribe the template provided in Figure 8.5 (without the flowchart and its associated steps) onto a whiteboard. On a large pad off to the side, agree on the name of the process. Then, give some careful thought to the objectives of the process—what is it that the process is supposed to accomplish? Envisioning outputs from the process will help. Document (write down) the process objectives. Then, list the stakeholders of the process (anyone who has an interest in the process or responsibilities related to completing the process). Using 3 × 5–inch Post-it® Notes, write down the names of the stakeholder groups and project groups involved in the process to be documented (one group per Post-it® Note) and place them across the top of the whiteboard. Our habit is to place the customer of the process on the left-hand side (leave space for a vertical column that will be either a set of the successive numbers of the steps of the process (starting with "1") or names specifying these steps. Typically, the names of the groups that are most involved in the process are placed next after the customers', and names of groups least involved in the process toward or at the right-hand side. Then, invite the participants in your process design workshop to suggest the tasks that need to be accomplished to perform the process. Initially, simply list each task on a separate Post-it® Note and place them on the whiteboard (anywhere). As you proceed with the identification of tasks, begin to organize the steps according to how the process should be done. [An alternative approach is to develop the process flowchart based on the existing way that the process is done (the "as-is process").] Don't concern yourselves yet with connecting the steps of the process with lines or with determining decision points— these refinements can be done off-line, after the workshop, by the person who has the primary responsibility for that process (we refer to this person as the process owner). Once you are satisfied that you have identified most or all of the tasks that need to be done in the process, refine your organization of the tasks into a logical flow (the process flowchart). You may find that one or more tasks need to be defined in more detail—you may choose to address this subprocess in a later workshop, or you may decide that it is so important that it needs to be defined first, before you complete the process flow that you started initially. Be very flexible. Have fun! Enjoy each other. Learn from one another. Consider inviting other stakeholders to join your group or create subgroups to define subprocesses (sometimes referred to as microprocesses of the macroprocess). Another approach, if you or someone else is very familiar with the process, is for that person to design a draft of the process flow independently and bring that draft work product to the process design workshop for refinement by the group in order to reach consensus.

For an example of a completed requirements process flowchart, refer to *Effective Requirements Practices* [3, pp. 110–124]. Write a narrative PD to accompany each flowchart (macro and micro). See Table 8.1 for a PD template. The PDs for the referenced flowcharts of the requirements process are available on my Web site (www.ralphyoung.net). The process owner should develop the PD off-line. I think of a defined process as including both the process flowchart and the narrative PD, because the information provided by both documents is required to understand the process.

Note that having a defined, documented process provides a basis for continuous improvement. As the process is being performed or "executed," suggestions for its improvement can be identified and provided to the process owner. The process owner should gather these suggestions and periodically invite stakeholders to participate in a process refinement workshop to consider suggestions. If it is decided to change ("update") the process flowchart or PD, the process owner should document the changes and release a new version of the process. A suggested naming convention is to use Version 1.1, 1.2, 1.3, and so forth, for minor updates and Version 2.0, 3.0, 4.0, and so forth, for major updates. This is important so that all stakeholders can identify and use the current version. An e-mail should be sent following the release of each new version so that all stakeholders are made aware of the current release.

Having taken responsibility for facilitating a process design or development workshop and creating a process flowchart and PD, you are a better-qualified RA or engineer. (Sometimes this type of work and related activities are referred to as process engineering.) Furthermore, you will find that teamwork is strengthened by these activities, because coworkers will become increasingly aware that they are dependent on others for work activities and for ideas and suggestions for improvement. Moreover, people will learn a lot about how the work should be done.

The industry literature reports a 7:1 ROI from process engineering activities. See [4–8] for several excellent reports. See [1, 9] for materials to help introduce and use QI techniques. I have experienced this return and other benefits at the Northrop Grumman IT DES business unit, and this has strengthened my commitment to process engineering and to achieving process maturity over the past dozen years [10].

Having successfully facilitated the process design workshop, follow it up with another venue: an informal brown-bag luncheon session where you present information about several simple, but powerful, QI techniques (these are described in [1]):

Table 8.1   Template for a PD

Name	Name of the process or subprocess
General information	
Process ID	Unique process identifier
Goal	Provide a brief description of the purpose and objective of the activity.
Standards	Identify the applicable process and product standards, including maturity-model references.
Related processes	Identify processes that are related to this process, especially if this process is part of a set that is normally viewed as a whole. List processes that either produce inputs or consume outputs of this process.
Version number	Include version history. For each version, include version number, approval date, and a summary of changes. As an example, the versions for this DID follow:
	3.0 broadened SW-CMM® to maturity models as a standard; added guidance on usage; changed to a table format; added guidance on indicators; changed footer to include version and date (10.14.02)
	2.0 version on PAL labeled 2.0.
	1.1 added reasons why organization or project goals and measurements may change
	1.0 updated process based on 7.1.99 peer review (7.12.99)
	0.1 initial version (1995)
Customer description	
Customer	Identify the internal and external stakeholders who benefit directly (receive products/services) from the results (outputs) of this process.
Requirements	List each of the legitimate requirements that have been negotiated and agreed to with the identified. These requirements should follow the RUMBA criteria in that they should be reasonable, understandable, measurable, believable, and achievable.
Interface description	
Entrance criteria	Identify the criteria that must be satisfied before the activity can be initiated. The criteria might say how to tell when a process can be started, for example at the conclusion of another activity or process.
Inputs	Identify the work products that are used at any point in the process.
Outputs	Identify the work products that are produced during the process.
Exit criteria	Identify the criteria that must be satisfied before the activity can be considered complete. Exit criteria summarize the salient measurable tasks of the process.
What to do	
Responsibilities	Describe the groups that participate in the process.
Tasks	Describe the tasks that must be accomplished within the process. For ease of reference, the tasks should follow the quality in daily work (QIDW) process diagram referenced as the main exhibit. If the process is procedural, describe the tasks in the order that they must be accomplished, numbering each task step. Parenthesize the responsible group to the left of the task, as shown below:
(<Participating group>)	*<Task description>*
	Use action verbs to describe the tasks. Reference by process ID all tasks that are further described elsewhere. Note any particular procedures, practices, or methods that are employed in any step.
Tools	Describe suggested or mandatory tools used during any step of the process.
Resources	Describe resources necessary to enact the process.

Table 8.1   Template for a PD (continued)

Name	Name of the process or subprocess
Measurement description	
Quality indicators	List and briefly describe those measurements that will be used to track the performance (or outcome) of this process in terms of the product or service delivered to the internal or external customer. These indicators should be linked closely to the valid customer requirements and should be used to monitor performance of the entire process. These measures should be measurable, verifiable, and cost effective.
Process indicators	List and briefly describe those measurements that are to be taken at critical points during the process and used to track and assess the effectiveness of the process itself. These in-process measures should also be measurable, verifiable, and cost effective.

Note: In organizational standard processes, quality and process indicators are suggested, but not mandatory.

Note: Projects determine process measurements during project planning and process improvement efforts. To reduce overhead, a project can designate process indicators as optional, to be collected if problem diagnosis is required.

(*Source:* Craig Hollenbach, a member of several of the CMMI® product development teams who contributed hugely to the development of the CMMI® products).

- Brainstorming;

- Multivoting;

- Fishbone (Ishikawa) diagrams;

- Pareto charts;

- PDCA;

- Rules of conduct;

- Defect prevention;

- Peer reviews;

- Inspections

- Action plans.

Invite members of your project or organization to start using them or to increase the frequency of use if these techniques are already known and used.

Your preparation for and facilitation of these workshops is itself a professional growth and development experience. I have found that the more that I present, the easier it is to do it.

Consider initiating an organizational requirements working group (RWG). Invite those who perform requirements-related work in on any of the organization's projects to participate. The RWG provides a mechanism (a way to get something done or to achieve a result) to coordinate requirements-related activities and for RAs to help each other. See Table 8.2 for a list of the advantages of having an RWG, and see [8] for other information.

Table 8.2   Advantages to Having an Organizational RWG

Allows the organization to benefit from the experience of its projects and the expertise of key staff members;
Seeds the organization with persons who share a common body of knowledge and have come to consensus on key topics;
Provides through its members a resource for the rest of the organization;
Facilitates use of the developed knowledge and artifacts for use in winning new business (proposals, lead marketing briefings, etc.);
Encourages a common way of doing things and supports repeatability and reuse;
Encourages and facilitates selection of appropriate methods and tools, as well as their deployment and implementation;
Encourages measurement of the effectiveness of the process and the benefits of institutionalization;
Allows participation in industry leading-edge efforts (transition packages).

Northrop Grumman IT has utilized this mechanism for seven years, and it has proven invaluable. Smaller companies may not have enough projects or RAs to form an RWG. In either case, companies should consider working with the SEI, local colleges or universities, or quality consortiums to share best local requirements practices (e.g., tools, techniques, ideas) among members and to serve as a networking forum.

Initially, a few active participants (approximately 6 to 8 of the 15 to 20 members of the RWG, depending on the particular meeting) designed an updated requirements (RE) process over a period of approximately four months. We used the abbreviation RE to distinguish the updated process from the previous version, which was an RM process (we wanted the updated process to address the full system life cycle, rather than only the software portion). Later, the RWG hosted several vendors over a period of four months, who provided demonstrations of the popular automated requirements tools, including DOORS (by Telelogic), RequisitePro ("ReqPro") by IBM (formerly Rational) Corporation, Caliber RM by Technology Builders (TBI) [now Star Team System Requirements by Starbase], CORE (by VITECH Corporation), RTM Workshop (by Integrated Chipware), and Vital Link (by Compliance Automation). As emphasized earlier, the RA must become familiar with and experienced in using an industry-strength automated requirements tool. (By industry-strength, I mean a requirements tool that provides the capabilities required to develop systems and software.) Participating in these demos provided the members of our RWG added insights into the use and value of automated tool support for requirements-related activities. Note that you can often download trial versions of many tools from the vendors' Web sites. Be sure that you are willing to commit some time to experimenting with the tool before you download it—the trial evaluation period passes very quickly in my experience, given your other responsibilities.

Over time, our organizational RWG has evolved into primarily an e-mail group that provides a mechanism to ask questions, get answers, share information, seek assistance with problems, proposals, or projects, find RAs for new assignments, and so forth. The RWG mechanism continues to be invaluable in many ways. A briefing that I presented at an industry conference concerning our RWG is available at my Web site [8].

Teamwork

I have been blessed to be a member of many empowered, high-performance teams in different organizations. A high-performance team really is more than the sum of its members. A high-performance team can accomplish most anything it sets out to do.

Teamwork evolves (or doesn't) based on a variety of factors. Here are some of the most important factors, from my experience:

1. A feeling of trust exists. I know that my manager believes that my intentions are good, even when I make mistakes.

2. Coworkers support one another. They treat each other as customers. A question from a coworker is not an interruption; rather, it's one of the reasons I'm there and an opportunity to help someone who is very important to me.

3. Meaningful, realistic (achievable), important objectives are given to the team. The objectives may be very ambitious, but they are achievable. The objectives are important to the organization's and project's business objectives.

4. Members of the team realize that each person has a unique role on the team and has special abilities (think of them as gifts) that he or she brings to the team effort.

5. Members of the team respect each other. They hold each other in high regard. They speak highly about one another to others.

6. A kick-off meeting is held to provide an official start to the team's efforts and to help inform others that the team effort is underway.

7. The team develops an action plan for its efforts, which defines specific tasks, planned completion dates, and who has the lead (the responsibility) for each task.

8. The team tracks and reports progress as compared with the plan. It considers itself a "mini project" responsible for using appropriate project planning and tracking techniques.

9. Members of the team feel supported by the project and the organization in carrying out their work. People know what the team is doing and are prepared to lend support ("help pull on the oars") when asked by the team or a member of the team.

10. The team agrees on a set of rules of conduct concerning how they will treat each other (see *Effective Requirements Practices* [3, p. 41] for a sample set of rules of conduct).

11. Management is interested in the progress of the team. Management provides time for periodic status reports from the team and wants to know what it can do to support the activities and efforts of the team. Management actively seeks opportunities to help the team and follows through on suggestions and commitments that it makes in status and review meetings.

12. The team and its members develop "work-arounds" when roadblocks and difficulties are encountered. They will not let barriers deter them from achieving the set objectives (or at least a realizable subset of the objectives).

13. The team and its members take time to celebrate progress and achievements along the way.

14. The team utilizes paraphernalia to foster increased spirit, motivation, and commitment, for example, coffee mugs or shirts with the team logo. The team is proud to use these and provides them to people outside the team who are helping.

15. The members of the team utilize proven QI techniques as the way they do their work (see the discussion of QI techniques earlier in this chapter).

16. Special celebrations take place when the team achieves a major milestone, for example, an end-of-day reception, a luncheon or dinner, recognition of the team at a senior management meeting, and letters of appreciation or commendation from managers or senior managers.

I trust that you get a sense from this discussion that having effective teamwork on a project and in an organization is powerful. It truly empowers the team, the project, and the organization. A high-performance team will (in my experience) accomplish seemingly impossible goals. Moreover, it is a joy to be a member of a high-performance team because of the satisfaction and fulfillment one derives.

Management can and must set the stage to allow its teams to be effective. Here are some of the ways management does this:

▸ Management communicates the business objectives of the organization, clearly articulating that each member of the organization is needed and depended upon to achieve these goals. Management convincingly expresses that it truly needs the able support of every member of the organization. Management requests the best efforts, ideas, suggestions, and energy of every person.

▸ Senior management involves subordinate managers in the decision process. The beliefs and concerns of managers are valued and utilized in making decisions. Managers feel needed and valued.

▸ Management provides support in the form of sponsorship, resources, its personal participation in kick-off and review meetings, time for status reports, recognition of efforts and milestones, commitment to follow through when requests are made, assistance in resolving issues and conflicts, and using good listening skills.

▸ Management maintains its interest in assignments given to people and teams and keeps people informed as priorities change, so that people don't feel they are doing unneeded or unimportant work.

▸ Management communicates in concert with representatives of other areas, such as marketing or systems engineering, for instance, by jointly sending an e-mail to the entire organization. This expresses a focus that might more clearly explain or communicate a topic in a way that overcomes the perceived agendas of individual departments.

When management chooses not to help in these and related ways, the probability of the organization's project teams being high-performance is greatly reduced, as we all know from our own experiences. We think, If my manager doesn't care and acknowledge what I'm trying to do, why bother?

As an RA, you can work to foster effective teamwork in your many roles described in Chapter 2. Teamwork is one of the ways that an integrated quality approach is instantiated.

Summary

An effective requirements process is necessary to have an integrated quality approach, and an integrated quality approach is required for the requirements (or any other) process to work best. Implementing an integrated quality approach involves:

▸ Familiarizing everyone in the organization with management's concern for quality and the value and importance of quality improvement to the organization's reason for being;

▸ Training people to lead QI teams;

▸ Training people in how to design work processes;

▸ Managing using a quality improvement approach.

RAs are in a strategic position to help projects and organizations deploy and use an integrated quality approach (review the roles of the RA suggested in Chapter 2 in this context). By doing so, they are helping to ensure an effective requirements process.

Case Study: An Example of Quality Improvement Sidetracked

A process engineer was called upon to assist a Canadian division of a large multinational company to leverage her extensive experience and expertise in process engineering and project management. The multinational company had recently made a commitment to use a process-engineering framework. The process-engineering consultant participated in a briefing presented by a vice president of the parent company to the division's technical staff of approximately 40 people. The briefing clearly communicated the critical importance of process improvement, demonstrated senior management sponsorship and commitment, and described the proven process improvement framework that would be used. The audience was extremely receptive and seemed to realize that something new and different was being offered to help them become more productive and effective. The consultant noticed looks of excitement on the faces of the technical staff. She was impressed by the degree of attention given to the presenter and by the number and thoughtfulness of follow-on questions and comments. The stage appeared to be set for a productive and effective process improvement initiative.

However, no significant progress was made in process improvement over the following three years. Why not? An analysis of this case study indicated the following problems:

- Although senior management at the parent company was convinced that process improvement would help the division achieve its business objectives, division management wasn't as convinced. There was no division management participation in the parent company's decision to initiate process improvement activities and no sponsorship or commitment to implementation. The process improvement initiative was, more or less, encouraged from the top down without sufficient time or preparation for lower-level acceptance. There was a lack of teamwork that prevented individuals at all levels of the organization from focusing on the common goal.

- The division's management used technicalities to delay process improvement. For example, one excuse for delay was that "the parent company's process improvement plan had not been finalized." In other words, the spirit of process improvement, which could have gone ahead in many ways with or without a final "approved" company-level process improvement plan, was easily sidetracked by adherence to the bureaucratic letter.

- A lot of money was spent by the parent company to develop a process improvement plan (PIP) and to engage experienced consultants to lend their experience and expertise. Training was provided to the division to familiarize the employees with the plan and with process improvement in general. However, these investments did not pay off. No significant changes were made in the organization and no major improvements in productivity or quality resulted.

Process improvement and quality improvement are as much cultural change issues as they are technical or managerial change issues. A better approach might have been for the parent company to issue a set of process improvement plans and overarching principles in stages. Early releases might have encouraged simple and effective process improvement activities, with more detailed plans released later. The company could then have monitored these early steps and encouraged the lower levels in the division to adopt the solution as their idea, rather than something that was forced down from above. The company could also have used feedback generated by closely monitoring the results of these initial steps to guide further development and identify specific technical or cultural barriers to be overcome within the division.

Your process design and improvement approach will become more detailed as your experience with it matures. That's great! The important thing is that the project or organization's essential processes are designed, documented, and continually improved by their stakeholders. By having an organizational standard process for needed activities, such as requirements, project planning, project tracking, peer reviews, CM, QA, DP, technology change management, and other needed processes, projects can reuse and tailor it as required. Having the processes (flowcharts, narrative PDs, and related artifacts such as templates for plans) available in an automated electronic library facilitates achieving repeatability in an organization. Using version control facilitates continuous improvement of the artifacts.

References

[1] Six Sigma Qualtec, *QI Story: Tools and Techniques, A Guidebook to Problem Solving,* 3d ed., 1999. Call (480) 586-2600 for information. See also www.ssqi.com/homepage.asp.

[2] Walton, M., *The Deming Management Method,* New York: The Putnam Publishing Group, 1986. The PDCA cycle is often attributed to Deming because he introduced it in Japan. Walter A. Shewhart originally conceived it. See pp. 86–88.

[3] Young, R. R., *Effective Requirements Practices,* Boston, MA: Addison-Wesley, 2001.

[4] Clark, B. K., "Effects of Process Maturity on Development Effort," Center for Software Engineering, University of Southern California, 1999, at www.ralphyoung.net.

[5] Northrop Grumman IT DES, "The Road to CMM(I) Level 3," white paper, available from ralph.young@ngc.com.

[6] Wiegers, K. E., *Creating a Software Engineering Culture,* New York: Dorset House Publishing, 1996.

[7] Young, R. R., "The Importance and Value of Process Improvement," at www.ralphyoung.net.

[8] Young, R. R., "The Value of an Organizational Working Group," at www.ralphyoung.net.

[9] GOAL/QPC materials, at www.goalqpc.com.

[10] Northrop Grumman IT DES press release concerning CMMI Level 5, at www.irconnect.com/noc/pages/news_releases.mhtml?d=35405.

A Vision for Requirements Engineering

A reasonable vision for requirements engineering is achieving the following goals:

1. Customers acknowledge that the system meets their expectations.

2. Systems and software engineers are fulfilled by their work.

3. Trained and experienced RAs are acknowledged to have made a positive difference.

4. Task and project requirements are complete and controlled to provide a stable basis for development.

5. Systems and software development projects incur less than 15% unplanned rework and less than 10% wasted resources.

6. An informed marketplace is developed, where a potential supplier's ability to define, implement, and support requirements-based development is valued.

7. Those who are masters in requirements, systems engineering, and project management tasks take personal responsibility for mentoring others.

These goals are achievable. Indeed, there are pockets of excellence where tasks, projects, and even organizations are already achieving these goals. There are organizations, projects, and tasks that perform at high levels of process maturity, as measured by industry standards such as the CMM® [1], the CMMI™ [2], and Six Sigma [3]. The SEI provides a Web page (www.sei.cmu.edu/sema) that reports on progress being achieved by organizations that use the CMM® and CMMI®. The industry average, however, is far lower than the high-maturity organizations being tracked by the SEI, as reported by organizations such as the Gartner Group and the Standish Group International.

It is clear that organizations have the *capability* to perform at higher levels of achievement, as measured by many of the goals provided above. Why don't they? Obviously, the answer to this question is complex. From Dr. Deming's perspective [4], it is a management issue: management often does not empower its work force or enable good to excellent performance in its organizations. Surely, management can be helped. Every person can make a difference.

This book suggests that requirements engineers and analysts can help a lot. Requirements are the basis for all of the work that is done in systems and software engineering. Industry results [5, 6] suggest that there is a lot of room for improvement in the practice of requirements engineering. It is clear that there is sufficient information available to enable significant improvement in achieving the goals I've enumerated. *The obvious need is for practitioners to use more effective requirements practices.* This requires knowledge and experience. I believe that you can further strengthen and improve your skills and be even more effective in the roles that you provide. As I indicated in Chapter 6, this requires a lot of hard work. As I communicate in workshops and seminars [7], things will get better only if we practitioners do some things differently. It's not that we don't know (or can't find out) *what* to do; it is that we do not persevere in doing things as well as we can do them. In my seminars, I encourage participants to create their own personal commitment list. I challenge them to listen closely and identify at least three things that they are willing to *commit* to doing differently in their work situations. Obviously, the key word here is "commit." I challenge them to work with their peers and managers to change a few things that will make a difference. If you have digested this book, I'm hopeful and confident that you have noted some things that you can do differently in your own work environment. Take the opportunity to follow through—to do the hard work that will improve the results of your tasks, project, and organization.

Table 9.1 provides some opportunities for RAs and engineers to improve project success rates. Think of these as *enablers* for the excellence we seek. More fundamentally, experience confirms that they are necessary conditions to achieving excellence in requirements engineering.

Requirements engineering is difficult. It is not just a simple matter of writing down what the customer says he wants. Customers and users have not thought through their real needs and aren't able to articulate them. Another fundamental problem in business is that requirements are inherently dynamic; they will change over time as our understanding of the problem we are trying to solve changes. The importance of good requirements and the underlying dynamic nature of the process mean that we must be as accurate as possible, and yet be flexible. Flexible does not mean "weak," but rather that we have a process for accommodating changed requirements as we clarify the real requirements of customers.

Table 9.1 Some Opportunities for RAs and Engineers to Improve Project Success Rates

Recognize that a productive work environment means supporting people, achieving effective teamwork, and establishing a value of continuous improvement. Take actions to create a more productive work environment so that requirements-related work is effective.

(Development) projects must be managed (continuous oversight is needed to ensure that the right things are being done properly and well). We must manage projects better and, by doing so, reduce requirements-related defects.

Train and use specialists in requirements engineering.

Have and use a requirements process that addresses full life-cycle requirements-related activities. Invest 8% to 14% of the total cost of the project development effort in requirements-related activities throughout the project life cycle.

Invest more time to identify the real requirements.

Use effective requirements practices.

Use an automated requirements tool to support the development effort.

Provide an effective process and mechanism to manage changes to requirements.

Take action when things aren't working. We know when things aren't working. Ensure that requirements-related efforts are effective.

Provide role models that consistently demonstrate effective work habits and disciplines, for example, creating and using a joint team to be responsible for the requirements.

This is not a job for the most junior member of the team or the least talented member of the group. It requires merging of excellent technical skills with domain knowledge, good people, and communications skills.

The following are some of the challenges we face in improving requirements engineering:

▸ PMs who are focused on daily activities and unable to address underlying human needs and long-term issues adequately. An industry study by the Standish Group concluded that 15% of projects failed outright in 2002, and another 51% were considered "challenged," that is, late, over budget, or completed with reduced functionality [5]. Only 54% of the originally defined features of a project are delivered, and of those delivered, 45% are never used! The Standish Group believes that the problem is rooted in poorly defined requirements. Significant root causes of project failures are attributable to project planning and tracking. Some PMs provide only lip service to quality, teamwork, and continuous improvement and are unwilling to invest in training and practice to create a "quality improvement culture."[1]

1. A good reference is Karl E. Wiegers, *Creating a Software Engineering Culture* (New York: Dorset House Publishing, 1996). See also, Rita Hadden, *Leading Culture Change in Your Software Organization* (Vienna, VA: Management Concepts, 2003).

Other PMs don't focus on satisfying the project requirements because they are focusing on being responsive to their three bosses: their managers (who do performance reviews and expect PMs to achieve revenue and profit goals); their customers (who are concerned with the expectations of users); and their project staffs (who are looking for direction). The PM must balance all of these needs and ensure that all parties are engaged in the project effort. Figure 9.1 provides some insights into the complex role of the PM. The PM must maintain a customer focus, be responsive to executive management, and provide an effective environment for developers. A good PM may have to depend upon a subordinate manager, such as the system engineer, to be responsible for the requirements.

- Developers who refuse to use improved techniques, even when these techniques have been demonstrated to yield better results; who have not learned requirements engineering techniques; and who have not been provided with expectations concerning how they are to work and what they are to do in different situations.

- Customers who believe they understand their needs (but let their egos force them to stake out an unmovable position), are impatient for short-term results, require use of risky techniques, and have limited experience working in a partnering[2] or team mode that requires common commitment to project success.

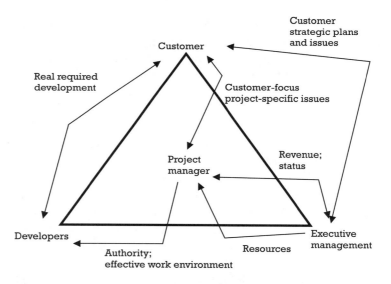

Figure 9.1 The challenges of the PM. (*Source:* Richard Raphael. Used with permission.)

2. See Frank Carr et al., *Partnering in Construction: A Practical Guide to Project Success* (Chicago: American Bar Association, 1999) for a thorough treatment of the partnering process. See www.facilitationcenter.com for a reference to a practitioner who is experienced in implementing the partnering process effectively.

All of these challenges hinder excellence as the standard for daily living, teamwork as the approach to excellence, and continuous improvement as the habit.

We (everyone who is involved in performing requirements-related activities on systems and software development projects) have a set of challenges we need to address. We must decide whether or not we are committed to improving performance and working toward higher achievement of the stated goals. Here are some examples of things that we should do in our daily work to live out our commitment.

How Should We Support PMs?

We should assist PMs in benefiting from the experiences of other projects. For example, most PMs in my experience would benefit from paying more attention to the human dimensions of projects. PMs could ask performers how things are going and then reflect on and incorporate input whenever possible. The point is that there is a wealth of information and advice available from the staff of any project that can further strengthen and improve the practices being used on the project. People put forward their best efforts when they are fulfilled and feel empowered[3] in their work environment. PMs need to find out what the team members want to do, encourage ideas for improvement, and seek advice on how to make their work environment more positive. They should create an atmosphere of trust and true interest in the opinions of team members and not be defensive about negative or unexpected feedback. Then, PMs should take actions to ensure the needed work is getting done *and* that people leave work most days feeling that they have accomplished things.

Another thing we should do for PMs is to provide resources about industry experience concerning requirements engineering and make specific recommendations to them about approaches that they might consider for a specific project. For example, recall the data from NASA noted in Chapter 1 that give a clear and powerful message: Projects that expended the industry average of 2% to 3% of total project development cost or effort on the (full life cycle) requirements process experienced an 80% to 200% cost overrun, while projects that invested 8% to 14% of total project cost or effort in the requirements process had a 0% to 60% overrun [8]. Further, we need to clarify for PMs that a portion of the one-third of project costs that is wasted[4]

---

3. By empowered, I mean that employees feel responsible not only for doing a good job, but also for making the whole organization work better. Teams work together to improve their performance continually, achieving higher levels of productivity. Organizations are structured in such a way that people feel that they are able to achieve the results they want, that they can do what needs to be done, not just what is required of them. See Cynthia Scott and Dennis Jaffe's *Empowerment: A Practical Guide for Success* (Menlo Park, CA: Crisp Publications, 1991).

4. As documented in *Effective Requirements Practices* (p. 79), 80% of all product defects are inserted in the requirements definition activities. Rework costs are estimated at 45% of total costs. By taking 80% of 45%, we learn that 36% (more than one-third) of total project costs (based on industry data) can potentially be avoided by driving requirements errors out of the work products.

can be redirected to pay for needed improvements in processes and practices. We need to show them how to track the ROI from specific improvements, so that they have the data to make good decisions ("manage by fact").

Projects should prioritize requirements. As we have discussed, all requirements are not equal—some are more important than others. Davis provides three case studies and offers 14 recommendations in his article "The Art of Requirements Triage" [9].

Projects need an effective process and mechanism to manage changes in requirements. We know from experience that this is where we lose control of many technical efforts. Let's take action not to let this happen again. For example, utilizing a joint customer/supplier team to maintain responsibility for the requirements throughout the development effort and having all change requests pass through a single channel will help. Another mechanism is controlling the sources of unofficial requirements [10]. Documenting the rationale for each requirement will also reduce the number of requirements (by as much as 50%, according to industry expert Ivy Hooks) [8].

How Should We Support Customers?

We should familiarize customers (and PMs and the project team) with industry experience that the initial set of written requirements is seldom (perhaps never) the set of real requirements. As explained in Chapter 1, customers need help from skilled RAs to identify the real requirements. The investment made to discover and evolve the real requirements will be more than repaid by avoiding downstream development work on an inadequate set of requirements. Let's not continue to relearn this lesson on every future project!

Are we really harnessing the power of effective teamwork? We should establish commitment to one another to allow any endeavor to be successful. We should find creative ways to make teamwork happen, even in environments that don't support it. For example, an integrated product team (IPT) approach [11] in which the customer is a member of the IPT facilitates communication and team effort.[5] We should advise customers, PMs, and organizations of successful approaches that have achieved effective teamwork and nurture the commitment that is required for any project to be successful [12].

How Should We Support Developers?

One way that we should assist developers is to listen to them and take action on what they say, to let them know that we are there for them. By this I

---

5. The DoD has started using the term *integrated team management* in lieu of IPT because of concerns that IPTs are not working as well as needed.

mean that it is management's job to provide a work environment that maximizes effectiveness. The bottom line is that success depends on people. We must provide an environment in which people can be effective and are fulfilled, where they can grow, and where they are appreciated and valued. Management must care deeply and show it.

Other ways in which we can assist developers are to put effective processes and practices in place (*and expect them to be applied*—see the next paragraph), to work at reducing rework, to create an environment of continuous improvement, and to work toward ever better quality in work products. If we don't do this, we risk people becoming frustrated and leaving the organization and projects.

Still another important thing we must do is make it clear to developers that we expect them to use the improved and proven policies, processes, mechanisms, methods, techniques, and tools that are the standards in the organization and on the project. Watts Humphrey's *"Why Don't They Practice What We Preach"*[6] details some reasons developers do not use improved techniques, even when they are provided with evidence that they achieve better results. We must make it clear that it's not acceptable for people to fall back on their old ways of doing things. We should provide role models that consistently demonstrate effective work habits and disciplines.[7] Einstein commented that the only rational way of educating is by example.

Whoever on the project is addressing requirements issues needs support. In addition to an effective automated requirements tool, requirements engineers need training in requirements engineering. What is a good requirement? Why must RAs not make requirements decisions? Why must I not gold plate (add features and capabilities that are not required)? We should create a set of expectations for the project staff concerning how they are to work and what they are to do in different situations. This can best be accomplished by training that is tailored to a particular project's environment and needs and presented by people who can really help. The training and advice to the staff must be presented in a way that respects people—we all have egos, and if mine is hurt, it's difficult for me to put forward my best efforts.

Summary

There are many things we can do to create a pathway to address requirements-related problems. I'm not pretending that this is easy or that it can be accomplished quickly. Achieving the defined vision for requirements engineering requires, however, that we do things differently. I hope that you will commit yourself to making some changes that will help.

---

6. Available at www.sei.cmu.edu/publications/articles/practice-preach/practice-preach.html.

7. Steve McConnell's *After the Gold Rush: Creating a True Profession of Software Engineering* (Redmond, WA: Microsoft Press, 1999) is full of ideas and suggestions to help with this situation. McConnell notes in his epilogue that common development problems won't be avoided without our support.

Case Study

There is a common misperception that Web sites are simple, can be built quickly, and don't require the planning and RM that real systems or software applications do. This is a trap for unsophisticated system owners and developers, and there are still many of those out there.

A requirements engineering consultant was called in to investigate why a Web site for a government agency was not being completed on schedule. The work was being done through a General Services Administration (GSA) schedule holder, but had been subcontracted to another company that had marketed the business. The prime contractor had not closely reviewed the proposal or the initial work, because it did not have in-house Web application development expertise. The work was fixed price, relations with the users were already strained, and the government had issued a "show cause" and was threatening to freeze the contractor's GSA schedule.

Reviewing the contractual materials, the consultant discovered that the solution was simply to put an existing Microsoft Access database on the Web, test it, and write a users guide and system documentation. There had originally been a task to do a database analysis, but all parties had agreed to a modification to reduce the cost of the project by removing this task. There was no requirement to develop a requirements document. Perhaps the agency users thought that would have been an unnecessary cost and delay. After all, they had a working system that represented their requirements. Or did they?

When the consultant reviewed the application (for this was an application, not just a static Web site), he discovered that the database had indeed been put on the Web. A front end had been written to accept selection criteria and produce on-line reports of the data. If the selections retrieved large amounts of data, after a wait, a large table would be generated on the screen that would force the user to scroll to the right as well as down to see all of it, despite the use of a small font. If the selections were too large, the retrieval would time out.

A different menu selection asked for a password and then provided a long series of data entry forms to allow the user to enter or update the data.

The developers considered the project essentially to be done, with the only work remaining being to (1) create a way to print the reports, and (2) fix the time outs and other errors that the user pointed out during testing. The existing database was on the Web, and it provided both a way to enter data and a flexible report generation capability that could generate any report the user would want.

Unfortunately, what the user wanted was a way to automate the previously manual process of collecting data from its offices in the field. The current process was for the offices to fill out forms or send in spreadsheets to headquarters, and another contractor would get the data into the Access database. The developers of the new system had not realized that the system owner had assumed that putting the database on the Web would provide them with the ability to have the field offices directly enter the data via the

Web. This would require a more sophisticated system than a single user password and set of data entry screens. In fact, the existing process turned out to incorporate workflow and approval before the data appeared at headquarters, and headquarters could have questions or even return it for rework before it would become part of the "official" database available to the public.

To make matters worse, many of the "errors" that the users complained about were related to data problems. The decade of existing data was fraught with inconsistent, missing, and erroneous data. The user would run reports on the existing system to compare with the Web-based system, but any minor change in query could yield different results. It turned out that the Access database had been used as it existed, without change, and that someone without a database background had developed it. No real database design had been performed. Numerous tables of similar data existed. Data elements had similar names. Text fields with inconsistent spellings were used for keys. The data was really a nightmare. However, reports generated from it had been submitted to Congress each year, and users should be able to duplicate them when they queried the Web site.

After a long process of meetings and negotiations with the government, the prime contractor agreed to build the access control and workflow aspects of the system and manage the quality control and testing, while the developer continued to improve the data retrieval and data entry aspects of the system. Additional programming resources were applied. Source code control was implemented. The system was coded, tested, documented, and ultimately accepted. The government appreciated the additional investment and effort made by the prime contractor, who was not terminated. The GSA schedule was restored.

The developer claimed that the data errors were not its contractual responsibility, and the government reluctantly agreed, but the prime contractor had to do a certain amount of data cleaning to get the system accepted anyway. Data cleaning and database design was really called for, but was not done because those funds had been removed from the contract. Changes to the database at that late point would also have required coding changes, and the prime contractor decided not to do that, although it would have resulted in a much simpler and more maintainable system.

Early attention to requirements could have averted this disaster. The divergence between what the government wanted (but never clearly articulated) and what the contractor felt it was responsible for was so great that the only way to recover was to rework the problem at almost a 100% overrun in cost!

The following requirements-related errors were made by the prime contractor, developer, and government client:

▸ Assuming that an existing system is a good representation of requirements for its replacement;

▸ Assuming that "put it on the Web" does not change "it" or require the development of any new business process or requirements;

‣ Agreeing to skip the data analysis, assuming that legacy data was clean and well structured;

‣ Forgetting about security, performance, maintainability, and other nonfunctional types of requirements.

The major lesson to be learned from this case is that system owners basically require that a system satisfy their envisioned business need, not that it meet the letter of the contractual requirements. Designing for the Web is no different. If the system does not meet the business need, it will be a failure. If the developers do not fully comprehend the business need, they cannot infer it from a legacy system, because the business processes that surround the legacy system are not documented in the system. In this case, they might have guessed that there was a requirement for workflow and multilevel approval of submitted data, but they might not have guessed that there was a requirement to replicate certain existing report outputs to avoid contradicting prior Congressional submissions.

A secondary lesson is that you should always assume that legacy data is "dirty" to at least some degree. It is extremely risky to assume that existing databases can be reused without redesign. In this case, skipping the data analysis was very costly to all parties and caused the eventual system failure.

Although some companies and government offices have been led to believe that Web sites can be prototyped and built in "Internet time," the requirements still need to be thought through. Because this work was contracted, and particularly because it was fixed price, the requirements should have been worked out and more explicitly documented. One way to avoid such surprises is to break the requirements and data analyses into a separately priced task, with its deliverables forming the basis for subsequent design and development.

Name withheld by request
Requirements-engineering consultant

References

[1]   Paulk, M. C., et al., *Capability Maturity Model for Software*, Version 1.1, February, 1993. SEI, Carnegie-Mellon University, Pittsburgh, PA, 1993, at www.sei.cmu. edu/publications/documents/93.reports/93.tr.024.html.

[2]   CMMI Product Team, *Capability Maturity Model Integration*, Version 1.1, December 2001. SEI, Carnegie-Mellon University, Pittsburgh, PA, 1993, at www.sei.cum. edu/cmmi.

[3]   Eckes, G., *Making Six Sigma Last: Managing the Balance between Cultural and Technical Change,* New York: John Wiley & Sons, Inc., 2001.

[4]   Deming, W. E., *Out of the Crisis,* Boston: MIT Center for Advanced Engineering Study, 1986.

[5]   The Standish Group, *CHAOS Chronicle 2003 Report,* West Yarmouth, MA: The Standish Group International, 2002, at www.standishgroup.com.

[6]   McGibbon, T., "A Business Case for Software Process Improvement Revised," Rome, NY: Data & Analysis Center for Software, September 30, 1999, at www.dacs.dtic.mil/techs/roispi2.

[7]   See "Tutorials, Conferences, Presentations, Workshops, and Discussions" at www.ralphyoung.net.

[8]   Hooks, I. F., and K. A. Farry, *Customer-Centered Products: Creating Successful Products through Smart Requirements Management,* New York: AMACOM, 2001.

[9]   Davis, A. M., "The Art of Requirements Triage," IEEE *Computer* (March 2003): 42–49.

[10] Weinberg, G. M., "Just Say No! Improving the Requirements Process," *American Programmer* 8(10) (October 1995): 19–23.

[11] U.S. Army Corps of Engineers Integrated Product Team, Web page, at www.usace.army.mil/ci/lcmis/lcmipt.html.

[12] A good reference concerning teamwork is P. R. Scholtes et al.'s *The Team Handbook,* 2nd ed. (Madison, WI: Oriel Inc., 2001). The authors' thesis is that in order to succeed in today's environment, the knowledge, skills, experience, and perspectives of a wide range of people must be brought together.

Contents

Moving Forward: Knowable Requirements, Manageable Risk

We have addressed topics in this book that are of great significance to the RA:

▸ Requirements are important, and leveraging requirements-related activities on a project has great power and effect (Chapter 1).

▸ Effective practices and documented, well understood processes are needed on projects of all sizes, not just for large-scale development (Chapter 1).

▸ Industry experience demonstrates the value of investing 8% to 14% of total project costs in the system life-cycle requirements process; data confirms that this level of investment produces the best results (Chapter 1).

▸ Criteria should be developed for a good requirement and each requirement should be evaluated against this list to clarify and restate the requirement (Chapter 1).

▸ Documentation of the rationale for each requirement (why it is needed) may eliminate up to half of the stated requirements (and a lot of costs) (Chapter 1).

▸ Differentiate between *stated* requirements and *real* requirements, and work collaboratively with your customers and users to identify the real requirements (Chapter 1).

▸ Planning the requirements effort and writing a requirements plan will pay good dividends (Chapter 1). (Watts Humphrey's books, *Introduction to the Personal Software Process* [1] and

Introduction to the Team Software Process [2] provide good insights into the value of planning.[1])

‣ All projects, with the possible exception of "tiny" projects, require an industrial-strength automated requirements tool (Chapters 2 and 5). Start the selection process for the tool of your choice early in the project planning phase, guided by a trade study to ensure that the selected tool supports your project's process and your customer's needs. Invest in formal training for the people who will use the tool the most.

‣ The biggest problem in computing and systems and software engineering is the failure to identify the real requirements before initiating other work, which results in costly rework (an average of 40% to 50% of total project costs, but the amount can be much higher, shading right into project cancellation), failure to meet budgets and schedules, poor quality of work products, customer dissatisfaction, and project failure (Chapter 5). A joint team can help overcome this problem. The second biggest problem in the systems and software development industry is the failure to control new requirements and changes to requirements (Chapter 5). Providing a formal mechanism can help overcome this problem.

‣ Although some requirements are not "knowable" at the beginning of a system or software development effort, an incremental development life cycle can be employed to manage the situation (Chapter 5). Also, using rapid application development and a spiral approach can help identify real requirements.

‣ Nine roles of the RA were identified. Suggestions and insights concerning how you can perform each role were provided (Chapter 2).

‣ Skills and characteristics needed by an effective RA were described (Chapter 3). An "RA's skills matrix" will help guide your professional development. Continuing your education can help you acquire expert knowledge of requirements engineering and use effective requirements practices.

‣ Several case studies were provided that help illustrate how requirements tasks can go wrong (all chapters). Requirements development and management is difficult. Applying processes, methods, techniques, and tools in the real world with diverse customers and users is particularly challenging.

‣ Various types of requirements were identified (Chapter 4). Recommended terminology to use and not to use was suggested, based on

---

1. One of the industry best practices that you might suggest to your organization is the Personal Software Process (PSP) and Team Software Process (TSP). Watts Humphrey has shown that data and planning are very powerful at the individual developer level and for teams of developers.

industry experience in using the various terms, to reduce confusion and facilitate effective communication. Using a project glossary and a project acronyms list will help.

> A requirements gathering checklist was provided that will help your project perform the needed work efficiently and effectively (Chapter 5). Having a documented procedure that you tailor to meet the needs of your project will help. We suggested that the effort be planned and that you take time out periodically to evaluate how you're doing in comparison with the plan (PDCA).

> You may find that you need to replan. In any case, we want to establish a value of continuous improvement and to capture the ideas and suggestions of coworkers every step of the way, fostering teamwork (Chapter 8).

> Your project should adopt a set of best practices for RAs (Chapter 6). There is a lot of talk and writing about best practices, but not enough actual implementation and institutionalization of their use. In fact, an endemic problem in computing and systems and software engineering is that we do not practice what we preach—*we need to make concerted efforts to actually use* (not just acknowledge) good practices, processes, mechanisms, methods, techniques, and tools at the individual, project, and organizational levels. The reason we don't do this is that it requires a lot of work. The issue is that we should strive to make our work efficient and effective, so that we can best support business and organizational objectives.

> Discussion of a set of RA's specialty skills provides insights into areas that may be critical at some point in your work (Chapter 7).

> An integrated quality approach is needed for processes (including the requirements process) to work most effectively (Chapter 8). RAs are in a strategic position to help projects and organizations.

> A vision for requirements engineering was provided that includes specific goals that are achievable (Chapter 9).

Where to Go from Here

We have covered a lot of ground in this book. Figure 10.1 shows the RA, engineer, or manager considering some of the tools available to help.

Consider the following topics in terms of some next steps. These are some courses of action that I hope you will consider:

1. Consider the roles that you provide in your current work assignments in the context of Chapter 2. Is it possible that you could expand on them, thus making a greater contribution, learning more, and being more fulfilled in your work activities?

Figure 10.1 There are good tools available to help. (*Source:* Richard Raphael. Used with permission.)

2.   Reflect on the skills you possess and the characteristics you exhibit in the context of Chapter 3. Perhaps in collaboration with your manager, develop a personal professional development plan that enables you to acquire additional skills that you believe are desirable. Consider taking steps to strengthen characteristics that will enable you to be a better coworker in the eyes of your peers.

3.   There is confusion on many projects concerning the types of requirements. If your project exhibits this confusion, what steps might you suggest to clarify it?

4.   Do you use a documented requirements process on your task or project? Has your work group taken advantage of some time together to consider possible improvements that can be made to the process? Might this be an opportunity to initiate or reinforce a habit of continuous improvement?

5.   Are the requirements gathering methods and techniques being used effective? Could some improvements be made based on industry experience with requirements gathering methods and techniques?

Would additional training concerning one or more methods or techniques help?

6. How many of the best practices for RAs described in Chapter 6 are in use on your project and in your organization? Are there any additional practices that it would make sense to consider using?

7. Is it advisable to invest some effort to strengthen any of the RAs' specialty skills described in Chapter 7?

8. Does an integrated quality approach exist on your task or project and in your organization? What are some steps that you can take to further strengthen and improve the approach? Might it be helpful to provide a briefing to your management groups to request additional support and sponsorship?

9. What is your vision for requirements engineering? How can you work toward achieving it?

Moving Forward

You may find (as I have) that reading stimulates your thoughts about moving forward. Reading doesn't necessarily require carefully digesting every sentence. You can grasp the essence of a work (book, article, Web site, conference presentation, etc.) through a cursory review, capturing some of the main ideas and reflecting on them through the lens of your own experience and beliefs.

I recommend not trying to change everything at once. Rather, select three to six practices or areas for your own personal commitment list. These are practices that you are willing to apply in your daily work habits in order to change in a committed way how you do things in your project and organizational environment. They may concern areas where your project or organization is experiencing feedback from a customer concerning needs for improvement, or areas where your project or organization is having some problems (these are sometimes referred to as "points of pain").

Here are some examples of candidate improvement areas that might help you create your own commitment list:

1. Implement a mechanism to identify real requirements. Persevere in making the mechanism successful and helpful.

2. Document the rationale for each requirement (why it is needed).

3. Prioritize the requirements for your project in collaboration with your customer and users. Establish those that are must-have, high, medium, and low priorities. Establish a product delivery strategy that is based on the established priorities. Assess the risk of each requirement, determining its magnitude.

4. Implement a mechanism to control changes to requirements and new requirements.

5. Provide formal requirements training for all persons involved in requirements-related activities on your project. Provide a requirements briefing for the project team and for your customer and users. A briefing is available on my Web site (www.ralphyoung.net) that you might tailor for this purpose.

6. Initiate peer reviews utilizing trained peer-review participants and peer-review moderators. Consider doing inspections of all requirements-related documents.

7. Initiate a partnering process in collaboration with your customer to gain commitment to project success.

8. Design or improve a process that seems particularly crucial to your work objectives and products in collaboration with the main stakeholders. Peer review the draft documented process and incorporate the peer review comments. Train the process, then deploy and implement it. Collect data and information concerning the results. After its been in use for three to six months, consider some improvement ideas (PDCA).

9. Quantify the estimated cost of rework on your project and commit to reducing rework by a reasonable percentage (say 20%) through implementing a set of process improvements. Develop and track data concerning the ROI of the process improvement initiative. Engage your management in the initiative.

10. Define and document a requirements policy for your project or organization. Peer review the draft documented policy and incorporate the peer review comments. Train the policy, then deploy and implement it. Collect data and information concerning results. Persevere in continuing use of the policy.

11. Consider selecting, getting training on, implementing, and using an automated requirements tool. Providing formal training concerning new automated tools is a good investment. Additionally, consider having the tool vendor provide a few days of consulting services to explain its use and to tailor it to the environment of the specific project and the needs of your team.

12. Consider using (or strengthening use of) bidirectional traceability of requirements using your automated requirements tool.

13. Provide a team-building training for your project or organization, perhaps facilitated by a trained facilitator from outside the organization. During the training, keep a list of ideas contributed by the participants concerning how the project or organization can improve. At the conclusion of the training session, gain consensus[2]

---

2. A technique to gain consensus is multivoting. See Six Sigma Qualtec's *QI Story: Tools and Techniques, A Guidebook to Problem Solving*, [3, pp. 47–48].

among the participants concerning the priority of each suggested idea. Implement the top one to six ideas (the number of ideas to be implemented is determined by the extent of management commitment to the ideas and the resources made available).[3]

14. Gain consensus on a set of "rules of conduct" that the members of your task or project agree to support. Document and publish your rules of conduct. Provide posters in each meeting room. Hold one another accountable to them.

15. Develop a requirements plan for your project. Peer review the draft requirements plan. Train the plan, being open to improvement suggestions from participants. Deploy and implement the plan. Collect data and information concerning results noted during its deployment and implementation. Assess the impact of creating and implementing a requirements plan, and consider initiating an organizational policy or procedure that requires or encourages development of a requirements plan for all new projects or efforts larger than a set number of person-months of effort.

16. Form an RWG in your organization. Share and assess the requirements policies, processes, mechanisms, practices, methods, techniques, and tools that have been most successful on each project. Document the results. Commit to expanded use of those that have been most successful. Over a period of time (one to three years), evolve a set of requirements best practices that work best in your organization. Consider having an e-mail group of the RWG members to provide a mechanism to ask questions and share information.

17. Address the topic of "Improving Communication within My Project" proactively. Brainstorm[4] suggestions for improving communications between and among project management and project members and teams, your customers, and major stakeholders. Consider establishing a project glossary and acronyms list.

18. Make a habit of "doing PDCA" at the end of each meeting and upon reaching milestones. Document the ideas and suggestions offered. Follow up on selected ideas and suggestions.

19. Further strengthen the acknowledgement of people for contributions made to the task, project, or organization. Establish a mechanism to celebrate team or project contributions. Form a habit of

---

3. A suggested implementation approach is to ask an advocate of the idea to write an action plan and to lead a QI team through the QI story. See Six Sigma Qualtec's *QI Story: Tools and Techniques, A Guidebook to Problem Solving,* [3, pp. 94–96 and 23–41].

4. Brainstorming is a valuable quality improvement tool to collect suggestions. See Six Sigma Qualtec's *QI Story: Tools and Techniques, A Guidebook to Problem Solving,* [3, pp. 43–46].

acknowledging people for new ideas and ongoing work products. Catch people doing things well.

20. Initiate or strengthen your project or organization's use of quality improvement tools such as brainstorming, multivoting, Pareto charts, fishbone (or Ishikawa) diagrams, PDCA, rules of conduct, barriers-and-aids analysis, countermeasures, and process flowcharts.

21. Review the reasons for requirements errors. Determine root causes. Brainstorm ideas and suggestions ("countermeasures") to tackle the root causes. Select a few countermeasures to implement, and track the results.

22. Examine whether you believe that your project's meetings are as effective as they can be. Consider ideas for making better use of meeting time.

23. Review the status of your personal study program and your project or organization's improvement program every six months. Ask, How am I (or how are we) doing? Do we need to reengage and recommit? Do we need to change our approach? Do we need to involve project or senior management and request stronger sponsorship or other actions? Perform PDCA on status and gain some consensus about where to go from there. Act on your findings. Establish near-term milestones and status them weekly.

24. Make sure that the requirements are used and that they do not become "shelf ware." Enlist the support of the developers, and with management, articulate the expectation that the requirements training provided to them is an integral element of the expected success.

25. Increase the visibility of requirements gathering—make sure that all developers know when they are seeing new or changing requirements and that they must communicate this information to the project CCB; otherwise, the project is in jeopardy of getting out of control.

A Requirements Mandala

A "mandala" is a diagram—a circle divided into four quadrants, each with symbology. It provides a map that sums up where an individual or organization is and where it is going.

Figure 10.2 provides a mandala related to requirements engineering.

The requirements mandala may help you visualize some next steps that you'll want to take. I purposely have not provided candidate lists of things to include for each quadrant—this should be your own creation. In the east quadrant, list some requirements practices you have used in the past or that have been applied on your project or in your organization. In the south quadrant, list some feeds to an improved situation—ideas about better

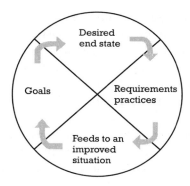

Figure 10.2 A requirements mandala.

practices that might be applied. In the west quadrant, list goals that you want to achieve by applying more effective practices. In the north quadrant, list characteristics of the desired end state—personal goals, project objectives, organizational goals, or business objectives you want to achieve or support.

This tool provides you an opportunity to reflect on all that you have done in previous and current experiences, as well as what you have read in this book and have learned in other ways. Each focal point provides an opportunity for questions and ideas. Take a few moments to list some things in each quadrant and reflect on them. In addition, have some discussions about this among the members of your task, project, or organizational team. This may lead to some useful directions. Perhaps everyone should take time to draw his or her own mandala.

Summary

RAs and engineers are in a strategic position to improve project results and success rates. Requirements are the basis for all of the follow-on work that is done on systems and software engineering projects. Improving the requirements practices being used can have a huge pay off. Be bold in offering your experience, energy, and insights.

Case Study

This case study is an example of how an effective RM process and adherence to it can make resolution of requirements interpretation issues go smoothly, even when the requirements change during the development effort.

A customer challenged the implementation of a software requirement as not meeting the intent of the higher-level system requirement during a design review on a project. The customer challenged the software requirement as being deficient against the parent system requirement, but acknowledged that the design did meet the software requirement. The software requirements for the system had already been through the software requirements review and approved by the customer following the project's RM process. The customer opened an action item in the design review as a mechanism to formally document the software requirement interpretation issue. At this stage of the design process, we knew more about the customer's environment and agreed (off the record) that they had a valid concern. We were too far along in the development process to make the design changes necessary to address this action item in this release of the product as the software requirements had already been approved. Our RM process dictated that an enhancement be submitted against the approved software requirement to be addressed in a future release of the product. This allows the project to continue against the current cost and schedule.

Following our system engineering process, we documented several solutions to address the problem. Solutions included modifying the design to address the new interpretation and proposing a manual process overlay with the existing design to address the issue opened by the customer. Cost and schedule estimates were laid out for each of the solutions. Senior engineering management was briefed on the issue, the original requirements, and the proposed solutions. Management agreed that we could not impact the approved schedule and budget given the design satisfied the approved software requirement. Our management team had gotten into trouble on a previous contract for trying to be too responsive to the customer's request, resulting in late delivery and cost overrun. Management was determined not to repeat that mistake.

We took the proposed solution to the action item back to the customer at the design review closure meeting. We pointed out via trace reports that we had formally decomposed the system requirements into software requirements. The decomposed requirements satisfied the intent to the best of our knowledge at the time of approval. The software requirements were approved as part of existing software requirements review. We presented the formal signature page as proof of this approval.

We had now established that the customer had ownership in this issue. When they saw the proposed options, they selected the one with the least amount of schedule and cost impact, the manual process overlay. The action was closed with a recommendation to propose the design change when the preplanned product improvement phase of the contract was bid. We acknowledged that the requirement did not address the customer's issue as raised during the design review, but the issue had not been raised during the requirement review.

By following our RM process we were able to avert a large cost and schedule impact to the program. The customer took ownership with us on the problem. We developed a short-term low-to-no cost plan and agreed to include the permanent solution in the next version of the product. It was tempting to say, "yes Mr. Customer, you have a valid point and we will modify the design to satisfy your need," but this would have deviated from our process and jeopardized contract completion within the planned schedule and cost. If it had been a critical requirement, we would have asked for approval from the customer for a cost and schedule replan as a new requirement was being raised after approval of the requirements.

Don Young
Requirements engineer
Telelogic Corporation

References

[1]   Humphrey, W. S., *Introduction to the Personal Software Process,* Reading, MA: Addison-Wesley, 1997.

[2]   Humphrey, W. S., *Introduction to the Team Software Process*, Reading, MA: Addison-Wesley, 2000.

[3]   Six Sigma Qualtec, *QI Story: Tools and Techniques, A Guidebook to Problem Solving,* 3rd ed, 1999. Copies can be ordered by calling (480) 586-2600.

Glossary

Allocation   Assigning each requirement to a component of the system where it will be implemented.

Application   The use of capabilities (services and facilities) provided by an information system to satisfy a set of user requirements, such as word processing.

Architecture   The underlying structure of a system.

Artifact   A document representing the result of effort. Artifacts are often referred to as examples of work products needed to provide evidence in support of assessments.

Attribute   A characteristic of a requirement that is useful in sorting, classifying, or managing requirements.

Baseline   A specification or product that has been formally reviewed and agreed on and thereafter serves as the basis for further development. It is changed only through formal change control procedures.

Business requirements   The essential activities of an enterprise. Business requirements are derived from business goals (the objectives of the enterprise). Business scenarios may be used as a technique for understanding business requirements. A key factor in the success of a system is the extent to which the system supports the business requirements and facilitates an organization in achieving them.

Business rules   The policies, conditions, and constraints of the business activities supported by a system; the decision processes, guidelines, and controls behind functional requirements (e.g., procedures, definitions, relationships and workflows in the business, and knowledge needed to perform actions).

Business scenario   A technique that can be used to understand an enterprise or organization. A business scenario describes the business process, application, or set of applications, the business and technology environment, the people and computing components that execute the scenario, and the desired outcome of proper execution.

Business system Hardware, software, policy statements, procedures, and people that together implement a business function.

Client An application component that requests services from a server.

Commercial-off-the-shelf An item of hardware or software that has been produced by a contractor and is available for general purchase.

Complexity The degree to which a system has requirements, a design, or an implementation that is difficult.

Configuration management A discipline that applies technical and administrative direction and surveillance to (a) identify and document the functional and physical characteristics of a configuration item; (b) control changes to those characteristics; and (c) record and report changes to processing and implementation status.

Constraint A necessary attribute of a system that specifies legislative, legal, political, policy, procedural, moral, technology, or interface limitations.

Customer The person(s) with the funds to pay for the project or its end product. The customer is not necessarily the user.

Customer need The set of requirements desired by a customer.

Decomposition Breaking apart the attributes of a customer need (the requirements of a system) so that they can be addressed.

Defect A variance from a desired product attribute.

Defect prevention Technologies and techniques (e.g., SPC) that minimize the risk of making errors in deliverables.

Defect removal Activities that find and correct defects in deliverables.

Defect removal efficiency The ratio of development defects to customer defects.

Derived requirement A requirement that is further refined from a primary source requirement or from a higher-level derived requirement, or a requirement that results from choosing a specific implementation or system element.

Design The process of defining the architecture, components, interfaces, and other characteristics of a system.

Design pattern A description of a problem and its proposed solution that indicates when to apply the solution and the consequences. See Gamma et al., *Design Patterns* (Reading, MA: Addison-Wesley, 1995).

Development The process of transforming a design into hardware and software components.

Domain expert An individual who has been working in a particular field for an extensive period of time and who is trained in that area. A domain expert is often referred to as a subject matter expert, or SME.

Enterprise　The highest level in an organization.

Feasibility study　An analysis that provides an initial understanding of the cost, viability, high-level technical architecture, and requirements of a capability or system.

Framework　A basic structure of ideas or frame of reference.

Function　A useful capability provided by one or more components of a system.

Function point　A measure of the complexity of software development.

Functional requirement　A necessary attribute in a system that specifies what the system or one of its products must do.

Functional specification or document　A comprehensive collection of the characteristics of a system and the capabilities it will make available to the users. It provides a detailed analysis of the data the system will be expected to manipulate. It may include a detailed definition of the user interfaces of the system.

Gold plating　Adding features and capabilities to systems when they are not required by the system specification or the real requirements.

Information system　The computer-based portion of a business system.

Information technology　An applied science utilizing hardware and software to support the transfer of ideas.

Institutionalization　The building of infrastructure and corporate culture that support methods, practices, and procedures so that they are the ongoing way of doing business, even after those who originally defined them are gone.

Interoperability　The ability of two or more systems or components to exchange and use information.

Iterate　To repeat a sequence of operations to yield results that are successively closer to a desired result.

Interface　The interaction or communication between independent systems or components of systems.

Integrated product team　A group that includes customers and developers and blends perspectives into a functioning or unified whole. The joint team recommended in this book is an example of an IPT.

Life cycle　The period of time that begins when a system is conceived and ends when the system is no longer available.

Life-cycle model　A framework of processes and activities concerned with evolving a system that also acts as a common reference for communication and understanding among the participants in the effort.

Major defect   A problem that precludes effective use of a work product, such as a design deficiency or discovery of conflicting requirements.

Mandala   A diagram that provides a mapping for an individual or an organization that sums up where one is and where one is going.

Measures of effectiveness   High-level indicators of how well the system performs its functions, defined in the terms and with the same dimensionality of the requirements document. For example, if we are dealing with a city's metro system, we may specify that a typical user during rush hour should not wait more than some period of time, on the average, for the next train.

Mechanism   A way to get something done or to achieve a result.

Method   A way, technique, process, plan, mechanism, body of skills or techniques, discipline, practice, system, model, framework, capability, or procedure for doing something.

Methodology   A body of methods, rules, and postulates employed by a discipline; a particular procedure or set of procedures.

Minor defect   A problem that doesn't preclude effective use of a work product, such as a formatting issue, spelling error, language usage problem, or acronym or definition not provided or explained.

Model   A representation of reality that is intended to facilitate understanding.

Nonfunctional requirement   A necessary attribute in a system that specifies how functions are to be performed, often referred to in systems engineering as the "ilities" (e.g., reliability, reusability, portability, maintainability, compatibility, verifiability, predictability, safety, information assurance, resource efficiency, completeness, and human factors).

Partnering   A structured process designed to create an atmosphere of commitment, cooperation, and collegial problem solving among organizations and individuals who will work together.

Performance requirement   A necessary attribute of a system that specifies how well the system or one of its products must perform a function, along with the conditions under which the function is performed.

Practice   The performance of work activities repeatedly so as to become proficient; the usual way of doing something so as to produce a good result.

Prioritized requirements   Categorization of the real requirements into subsets according to criticality of need for a system or capability.

Problem frame   The definition of a problem class. A problem frame consists of a frame diagram, domain characteristics, and the frame concern. See Michael Jackson, *Problem Frames: Analysing and Structuring Software Development Problems* (New York: Addison-Wesley, 2000).

Process   A set of activities that results in the accomplishment of a task or achieving of an outcome.

Process capability   The range of expected results that can be achieved by following a process.

Process description   A document that describes a process, including, for example, its purpose, customers, customer requirements, entrance criteria, inputs, outputs, exit criteria, tasks involved and who is responsible for each, measurement indicators, resources needed, and version.

Process flowchart   A diagram that shows a step-by-step series of actions through a procedure using connecting lines and a set of standard symbols adopted by an organization.

Process model   A framework for identifying, defining, and organizing the functional strategies, rules, and processes needed to manage and support the way an organization does or wants to do business. The process model provides a graphical and textual framework for organizing the data and processes into manageable groups to facilitate their shared use and control throughout the organization.

Project   An undertaking focused on developing or maintaining a product. Typically a project has its own funding, accounting, and delivery schedule.

Project champion   An advocate who is very familiar with the set of real customer needs for a system who provides an active role in the development effort, facilitating the tasks of the development team.

Project or program manager   The role with total business responsibility for a project, ultimately responsible to a customer.

Prototyping   A technique for building a quick and rough version of a desired system or parts of that system. The prototype illustrates the capabilities of the system to users and designers. It serves as a communications mechanism to allow reviewers to understand interactions with the system. It enables them to identify problems and consider ways to improve a system. It sometimes gives an impression that developers are further along than is actually the case, giving users an overly optimistic impression of completion possibilities!

Quality   Meeting real customer needs.

Quality culture   The presence of an attitude of continuous improvement and customer satisfaction throughout an organization.

Quality function deployment   A methodology originally conceived in Japan in the 1970s that provides an opportunity for the user and developer of a system to understand requirements more fully and to prioritize them.

Rational Unified Process   A methodology advocated by Rational Software, Inc. (now IBM, Inc.)

Real requirements   Requirements that reflect the verified needs for a particular system or capability.

Requirement   A necessary attribute in a system; also a statement that identifies a capability, characteristic, or quality factor of a system in order for it to have value and utility to a user.

Requirements allocation   Assignment of requirements to architectural components of a system (e.g., a hardware or software configuration item, training, or documentation). Sometimes referred to as flowdown.

Requirements analysis   A structured (organized) method to understand the attributes that will satisfy a customer need.

Requirements baseline   The set of requirements associated with a particular release of a product or system.

Requirements definition   A detailed description in general, rather than functional, terms of the attributes needed in a system.

Requirements derivation   Obtaining requirements for a system from sources provided by the customer.

Requirements document   A repository of the attributes in a system.

Requirements elicitation   The process of drawling forth and bringing out requirements based upon information provided by the customer.

Requirements engineering   An area within the broader field of systems and software engineering that focuses on the RE process.

Requirements leakage   The addition or leaking in of unofficial requirements to the requirements specification, when the requirements are not really needed.

Requirements management   Tracking requirements status and change activity and tracing requirements to the various phases and products of the development effort.

Requirements pattern   A framework for the requirements set that supports the product or service needs, minimizing gaps in knowledge that might cause project failure. The requirements pattern helps to capture all types of requirements, independent of the kind of design, implementation, or method used to capture and identify the requirements. See P. Ferdinandi, *A Requirements Pattern: Succeeding in the Internet Economy* (Boston: Addison-Wesley, 2002).

Requirements process   A full system life-cycle set of actions concerning the necessary attributes of systems. The requirements process involves understanding customer needs and expectations (requirements elicitation), requirements analysis and specification, requirements prioritization, requirements derivation, partitioning and allocation, requirements tracing, requirements management, requirements verification, and requirements validation.

Requirements traceability   The ability to determine the customer need to requirement relationship or connectivity, or the relationship of a parent requirement to a child and vice versa. The ability to trace a requirement throughout the system development process, from requirements specification to design, to system component through testing and system documentation. Absolutely critical for all systems.

Requirements verification   Independent assurance that requirements are addressed and met in a system.

Requirements verification matrix   An analysis that shows the verification method for each requirement.

Reuse   Reuse has two meanings: (1) to take object X (e.g., an object, subroutine, or COTS software) that was done by Y and use it directly in another project; and (2) to tailor a developed work product (a specification, a plan, or process for example).

Risk   The possibility of suffering loss.

Robust architecture   An underlying structure of a system that can readily meet and adapt to real requirements.

Role   A set of defined responsibilities that may be assumed by one or more individuals.

Scalability   The capability to grow to accommodate increased work loads.

Scenario   A technique used for understanding requirements.

Senior management   A role sufficiently high in the organization that its primary focus is on the long-term vitality of the organization.

Software quality   Software that combines the characteristics of low defect rates and high user satisfaction.

Specification   A document that describes technical requirements and verification procedures for items, materials, and services. An output of the requirements analysis process.

Stakeholder   Anyone who has an interest in a system or in its possessing qualities that meet particular needs.

Stated requirements   Requirements provided by a customer at the beginning of a system or software development effort. To be distinguished from real requirements.

Subject matter expert   An individual who has been working in a particular field for an extensive period of time and who is trained in that area. A subject matter expert is often referred to as a domain expert.

Supplier   An organization that contracts with a buyer to provide a system.

System   An integrated set of people, products, and processes that provide a capability to satisfy a customer need.

System life cycle   The set of activities involved in understanding a customer need, defining and analyzing requirements, preparing a design, developing a system, and testing, implementing, operating, and maintaining it, ending in its retirement.

Systems engineering   A technical and management discipline that translates a customer need into a system that meets the customer need. Another source states system engineering is the iterative, but controlled, process in which user needs are understood and evolved into an operational system. The role of systems engineering is: technical authority on a project; single interface to customer and project; architecture and system design; requirements derivation, allocation and interpretation; and others.

Tailoring   The activity of modifying, elaborating, or adapting a process or document for another use. Reuse of tailored artifacts saves time and money and is an advantage of a process-oriented approach.

Teamwork   Proactive support of one another; necessary for success of any significant undertaking. Physical collocation facilitates teamwork and may be a prerequisite to success.

TEAMWORKS   An environment or work setting where working together as an effective team is valued and appreciated

Technical performance measures   Indicators of how well the system works and how well the requirements are met; estimates or measures of the values of essential performance parameters. Technical performance measures are used to evaluate the impact to cost, schedule, and technical effort.

Technical specification   A comprehensive collection of the details of how a system will be implemented, including the technical architecture (hardware and software), decomposition of the system into subsystems, identification of common modules that will be developed, and other details requiring definition in order to allow development of the system.

Technique   A set of rules to follow to accomplish a task, a treatment of technical details, a body of technical methods, or a method of accomplishing a desired aim.

Technology insertion   Adding new technology to a system throughout the system life cycle.

Tool   Something used to facilitate performing an operation or practicing a process or activity.

Trade study   An analysis of alternative courses of action in which a balancing of factors, all of which are not obtainable at the same time, is performed.

Unified Modeling Language (UML)   A general-purpose notation (a way to document) that describes the static and dynamic behavior of a system. It is not a design method or a development process.

Use case   A picture of action(s) a system performs depicting the actor(s).

Use case driven   Describing the behavior of a system based on how the users interact with the system.

Use case model   A description of the functional behavior of a system that includes all of the actors and all of the use cases through which the actors interact with the system.

User   The individual or group who uses a system in its environment.

User friendly   Easy to use.

User perspective   Maintaining the view of what the user wants, needs, prefers, is happy with, and can use.

User satisfaction   Quality of clients being pleased with a vendor's products, quality levels, ease of use, and support.

Validation   A process for confirming that the real requirements are implemented in the delivered system.

Verification   A process for assuring that the design solution satisfies the requirements.

Verification methods   The approaches used to perform verification: test, inspection, demonstration, and analysis.

View   A perspective of a system, such as the functional, implementation, or physical view.

Work product   Something produced or created as a result of systems or software development activity.

List of Acronyms

AI	action item
AKA	also known as
AP	action plan
APM	Association of Project Managers (in the UK)
BOE	basis of estimate
BSI	British Standards Institute
BT	British Telecommunications
CARE	Computer-Aided Requirements Engineering, a requirements tool marketed by Sophist Technologies (Germany)
CCB	configuration control board or change control board
CM	configuration management
CMM®	Capability Maturity Model
CMMI®	Capability Maturity Model Integration
CMP	configuration management plan
CMWG	configuration management working group
CONOPS	concept of operations
CORE	a requirements tool marketed by Vitech Corporation
COTS	commercial off-the-shelf software
CR	change request
DACS	Data and Analysis Center for Software
DAR	decision analysis resolution
DES	Defense Enterprise Solutions
DoD	U.S. Department of Defense
DOORS	Dynamic Object-Oriented Requirements System, a requirements tool marketed by Telelogic Corporation
DP	defect prevention

EIA	Electronic Industries Association (industry standards group)
EPG	engineering process group
EPI	engineering process improvement
EPIP	engineering process improvement plan
ESE	engineering software environment
FD	functional document
FP	function point
FPA	function point analysis
GSA	General Services Administration
GUI	graphical user interface
ICRE	IEEE Conference on Requirements Engineering
IDEF	integrated definition for functional modeling
IE	impact estimation
IEEE	Institute of Electrical and Electronic Engineers
IFPUG	International Function Points User Group
ILS	integrated logistics support
INCOSE	International Council on Systems Engineering
IT	information technology
ISO	International Standards Organization
IV&V	independent verification and validation
JAD	joint application development
JT	joint team
KPA	key process area
MDD	model-driven development
MQ	maturity questionnaire
NGC	Northrop Grumman Corporation
O&M	operation and maintenance
OMA	Object Management Architecture
OMG	Object Management Group
OO	object oriented
OOSE	object-oriented software engineering
OSD/ AT&L	Office of the Secretary of Defense, Acquisition, Technology, and Logistics
PA	process area

PAL	process asset library; purpose, agenda, and limit (in connection with a meeting)
PBS	product breakdown structure
PD	process description
PDCA	plan-do-check-act
PI	process improvement
PIP	process improvement plan
PM	program manager, project manager
PMP	program management plan, project management plan
PP	project planning or program plan
PR	peer review
PRINCE	a registered project management methodology supported by the APM, closely allied with the British Standards Institute
PSP	personal software process
QA	quality assurance
QAI	Quality Assurance Institute
QFD	quality function deployment
QI	quality improvement
QIDW	quality in daily work (also referred to as process management)
QM	quantitative management
QMB	quality management board
R&D	research and development
RA	requirements analyst
RAD	rapid application design, rapid application development
RD	requirements document; requirements development (a process area in the CMMI®)
RDM	requirements-driven management
RE	requirements
REQM	requirements management (acronym used in the CMMI® for this process area)
RESG	Requirements Engineering Specialist Group (in the UK)
RFC	request for change
RFI	request for information
RFP	request for proposals

RFQ	request for quote
ReqPro	Requisite Pro (a requirements tool marketed by IBM [formerly Rational] Corporation)
RM	requirements management
RMA	Risk Manager's Assistant (a risk tool)
ROI	return on investment
RP	requirements plan
RRB	requirements review board
RT	Requirements Tracer, a requirements tool marketed by Teledyne Brown Engineering (aka Xtie-RT)
RTM	requirements traceability matrix
RTM Workshop	a requirements tool marketed by Integrated Chipware
RUP	rational unified process
RWG	requirements working group
S&PE	Systems and Process Engineering Organization in DES, NGC
SA	system architecture
SCAMPI	Standard CMMI® Assessment for Managing Process Improvement
SCE	software capability evaluation
SDP	software development plan
SE	systems engineering
SE-CMM®	System Engineering Capability Maturity Model (EPIC)
SEI	Software Engineering Institute
SEMP	systems engineering management plan
SEP	systems engineering process
SEPG	systems or software engineering process group
SLA	service-level agreement
SLATE	an automated requirements tool
SLC	systems life cycle
SME	subject matter expert
SOW	statement of work
SPE or PE	software product engineering
Spec	specification
SPI	software process improvement
SPIP	software process improvement plan

SPR	Software Productivity Research, a wholly owned subsidiary of Artemis Management Systems
SS	system specification
STD	standard
SRR	system requirements review
SRS	system or software requirements specification
SSQ	Society for Software Quality
STQE	*Software Testing & Quality Engineering* (a periodical;. see www.stqemagazine.com.
SUNA	scenario-based user needs analysis
SW	software
SW-CMM®	capability maturity model for software (developed by the SEI)
SWE	software engineering
Synergy RM	a requirements tool marketed by CMD Corporation
TBQ	taxonomy-based questionnaire
TQM	total quality management
TSP	team software process
UBL	Universal Business Language
UML	Unified Modeling Language
URL	uniform resource locator
V&V	verification and validation
Vital Link	a requirements tool marketed by Compliance Automation
WBS	work breakdown structure
Xtie-RT	requirements tracer, a requirements tool marketed by Teledyne Brown Engineering
ZF	Zachman framework

Bibliography

ABT Corporation, "Core Competencies for Project Managers," White Paper, 2000. See www.tsepm.com/may00/art5.htm.

Adams, James L., *Conceptual Blockbusting: A Guide to Better Ideas* (3rd ed.), Reading, MA: Perseus Books, 1986.

Adhikari, Richard, "Development Process is a Mixed-Bag Effort," *Client/Server Computing*, February 1996, pp. 65–72.

Afors, Cristina, and Marilyn Zuckermann Michaels, "A Quick Accurate Way to Determine Customer Needs," American Society for Quality: *Quality Progress*, July 2001, pp. 82–87.

Alexander, Ian, Web site, easyweb.easynet.co.uk/~iany/index.htm.

Alexander, Ian F., and Richard Stevens, *Writing Better Requirements*, London, UK: Addison-Wesley, 2002.

Alexander, Ian, and Andrew Farncombe, John Boardman Associates (JBA), Stakeholder Analysis Template, Systems Engineering Foundation Course, 2003.

American Society for Quality (ASQ) Web site: www.asq.org/.

Andriole, Stephen J., *Managing System Requirements: Methods, Tools, and Cases*, New York: McGraw Hill, 1996.

Bach, James, "James Bach on Risk-Based Testing: How to Conduct Heuristic Risk Analysis," *Software Testing and Quality Engineering (STQE) Magazine*, November/December 1999, pp. 23–29.

Bachmann, Felix, Len Bass, Gary Chastek, Patrick Donohoe, and Fabio Peruzzi, *The Architecture Based Design Method*, Software Engineering Institute, Technical Report CMU/SEI-2000-TR-001, ESC-TR-2000-001, 2000.

Bass, Len, Paul Clements, and Rick Kazman, *Software Architecture in Practice*, Reading, MA: Addison-Wesley, 1998.

Bennis, Warren, and Patricia Ward Biederman, *Genius: The Secrets of Creative Collaboration*, Reading, MA: Perseus Books, 1997.

Bentley, Colin, *PRINCE® 2: A Practical Handbook*, Woburn, MA: Butterworth-Heinemann, 1997.

Berezuk, Steven P., with Brad Appleton, *Software Configuration Management Patterns: Effective Teamwork, Practical Integration*, Boston, MA: Addison-Wesley, 2003.

Bicknell, Barbara A, and Kris D., Bicknell, *The Road Map to Repeatable Success: Using QFD to Implement Change*, Boca Raton, FL: CRC Press, 1995.

Boehm, Barry W., *Software Engineering Economics*, Englewood Cliffs, NJ: Prentice Hall, 1981.

Boehm, Barry, "Spiral Model of Software Development and Enhancement," *IEEE Computer*, May 1988 (also published in Barry Boehm, *Software Risk Management*, IEEE Computer Society Press, 1989, p. 26).

Boehm, Barry W., WinWin Spiral Model & Groupware Support System, University of Southern California, 1998. Available at sunset.usc.edu/research/WINWIN/index.html.

Boehm, Barry, Alexander Egyed, Julie Kwan, Dan Port, Archita Shah, and Ray Madachy, "Using the WinWin Spiral Model: A Case Study," IEEE *Computer*, July 1998, pp. 33–44.

Boehm, B. W., and Hoh In, "Identifying Quality-Requirements Conflicts," *IEEE Software*, March 1996, pp. 25–35.

Boehm, Barry W., and Kevin J. Sullivan, "Software Economics," *CrossTalk, The Journal of Defense Software Engineering*, December 1999. See www.stsc.hill.af.mil/.

Boehm, Barry, and Richard Turner, "Observations on Balancing Discipline and Agility," Excerpted from *Balancing Agility and Discipline: A Guide to the Perplexed*, Boston, MA: Addison-Wesley, 2003.

Boehm, Barry, and Wilfred J. Hansen, "The Spiral Model as a Tool for Evolutionary Acquisition," A joint effort of the University of Southern California Center for Software Engineering and the Software Engineering Institute (SEI), *CrossTalk*, May 2001, pp. 4–11.

Brodman, Judith G., and Donna L. Johnson, *The LOGOS Tailored CMM for Small Businesses, Small Organizations, and Small Projects*, LOGOS International, Inc. www.tiac.net/users/johnsond.

Brodman, Judith G., and Donna L. Johnson, "Return on Investment (ROI) from Software Process Improvement as Measured by U.S. Industry," *Software Process Improvement and Practice*, Sussex, England: John Wiley & Sons Ltd., 1995, pp. 35–47.

Buede, Dennis M., *The Engineering Design of Systems: Models and Methods*, New York: John Wiley & Sons, 2000.

Butler, K., "The Economic Benefits of Software Process Improvement," *CrossTalk*, 1995, pp. 28–35.

Capability Maturity Model Integration (CMMI) Project. See www.sei.cum. edu/cmmi/.

Carr, Frank et al, *Partnering in Construction: A Practical Guide to Project Success*, Chicago, IL: American Bar Association Publishing, 1999.

Clark, Bradford K., "Effects of Process Maturity on Development Effort," Available at www.ralphyoung.net/goodarticles/.

Cockburn, Alistair, *Writing Effective Use Cases*, Boston, MA: Addison-Wesley, 2001.

Data & Analysis Center for Software (DACS), DACS Technical Reports. See www.dacs.dtic.mil/techs/tr.shtml.

Daughtrey, Taz (ed.), *Fundamental Concepts for the Software Quality Engineer*, Milwaukee, WI: ASQ Quality Press, 2002.

Davis, Alan M., *Just Enough Requirements Management* (Redmond, WA: Microsoft Press, forthcoming).

Davis, Alan M., "The Art of Requirements Triage," *IEEE Computer*, IEEE Computer Society Press, Vol. 36, No. 3, March 2003, pp. 42–49.

Davis, Alan M., *Software Requirements: Objects, Functions, & States*, Upper Saddle River, NJ: Prentice Hall PTR, 1993.

Deming, W. Edwards, *Out of the Crisis*, MIT Center for Advanced Engineering Study, 1986.

Dion, R., "Process Improvement and the Corporate Balance Sheet," IEEE Software, October 1993, pp. 28–35.

Eckes, George, *Making Six Sigma Last: Managing the Balance Between Cultural and Technical Change*, New York: John Wiley & Sons, Inc., 2001.

Electronic Industries Alliance (EIA), *EIA Standard 632 Processes for Engineering a System*, Arlington, VA, 1998.

Electronic Industries Association (EIA), EIA Standard 649, National Consensus Standard for Configuration Management, Arlington, VA, 2001.

Engineering Process Improvement Collaboration (EPIC), *A Systems Engineering Capability Maturity Model*, Version 1.1. Pittsburgh, PA: Software Engineering Institute, Carnegie-Mellon University, 1995, Available at www.sei.cmu.edu/pub/documents/95.reports/pdf/mm003.95.pdf.

Federal Information Processing Standards Publications (FIPS PUBS) 183, Integration Definition for Function Modeling (IDEF0). Available from www.itl.nist.gov/fipspubs/idef02.doc.

Feldmann, Clarence G., *The Practical Guide to Business Process Reengineering Using IDEF0*, New York: Dorset House, 1998.

Ferdinandi, Patricia L., *A Requirements Pattern: Succeeding in the Internet Economy*, Boston, MA: Addison-Wesley, 2002.

Fowler, Martin, *Analysis Patterns: Reusable Object Models*, Reading, MA: Addison-Wesley, 1996.

Fowler, Martin, *UML Distilled: Applying The Standard Object Modeling Language*, Reading, MA: Addison Wesley, 1997.

Gaffney, Steven, *Just Be Honest*, Arlington, VA: JMG Publishing, 2002.

Gaffney, Steven Web site, www.StevenGaffney.com.

Gamma, Erich, et al, *Design Patterns*, Reading, MA: Addison-Wesley, 1995.

Garmus, David, and David Herron, *Function Point Analysis: Measurement Practices for Successful Software Projects,* Reading, MA: Addison-Wesley, 2001.

Gilb, Tom, *Impact Estimation Tables: Understanding Complex Technology Quantitatively*, November 1997. White Paper available at Gilb's Web site: www.gilb.com.

Gilb, Tom, "Planning to Get the Most Out of Inspection," in *Fundamental Concepts for the Software Quality Engineer*, Taz Daughtrey (ed.), p. 178.

Gilb, Tom, *Principles of Software Engineering Management*, Harlow, England: Addison-Wesley, 1988.

Gilb, Tom, and Dorothy Graham, *Software Inspection*, Boston, MA: Addison-Wesley, 1993.

GOAL/QPC materials. See www.goalqpc.com.

Gottesdiener, Ellen, *Requirements by Collaboration*, Reading, MA: Addison-Wesley, 2002.

Gottesdiener, Ellen, "Top Ten Ways Project Teams Misuse Use Cases—and How to Correct Them," Available at www.therationaledge.com/content/jun_02/t_misuseUseCases_eg.jsp.

Gottesdiener, Ellen, and Jim Bruce, "The Value of Standardization of Business Rules," Available at www.ebgconsulting.com/BusRulesObjectMagsHTML.html.

Gottesdiener, Ellen, "Capturing Business Rules," *Software Development Magazine*, Vol. 7, No. 12, December 1999. Available at www.sdmagazine.com/.

Gottesdiener, Ellen, "Turning Rules Into Requirements," *Application Development Trends*, July 1999. Available at www.adtmag.com/ print.asp?id=3806.

Grady, Jeffrey O., *System Validation and Verification*, Boca Raton, FL: CRC Press, 1997.

Grady, Jeffrey O., *Systems Requirements Analysis*, New York: McGraw-Hill, 1993.

Hadden, Rita, *Leading Culture Change in Your Software Organization*, 2003.

Hadden, Rita, "How Scalable Are CMM Key Practices?" *CROSSTALK*, April 1998, pp. 18–23. See also www.ppc.com.

Hall, David C., "Best Practices: Using a Risk Management Maturity-Level Model," *Software Quality Magazine*, Vol. 2, No. 4., October 2002, Available at www.sqmmagazine.com/issues/2002-04/maturity.html.

Harmon, Paul, and Mark Watson, *Understanding UML: The Developers Guide*, San Francisco, CA: Morgan Kaufman Publishers, Inc, 1997.

Hay, David C., *Data Model Patterns: Conventions of Thought*, New York: Dorset House, 1996.

Hay, David C., *Requirements Analysis: From Business Views to Architecture*, Upper Saddle River, NJ: Prentice Hall PTR, 2003.

Hay, John, *Requirements Analysis—From Business Views to Architecture*, Englewood Cliffs, NJ: Prentice Hall, 2002.

Herbsleb, James, Anita Carlton, James Rozum, Jane Siegel, and David Zubrow, *Benefits of CMM-Based Software Process Improvement: Initial Results*, Technical Report CMU/SEI-94-TR-013, Pittsburgh, PA: Software Engineering Institute, August 1994.

Higgins, Stewart A., et al, "Managing Requirements for Medical Information Technology Products," *IEEE Software* 2003: 20(1), 26–33. See www.computer.org/software.

Hooks, Ivy F., and Kristin A. Farry, *Customer-Centered Products: Creating Successful Products through Smart Requirements Management*, New York: AMACOM (publishing arm of The American Management Association), 2001.

Hooks, Ivy, "Writing Good Requirements: A One-Day Tutorial," Sponsored by the Washington Metropolitan Area (WMA) Chapter of the International Council on Systems Engineering (INCOSE), McLean, VA: Compliance Automation, Inc., June 1997.

Humphrey, Watts S., *Introduction to the Personal Software Process*, Reading, MA: Addison-Wesley, 1997.

Humphrey, Watts S., *Introduction to the Team Software Process*, Reading, MA: Addison-Wesley, 2000.

Humphrey, W. S., et al, "Software Process Improvement at Hughes Aircraft," IEEE Software, August 1991, pp. 11–23.

Inmon, W. H., John A. Zachman, and Jonathan C. Geiger, *Data Stores, Data Warehousing, and the Zachman Framework: Managing Enterprise Knowledge*, New York: McGraw Hill, 1997.

Institute of Electrical and Electronics Engineers (IEEE), IEEE Conference on Requirements Engineering (ICRE) Web site: conferences.computer.org/RE/.

Institute of Electrical and Electronics Engineers (IEEE), IEEE 1220, *IEEE Guide for Information Technology-System Definition-Concept of Operations (ConOps) Document*, IEEE, New York, 1998.

Institute of Electrical and Electronics Engineers (IEEE), IEEE 1320.1, *IEEE Standard for Functional Modeling Language—Syntax and Semantics for IDEF0,* IEEE Computer Society, 1998.

Institute of Electrical and Electronics Engineers (IEEE), J-STD-016-1995, *Standard for Information Technology Software Life Cycle Processes Software Development Acquirer-Supplier Agreement* (Issued for Trail Use), New York: The Institute of Electrical and Electronics Engineers, Inc., 1995.

Institute of Electrical and Electronics Engineers (IEEE) Software Engineering Standards Committee, IEEE STD 830-1998, *IEEE Recommended Practice for Software Requirements Specifications,* IEEE Computer Society, June 25, 1998.

Institute of Electrical and Electronics Engineers (IEEE) Software Engineering Standards Committee, IEEE Std 1233a-1998, *IEEE Guide for Developing Software Requirements Specifications,* IEEE Computer Society, December 8, 1998.

Institute of Electrical and Electronic Engineers (IEEE) Standard 12207, Software Life Cycle Processes, New York: IEEE, 1998.

International Association of Facilitators Web site: www.iaf-world.org/.

International Council on Systems Engineering (INCOSE), INCOSE *INSIGHT* (*Journal of Systems Engineering*) Web site: www.incose.org/insight.html.

International Council on Systems Engineering (INCOSE), INCOSE national organization's Web site: www.incose.org/se-int/.

International Council on Systems Engineering (INCOSE), INCOSE Washington Metropolitan Area (WMA) Chapter Web site: www. incose-wma.org/info/.

International Function Point Users Group (IFPUG) Web site: www.ifpug.org.

Jackson, Michael, *Problem Frames: Analyzing and Structuring Software Development Problems,* London, UK: Addison-Wesley, 2001.

Jones, Capers, *Assessment and Control of Software Risks,* Englewood Cliffs, NJ: Prentice Hall, 1994.

Jones, Capers, *Estimating Software Costs,* New York: McGraw Hill, 1998.

Jones, Capers, "Positive and Negative Factors That Influence Software Productivity," Burlington, MA: Software Productivity Research, Inc., Version 2.0, October 15, 1998.

Jones, Capers, *Software Assessments, Benchmarks, and Best Practices,* Reading, MA: Addison-Wesley, 2000.

Jones, Capers, "Software Project Management in the 21st Century," *American Programmer,* Vol. 11, No. 2, February 1998. Also available at spr.com/news/articles.htm.

Jones, Capers, *Software Quality: Analysis and Guidelines for Success,* London: International Thomson Computer Press, 1997.

Jones, Capers, *Software Quality in 2000: What Works and What Doesn't*, January 18, 2000.

Jones Capers, "What It Means To Be 'Best in Class' for Software," Burlington, MA: Software Productivity Research (SPR), Inc., Version 5, February 10, 1998.

Korson, Timothy, "The Misuse of Use Cases: Managing Requirements," Available at www.korson-mcgregor.com/publications/korson/Korson9803 om.htm.

Kotonya, Gerald, and Ian Sommerville, *Requirements Engineering: Processes and Techniques*, Chichester, UK: John Wiley & Sons, 1998.

Kulak, Daryl, and Eamonn Guiney, *Use Cases: Requirements in Context*, New York: ACM Press, 2000.

Leffingwell, Dean, and Don Widrig, *Managing Software Requirements: A Unified Approach*, Reading, MA: Addison-Wesley, 2000.

Markert, Charles, *Partnering: Unleashing the Power of Teamwork*, 2002, briefing available from markert@facilitationcenter.com.

McConnell, Steve, *Software Project Survival Guide*, Redmond, Washington: Microsoft Press, 1998.

McGibbon, T., "A Business Case for Software Process Improvement Revised: Measuring Return on Investment from Software Engineering and Management," Contract Number SP0700-98-4000, Data & Analysis Center for Software (DACS), ITT Industries, Advanced Engineering and Sciences Division, Rome, NY, September 30, 1999. Available at www.dacs.dtic. mil/techs/roispi2/.

McKinney, Dorothy, "Six Translations between Software-Speak and Management-Speak," *IEEE Software* 2002: 19(6) 50–52. See www.computer. org/software.

Northrop Grumman Information Technology Defense Enterprise Solutions Press Release concerning CMMI Level 5. See www.irconnect.com/noc/pages/news_releases.mhtml?d=35405.

Northrop Grumman Information Technology Defense Enterprise Solutions, "The Road to CMM(I) Level 3," White Paper available from ralph.young@ngc.com.

Object Management Group (OMG), Introduction to the UML. See www. omg.org/gettingstarted/what_is_uml.htm.

Object Management Group (OMG), OMG Unified Modeling Language Specification, Version 1.4, September 2001 (566 pages). Available at www.omg.org/technology/documents/formal/mof.htm.

Palmer, James D., "Traceability," *Software Requirements Engineering*, R. H. Thayer and M. Dorfman (eds.), 1997, pp. 364–374.

Paulk, M. C., "Using the Software CMM with Good Judgment," ASQ *Software Quality Professional* Vol. 1, No. 3, June 1999, pp. 19–29. Available at www.sei.cmu.edu/publications/articles/paulk/judgment.html.

Paulk, Mark C., "Using the Software CMM with Good Judgment: Small Projects & Small Organizations," Presentation at the Washington, DC Chapter, Society for Software Quality (SSQ) Roundtable 1998, January 26, 1998.

Paulk, Mark C., Bill Curtis, Mary Beth Chrissis, and Charles V. Weber, *Capability Maturity Model for Software*, Version 1.1, February, 1993, Software Engineering Institute (SEI), Carnegie-Mellon University, Pittsburgh, PA, 1993. See www.sei.cmu.edu/publications/documents/93.reports/93.tr.024.html.

Porter-Roth, Bud, *Request for Proposal: A Guide to Effective RFP Development*, Boston, MA: Addison-Wesley, 2002.

Requirements Engineering Specialist Group (RESG) (in the UK) Web site: www.resg.org.uk/.

Robertson, Suzanne, and James Robertson, *Mastering the Requirements Process*, Harlow, England: Addison-Wesley, 1999.

Rogers, Everett M., *Diffusion of Innovations* (4th ed.), New York: The Free Press, 1995.

Ross, Jeanne W., and Peter Weill, "Six IT Decisions Your IT People Shouldn't Make," *Harvard Business Review*, November 2002, pp. 85–91.

Sabourin, Rob Web site, www.amibug.com/index.shtm.

Scholtes, P., B. Joiner, and B. Streibel, *The Team Handbook* (2nd ed.), Madison, WI: Oriel Inc., 2001.

Scott and Jaffee, *Empowerment: A Practical Guide for Success*.

Sharp, Helen, et al, "Stakeholder Identification in the Requirements Engineering Process," IEEE, 1999, pp. 387–391.

Six Sigma Qualtec, *QI Story: Tools and Techniques, A Guidebook to Problem Solving*, Third Edition, 1999. Call 480-586-2600 for information. See also www.ssqi.com/homepage.asp.

Smith, Preston G., and Donald G. Reinertsen, *Developing Products in Half the Time* (2nd ed.), New York: John Wiley & Sons, Inc., 1998.

Society for Software Quality Web site: www.ssq.org/.

Software Development Magazine, Web site: www.sdmagazine.com/.

Software Engineering Institute (SEI), *Taxonomy-Based Risk Identification*, Technical Report CMU/SEI-93-TR-6, Pittsburgh, PA: SEI, June 1993. See www.sei.cmu.edu/pub/documents/93.reports/pdf/tr06.93.pdf.

Software Productivity Research, Inc. Web site, www.spr.com.

Sommerville, Ian, *Software Engineering* (6th ed.), Reading, MA: Addison-Wesley, 2001.

Sommerville, Ian, and Pete Sawyer, *Requirements Engineering: A Good Practice Guide*, New York: John Wiley & Sons, 1997.

Sommerville, I., P. Sawyer, and S. Viller, "Viewpoints for Requirements Elicitation: A Practical Approach," *Proceedings of the 1998 International Conference on Requirements Engineering* (ICRE '98), April 6–10, 1998, Colorado Springs, CO, New York: IEEE Computer Society, 1998, pp. 74–81. See computer.org/proceedings/icre/8356/8356toc.htm.

Sorensen, Reed, *Comparison of Software Development Methodologies*, Software Technology Support Center, Jan 1995. Available at www.stsc.hill.af.mil/crosstalk/1995/jan/comparis.asp.

Thayer, Richard H., and Merlin Dorfman (eds.), *Software Requirements Engineering* (2nd ed. Revised), Los Alamitos, CA: IEEE Computer Society Press, 2000.

Thayer, Richard H., and Mildred C. Thayer, "Software Requirements Engineering Glossary," *Software Requirements Engineering* (2nd ed.), Richard H. Thayer and Merlin Dorfman (eds.), Los Alamitos, CA: IEEE Computer Society Press, 1997.

The Standish Group International, Inc., *CHAOS Chronicles 2003Report*, West Yarmouth, MA: The Standish Group International, Inc., 2002. See www.standishgroup.com.

The Standish Group International, Inc, *What are Your Requirements? 2003*, West Yarmouth, MA: The Standish Group International, Inc., 2002.

U.S. Army Corps of Engineers Integrated Product Team Web page. See www.usace.army.mil/ci/lcmis/lcmipt.html.

Walton, Mary, *The Deming Management Method*, New York: The Putnam Publishing Group, 1986.

Watts, F. B., *Engineering Document Control Handbook: Configuration Management in Industry* (2nd ed.), Park Ridge, NJ: Noyes Publications, 2000.

Waugh, Penny, Peer Review Participant and Peer Review Moderator Training Materials, Northrop Grumman Information Technology Defense Enterprise Solutions, 2002. Contact her at PWaugh@ngc.com.

Webster Bruce F., *Pitfalls of Object-Oriented Development*, M&T Books, 1995.

Weinberg, Gerald M., "Just Say No! Improving the Requirements Process," *American Programmer* (10) 1995:19–23.

Whitten, Neal, "Meet Minimum Requirements: Anything More Is Too Much," *PM Network*, September 1998.

Wiegers, Karl E., Web site, www.processimpact.com/.

Wiegers, Karl E., *Software Requirements* (2nd ed.), Redmond, WA: Microsoft Press, 2003.

Wiegers, Karl E., "Do Your Inspections Work?" *StickyMinds.com*, June 24, 2002. See www.stickyminds.com.

Wiegers, Karl E., *Peer Reviews in Software: A Practical Guide*, Boston, MA: Addison-Wesley, 2002.

Wiegers, Karl E., "Inspecting Requirements," *StickyMinds.com*, July 30, 2001. See www.processimpact.com/.

Wiegers, Karl E., "Habits of Effective Analysts," *Software Development Magazine*, Vol. 8, No. 10 (October 2000), pp. 62–65.

Wiegers, Karl, "10 Requirements Traps to Avoid," *Software Testing and Quality Engineering Magazine*, January/February 2000. See www.stqemagazine.com/featured.asp?id=8.

Wiegers, Karl E., "First Things First: Prioritizing Requirements," *Software Development Magazine*, Vol. 7, No. 9, September 1999, pp. 24–30.

Wiegers, Karl E., "Automating Requirements Management," *Software Development*, July 1999.

Wiegers, Karl E., *Creating a Software Engineering Culture*, New York: Dorset House Publishing, 1996.

Wiley, Bill, *Essential System Requirements: A Practical Guide to Event-Driven Methods*, Reading, MA: Addison-Wesley, 2000.

Wood, Jane, and Denise Silver, *Joint Application Development*, New York: John Wiley & Sons, 1995.

Young Ralph R., "Early Project Requirements Briefing," Web site: www.ralphyoung.net.

Young, Ralph R., *Effective Requirements Practices*, Boston, MA: Addison-Wesley, 2001. .

Young, Ralph R., "Recommended Requirements Gathering Practices," *CrossTalk*, 15(4), April 2002, pp. 9–12.

Young, Ralph R., Requirements Plan Template and Sample Requirements Plan. See www.ralphyoung.net.

Young, Ralph R., "Requirements Tools Trade Study," Available at www.ralphyoung.net/publications/Requirements_Tools_Trade_Study1.doc.

Young, Ralph R, "The Importance and Value of Process Improvement." Available at www.ralphyoung.net.

Young, Ralph, "The Value of an Organizational Working Group." Available at www.ralphyoung.net.

Zachman Framework Web sites, e.g., see www.zifa.com/.

About the Author

Dr. Ralph R. Young is an active leader and contributor in systems, software, and process engineering. His primary interest is to bring a sound working knowledge of the best practices to a wide professional and academic community. In this pursuit, he teaches requirements and process engineering courses and workshops, is a frequent speaker at meetings and conferences, and maintains regular contact with industry experts. He has been awarded teamwork, leadership, continuous improvement, and publishing awards and is often recognized for his contributions in process management and improvement. He has created a seven-text series that covers the full spectrum of achieving his vision of requirements engineering that is described in Chapter 9. This is the second book in the series; his first book, *Effective Requirements Practices* (Addison-Wesley, 2001), found a receptive audience with RAs in computing and engineering, developers, and managers, and led to a number of speaking and workshop presentation requests and other writing opportunities.

Dr. Young is the director of engineering process improvement, systems and process engineering, Defense Enterprise Solutions (DES), at Northrop Grumman Information Technology, a leading provider of systems-based solutions. Dr. Young helped lead his former business unit (Litton PRC) to CMM® Level 5 and his current business unit (DES) to CMMI® Level 5. He supports internal and external projects to improve their capabilities to utilize process improvement techniques, implement effective requirements practices, and develop innovations to facilitate project management. He leads a requirements working group that involves over 50 requirements engineers from projects in his business unit.

Dr. Young is a graduate of the University of New Hampshire and earned an M.A. in economics and a doctorate in business administration at George Washington University in Washington, D.C. He has been involved in systems and software development activities for more than 35 years. In 1972, he was appointed director of the Systems Development Branch for Fairfax County, Virginia, where a group of 45 highly qualified developers provided state-of-the-art systems for local government functions. Subsequently, he was involved in and managed various systems and software activities at

Martin Marietta Corporation, TRW, PRC, Inc., Litton PRC, and Northrop Grumman Information Technology.

He and his wife, Judy, have been married for 37 years. Judy is an association executive and leader in sports and physical activity, and thus has Ralph out walking at an early hour every day! Ralph enjoys family activities with children and grandchildren, music, singing, nature, the outdoors, and the wilderness. A priority in his life is active involvement in the faith communities of local churches. After retirement, Judy and Ralph have a dream of living aboard a trawler and traveling extensively.

Index

For further information on these and other Artech House titles, including previously considered out-of-print books now available through our In-Print-Forever® (IPF®) program, contact:

Artech House
685 Canton Street
Norwood, MA 02062
Phone: 781-769-9750
Fax: 781-769-6334
e-mail: artech@artechhouse.com

Artech House
46 Gillingham Street
London SW1V 1AH UK
Phone: +44 (0)20 7596-8750
Fax: +44 (0)20 7630-0166
e-mail: artech-uk@artechhouse.com

Find us on the World Wide Web at:
www.artechhouse.com